THE SOCIAL CHALLENGE OF AGEING

THE SOCIAL CHALLENGE OF AGEING

EDITED BY DAVID HOBMAN

CROOM HELM LONDON

Croom Helm Ltd, 2-10 St John's Road, London SW11

ISBN 0—85664—428—5

Printed in Great Britain by Biddles Ltd, Guildford, Surrey

CONTENTS

PREFACE

David Hobman

The great majority of people accomplish the process of ageing with little or no recourse to their medical advisers and none to the social services. Old age is not a disease nor is it a social problem.

However, attitudes towards the elderly suggest that western society considers them to be sick or socially incompetent. This is expressed in a letter written by a sixty-year-old Englishwoman to a Sunday newspaper about her feelings on having reached the statutory retirement age. Her letter read:

> Pensioners are being got at. We must prepare to do battle to main-
> tain our independence and preserve our attractive personalities . . .
> now I am haunted by the fear that if I cannot dispel the assumption
> that I am a senior citizen, the following events may reasonably occur.
> (i) I shall have a gang of young thugs sent to my home to paint my
> kitchen instead of going to prison; (ii) I shall have patients from the
> local mental hospital drafted to dig my garden; (iii) I may be forced
> to go to suitable entertainments, drink tea and wear a paper hat;
> (iv) I may receive vast boxes of assorted food to which I feel I am
> not entitled. We pensioners are in a terrifying position. We are
> *recipients* . . . hands off, please. *I* am in charge of my life.

The writer of this passage recognises, but neither accepts nor relishes, one widely held image of ageing — one full of assumptions and value judgements, with its underlying theme of patronising attitudes setting the elderly as a race apart, to be pitied as people who are no longer capable of managing their own lives. This image assumes that ageing is synonymous with a changing personality, and that the retired adopt common characteristics with an incompetent level of social functioning, and with cultural and intellectual thresholds devoid of critical faculties, whatever previous socio-economic, personal, intellectual or other status they had before.

This image suggests the old are incapable of exercising informed or rational choice, or of maintaining a degree of control over their circumstances; it also implies that they do not have sufficient resources to meet their own needs for recreation or welfare when, in fact, in

11

many societies the young retired represent a very important resource and could well make a substantial contribution to the health and social well-being of the community as a whole.

At about the time the English newspaper published its comment by a young retired woman, an American journal published a contribution from a retired journalist. He had said, in a circular letter to his friends 'at 86 Rosie (my wife) and I live by the rules of the elderly. If the toothbrush is wet, you have brushed your teeth. If the bedside radio is warm in the morning, you left it on all night. If you are wearing one black shoe and one brown shoe, you have a pair like it somewhere in the closet . . . I stagger when I walk and small boys follow me, making bets on which way I will go next. This upsets me. Children should not gamble.'

This American octogenarian's acute perception of the ageing process within himself provides an important reminder that unlike the images of youth, those usually associated with ageing represent a very limited perspective leading to the creation of stereotypes which seem likely to *influence* behavioural patterns rather than simply to reflect them.

Stereotypes influence the attitudes of the young, of the middle-aged (both in relation to old people they observe and their *own* ageing), and of the old themselves. It has been suggested that any old person who was to try to present a more positive, outgoing, involved and lively image, would in effect have to violate society's norms of social behaviour for the elderly — a stance that would indeed be courageous. If this is true, the role and status ascribed by society to the old is the role and status that the old will tend to assume.

This may lead to a smooth-running society but it can also become a prison for the old person.

Hence, the need for a massive programme of public education about ageing and the publication of this book in order to help us understand the process within ourselves, as well as in others and in recognition of the fact that when the elderly do encounter difficulties they are likely to be complex. Multidimensional problems can only be resolved through the discovery of interdisciplinary solutions.

INTRODUCTION

Although all recorded societies have contained a few people of extreme old age; they have been the exception, rather than the rule. The possibility of one fifth of the total population in retirement from active employment would have been unthinkable at the beginning of the twentieth century and even recent social planning has made no adequate provisions for a society in which one in every twenty-five people will be over seventy-five, and one in every hundred over eighty-five within less than a decade.

In Great Britain, however, and in many other industrialised societies, this is now a reality. Even in the Third World there is evidence of a rapidly ageing population and it has been estimated that one third of the people who have reached the age of sixty-five in the last 2,000 years are alive today.

According to figures compiled for the United Nations (in 1970), the world's population of over-sixties was 291 million, an increase of 100 million in twenty years. If future predictions are accurate; they will number 585 million by the year 2,000, a growth rate of almost 100 per cent in thirty years.

Ageing therefore will represent the major social challenge for the remainder of the twentieth century when vast resources will need to be directed towards the support, care and treatment of the old.

In the past, the relatively small group of people who achieved great age would almost certainly have had their needs met within the network of the extended family where they would have maintained their role and status. For a variety of reasons, this is now no longer possible for many. New technology has replaced the transmission of skills from generation to generation. Social mobility, the nuclear family, changed styles of building, and the growth of vast metropolitan areas have combined to lead to isolation and poverty amongst many old people. For example, in Great Britain there are two million single person pensioner households and about the same number claim supplementary income benefits.

Just over half all adult hospital beds, and just under half all psychiatric patients are over retirement age; but the training of doctors, social workers and others in the caring professions has paid very little atten-

tion to ageing. Whilst a growing body of knowledge based upon biological and clinical studies of the ageing process has been accumulated
in recent years, only a modest investment has been made in social
gerontology.

Where professional courses have involved sequences of teaching
about ageing, they have often been short, and peripheral to the main-
stream of medical and social studies, with very little recognition of the
fact that many of the problems facing the elderly are multidimensional
and demand interprofessional approaches. As a result, many practitioners have failed to recognise and relate the wide range of skills which
are needed for the support, care and treatment of the old. Many of
them have also been largely ignorant of the social forces and agencies
within society which could, or should, be concerned with meeting the
needs of old people. Attitudes cultivated during training have resulted
in tension between professional groups in practice so that even when
new generic systems have been evolved, there have still been communication failures.

The Social Challenge of Ageing provides a multidisciplinary
textbook for medical, social work, clergy and other students in the
caring professions as well as for planners and architects whose decisions
and designs affect the lives of the elderly. It is written for both undergraduate and post-professional students.

The book is divided into three parts. The first provides a sociological, demographic and cultural background to the place of old people
in western and eastern societies. The second explores the relationship
which exists (or should exist) between a number of professional
disciplines and part three considers an interdisciplinary model in
practice.

1 AGEING IN WESTERN SOCIETY

Robert Havighurst

In this description of ageing in western societies, the USA is used as the principal source of data, but material on Western Europe is presented for background information, and to correct a possibly over-simple picture that might seem to emerge from the concentration on North America. The Western European countries are more 'mature' in their evolution from agriculture to industry as the principal base for the economy and social structure. They may be somewhat farther along on the course of demographic development.

Age Structure of the Population. The well-known increase in the proportion of older persons in the total population is documented in Table 1. In general, the proportion of persons over 65 years of age starts at 4 or 5 per cent in the middle of the nineteenth century, and even at the beginning of the twentieth century for some countries, including the USA. This proportion increases to approximately 10 to 12 per cent by 1970, and will remain at that level for the remainder of the twentieth century. Causes for the increased proportions of elderly

Table 1: Percentage of Population 65 Years Old and Over for
Selected Countries: 1850 to 1970-75

Country	1850	1860	1880	1900	1920	1930	1940	1950	1970-75
France	6.5	6.9	8.1	8.2	9.1	9.4	–	11.8	13.6
United Kingdom	4.6	4.7	4.6	4.7	6.0	7.4	9.0	10.8	13.8
Sweden	4.8	5.2	5.9	8.4	8.4	9.2	9.4	10.3	14.5
Germany*	–	–	4.7	4.9	5.8	7.4	–	9.3	13.9
United States	–	–	–	4.1	5.7	5.4	6.9	8.1	10.3
Italy	–	4.2	5.1	6.2	6.8	–	7.4	–	10.9
Canada	–	–	–	5.1	4.8	5.6	6.7	7.8	8.3
Netherlands	4.8	4.9	5.5	6.0	5.9	6.2	7.0	7.7	10.4
Czechoslovakia	–	–	–	–	–	6.6	–	7.6	11.6

* West Germany after 1950.
Source: United Nations, *Demographic Yearbook*, 1974; United Nations, *The Aging of Populations*, Population Studies, no. 26, 1956.

persons are three: the saving of lives of children due to improved medical service; a decreasing birthrate in many countries; and a reduction of immigration to North America.

Increased Life Expectancy. Improved medical health service had its greatest effect on population structure in the early years of the twentieth century, when medical advances produced innoculations against the diseases that killed many children. Then, around 1940, the sulfa-drugs were put into use to save lives from pneumonia and other diseases that kill adults. The result of these advances in medical science has been a major increase in life expectancy. This is usually thought of as the average age of death for persons born in a certain calendar period. Technically, it is measured by applying the mortality rates for each age at a given date, such as 1977. The mortality rates for each age, in the year 1977, are applied to a thousand persons born in that year. The average age of death of the people born in that year, is their life expectancy, assuming that the current death rates continue unchanged for this age cohort. Table 2 gives the latest life expectancy data on people in various countries, and shows that the greatest gain in life expectancy is between people born around 1950. Since 1950, there have been very slight increases in life expectancy. However, changes in life expectancy after age 60 or 65 have a good deal of meaning for elderly people, because a year or two more after those ages amounts to a 10 or 15 per cent increase in years left for them to live.

The difference between the sexes in life expectancy varies from one country to another, with women ahead of men in all modernised societies. Even at age sixty-five, women have a one to three year greater life expectancy than men. This, alone, would produce more widows than widowers. And the fact that men marry women on the average two to four years younger increases the probability of widowhood for women. Thus, in the USA in 1970, 28 per cent of men aged seventy-five or over were widowed, compared to 68 per cent of women at that age. In the 1950s, approximately 26 per cent of European men aged sixty-five or over were widowed, compared with 45 per cent of women in the countries not affected by male deaths of World War II or I.

Urban versus Rural Residence. As the proportion of people working in agriculture has decreased substantially in most modern countries within the past hundred years, the elderly population has become

Table 2: Expectation of Life at Specified Ages for Nine Selected
Countries by Sex, in or around 1900, 1930, 1950 and 1970

Country and Year	Life-expectancy for given sex and age							
	Male				Female			
	0	20	40	65	0	20	40	65
France:								
1898–1903	45.3	41.0	26.7	10.5	48.7	43.6	29.1	11.5
1928–33	54.3	43.3	27.6	10.9	59.0	47.4	31.4	12.6
1950–1	63.6	48.4	30.4	11.9	69.3	53.4	35.0	14.4
1972	68.6	50.5	32.2	13.1	74.4	57.9	38.7	17.1
England and Wales:								
1901–10	48.5	43.0	27.0	10.8	52.4	45.8	29.4	12.0
1930–2	58.7	46.8	29.6	11.3	62.9	49.9	32.6	13.1
1951	65.8	49.1	30.5	11.2	70.9	53.5	34.7	13.8
1970–2	68.9	52.0	31.9	12.1	75.1	56.8	37.4	16.0
Sweden:								
1901–10	54.5	45.9	30.8	12.8	57.0	47.7	32.5	13.7
1931–5	63.2	49.4	32.5	13.2	65.3	50.6	33.5	13.7
1946–50	69.0	52.1	33.8	13.5	71.6	54.0	35.3	14.3
1973	72.1	53.5	30.1	14.0	77.7	58.8	34.7	17.1
Germany:								
1901–10	44.8	42.6	26.6	10.4	48.3	44.8	29.2	11.1
1932–4	59.9	48.2	30.8	11.9	62.8	49.8	32.3	12.6
1949–55*	64.6	50.3	32.3	12.8	68.5	53.2	34.7	13.7
1971–3*	67.6	50.2	31.8	12.1	74.1	56.0	36.8	15.2
United States:								
1900–02	47.9	38.4	27.7	11.5	50.7	39.9	29.1	12.2
1929–31	57.7	44.9	28.7	11.7	61.0	47.2	30.9	12.8
1949–51	65.5	48.9	30.8	12.7	71.0	53.7	35.1	15.0
1972	67.4	49.7	31.6	13.1	75.2	56.9	37.9	12.0
Italy:								
1901–11	42.2	43.3	28.2	10.7	44.8	43.7	29.2	10.8
1930–2	53.8	46.8	30.4	11.9	56.0	46.8	32.1	12.7
1970–3	69.0	52.0	33.2	13.3	74.9	57.3	38.1	16.2
Canada:								
1930–2	60.0	49.1	32.0	13.0	62.1	49.8	33.0	13.7
1950–2	66.3	50.8	32.5	13.3	70.8	54.4	35.6	15.0
1970–2	69.3	51.7	33.2	13.7	76.4	58.2	39.0	17.5
Netherlands:								
1900–09	51.0	45.7	29.5	11.6	53.4	46.9	30.8	12.3
1931–40	65.5	50.8	32.8	12.8	67.2	51.5	33.3	13.3
1950–2	70.6	53.7	34.9	14.1	72.9	55.4	36.3	14.7
1973	71.2	53.0	34.0	13.6	77.2	58.6	39.1	17.0
Czechoslovakia:								
1929–32	51.9	45.3	29.0	11.3	55.2	47.4	31.0	12.1
1972–3	70.8	50.0	30.6	11.6	76.3	55.2	35.9	14.5

* For West Germany.

Source: United Nations, *Demographic Yearbook.*

more urbanised. However, in the villages and smaller cities in the USA
and in Western Europe, there has been a tendency for young adults
to migrate to cities and industrial centres leaving their parents behind
to round out their lives in those semi-rural communities. For example,
the several West North Central American states, including Iowa and
Missouri, which have a relatively large farm and small town population,
had 12.5 per cent population over sixty-five, compared with 10.5 per
cent for the country as a whole in 1975.

On the other hand, there has been a general increase of elderly
population in the 'urbanised areas' of the USA. Such an area contains
a city of 50,000 population or more plus the surrounding closely
settled areas. The elderly population in 1950 was 44 per cent in
urbanised areas; in 1970 this had grown to 56 per cent.

Elderly in the Labour Force. In an agricultural country where the
bulk of the population live and work on farms, the entire family, from
grandparents to grandchildren, is generally occupied full-time or part-
time, and it is difficult to get strictly reliable data on participation in
the labour force. But the Western European countries and the USA have
all become more industrialised during the twentieth century, and their
data on labour force participation have become more nearly comparable. Table 3 shows the percentages of men and women aged 60-64
and 65-69 in a number of western countries who were in the labour
force about 1950. By this time labour-force participation of women,
and especially of women over forty, was a growing force. This has
continued to grow, and Table 4 provides the data on increasing
participation of women, and of older women, in the American labour
force.

Economic Status of the Elderly. The economic status of the elderly
part of the population only becomes an important concept and problem when the older adult generation lives and cares for itself
separately from its middle-aged adult children. This is characteristic
of an urbanised, industrial society, and therefore has become socially
important first in Western Europe and then in North America.

The older generation, which consists of many people who are no
longer employed, needs a 'retirement income'. This may be self-
provided by those who have been able to save money and to acquire
property, but the great majority of people, especially manual workers,
do not save much money during their middle adult years, when
expenses are at a peak for current living costs, and the cost of

Table 3: Participation in the Labour Force for Older Men and Women: Selected Countries

		Men			Women	
	Total	60-64 years	65-69 years	Total	60-64 years	65-69 years
United Kingdom:						
1951	88	88	49	35	14	9
1971	81	87	31	43	28	13
Australia:						
1947	65	80	50	19	10	7
1971	80	76	18*	37	16	3*
New Zealand:						
1951	58	64	40	18	9	5
1971	81	72**	42**	42	34**	15**
Sweden:						
1950	65	80	56	23	19	12
1971	69	76	32	37	26	8
Finland:						
1950	88	87	NA	52	42	NA
1970	74	63	20	49	29	7
France:						
1946	86	76	67	46	40	31
1968	73	66	15*	36	32	6*
Austria:						
1951	64	70	44	35	26	19
1971	74	45	4*	39	13	2*
Switzerland:						
1950	67	88	66	26	24	17
1970	84	87	50	42	30	17
United States:						
1950	79	79	60	29	21	13
1970	73	73	39	40	36	17

Worker rates across the Men and Women column groups.

NA = Not available.

* Estimated, from data on 65 plus.

** 1966 data.

Total is the percentage economically active in the age range fifteen years of age and older.

Source: United Nations, *Demographic Yearbook*, 1956, 1973.

Table 4: Elderly Persons in the American Labour Force, by Sex 1950 to 1990

	1950	1960	1970	1975	1980*	1990*
	Percentages of the non-institutional population					
Men						
55 – 64	87	87	83	76	75	70
55 – 59	NA	92	90	84	83	81
60 – 64	NA	81	75	66	63	57
65 and over	46	33	27	22	20	17
65 – 69	NA	47	42	32	30	26
70 and over	NA	24	18	15	13	10
16 and over	82	84	81	79	79	78
Women						
55 – 64	27	37	43	41	42	43
55 – 59	NA	42	49	48	49	51
60 – 64	NA	31	36	33	33	33
65 and over	9.7	10.8	9.7	8.3	8.0	7.5
65 – 69	NA	17.6	17.3	14.5	14.4	13.9
70 and over	NA	6.8	5.7	4.9	4.4	4.1
16 and over	33	38	43	46	48	52
Both sexes						
16 and over	59	60	61	62	63	64

NA = Not available.
* Estimated.

Source: US Bureau of the Census, *Current Population Reports*, Series P-23, no. 59, May 1976. Statistical Abstract of the United States, 1974.

education of adolescent children may be rather heavy.

The experience of European countries led them to provide pensions from government funds for their older citizens, commencing as early as 1889 in Germany. Denmark, Great Britain, Sweden were next in order, with national old age assistance programmes. When the United States Congress established an Old Age Assistance programme as part of the Social Security Act of 1935, there were already such programmes in twenty-two of the twenty-seven European countries. Some were financed out of general government funds, and were simply regarded as part of the cost of government provision for the socio-economic needs of the population. Others were financed from a tax on the earnings of people, with the funds going into an insurance trust fund. These latter were generally called Old Age Insurance rather than Old Age Assistance programmes.

Thus the concept of a retirement income has come into use, following the principle that retirement incomes should amount to something like 50 to 70 per cent of the average income during the five to ten years before retirement.

The northern European and Scandinavian countries have created the most stable and advantageous retirement fund levels. The American system of social security benefits is inadequate as retirement income, and must be supplemented either by personal savings, or by pension funds maintained by employers, or by welfare payments from the state or federal governments.

The Place of the Elderly in Society

The twentieth century has transformed the elderly from an almost invisible group sheltered by the extended family to a highly visible group with a life of its own, with moral and legal claims on society, and with a certain amount of social and political power. This transformation has disadvantages and advantages for the persons involved. The disadvantages have been stated cogently by Ernest W. Burgess the American sociologist who was one of the creators of the discipline of social gerontology. He pointed out that modern industrial society has shifted responsibility for the elderly away from the family. He wrote:

The full force of these shifts has fallen heaviest on the older person. He can no longer count as a matter of right and of moral and legal obligation on economic support by his children. He is less and less likely, if widowed, to be offered a home by a son or a daughter. If ill, particularly with a chronic ailment, his children are more and more disposed to shift his care to a hospital rather than to provide a bed in their home. If lonely, he must more and more look elsewhere than to his descendants to provide companionship and sociability. In short, he must seek elsewhere for the satisfaction of his needs — financial, health, and social. In Western cultures he turns to the government or to other organisations.

The older person, like those in all age groups in modern society, must rely less upon the family and more on organisations for support and for fulfilment of his desires. Organisations in Western countries are taking the primary place which the family had held from the beginning of human history.[1]

Burgess had a rather negative view of the results of these changes. He went on to say:

Modern economic trends have brought losses as well as gains to all age groups in the population. But the full impact of their adverse effects has been experienced by the ageing. Let us recapitulate the series of blows which struck them one after another. First, they lost their economic independence. They were demoted from the status of employer to that of employee. Their place of work was no longer the home but the factory or office. Second, in increasing numbers they had to give up rural residence for urban living. Third, they were now forced to retire from work by the decision of the employer rather than of their own free will as in the past. Fourth, they lost their former favored position in the extended family. No longer were the grandfather and the grandmother the centre of the absorbing social life of their descendants but often became un-wanted hangers-on, taking part by sufferance in the activities of their children and grandchildren. Fifth, deprived of the society of their family and having lost associates on the job and other friends by death or departure to other communities, they found them-selves cursed instead of blessed by leisure time in abundance and little or nothing to do with it.

In short, the retired older man and his wife are imprisoned in a role-less role. They have no vital function to perform such as they had in rural society. This is doubly true of the husband, because a woman as long as she is physically able retains the role and satis-factions of homemaker. Nor are they offered a ceremonial role by society to make up in part for their lost functional role.

This role-less role is thrust by society upon the older person at retirement, and to a greater or lesser degree he has accepted it or become resigned to it.

This rather pessimistic view of the fate of the elderly in western societies will be challenged in the next section of this chapter. The elders of society have found many advantages in their situation as 'senior citizens'. They have discovered or created roles for themselves which have some rewards.

The Contemporary Situation: 1970-80

It may be said with some caution that the socio-economic situation of the elderly population has become fairly stable and will remain so for the remainder of this century. This is true for population structure, though questionable for the labour force participation and the economic status of the elderly people. For instance, continued monetary inflation at 1975-8 rates (rise in the cost of living) will create problems, as will any tendency to push older people out of employment – and both of these are likely to occur.

Population projections for the USA are shown in Table 5. These are based on assumptions concerning future death rates and birth rates, and they represent the consensus of contemporary demographers. A slight reduction of death rates for people over fifty is generally expected, but not a major breakthrough by a discovery of some substance that will slow down the rate of ageing of the body and thereby extend the average life-span by ten or fifteen years. There is more question about the future birthrate. The most general expectation is that the fertility rate of women in Western Europe and North America will stabilise at the 'replacement level' of 2.1 children per woman who lives through her child-bearing years. At present this rate is below replacement level in the USA, and it has fluctuated around this level in several European countries. However, the American birth rate was quite high from 1950 to 1965, thus producing an unusually large cohort of women who will be bearing children from 1970 to 2010. With methods of contraception easily available, with abortion available on request in many countries, and with a generally favourable attitude toward a policy of zero population growth in the western societies, the projections of Table 5 seem to be reasonable ones. They lead to a stable USA population of about 318 million around the year 2050, with approximately 16 per cent over sixty-five years of age. For western and northern Europe, there may even be a slow decline of population, since there is little or no immigration, a force that probably will continue in the USA for some decades.

Family Structure and Living Arrangements of Older People

The most generally desired living arrangement for elderly people in the modern western countries is for husband and wife to live together but not with their children, who, they hope, will live within easy visiting distance. (The Harris Poll of 1974 in the USA found that 81 per cent of the elderly people who had living children had seen some of their children within 'the last week or so'.) Table 6 shows data on

Table 5: Population Projections, USA; 1975—2050

Age Group	Number in millions				
	1975	1990	2000	2025	2050
Under 20	74.6	74.9	79.2	83.2	87.5
15-24	40.2	34.8	38.8	40.9	43.3
20-64	116.6	141.3	152.6	168.4	179.7
55 +	42.1	49.4	53.5	82.2	87.4
65 +	22.3	28.9	30.6	48.1	51.2
75 +	8.4	11.4	13.5	18.0	22.1
Total	213.5	245.1	262.5	299.7	318.4
Per cent under 20	35.0	30.6	30.1	27.7	27.4
Per cent 65 and over	10.4	11.8	11.7	16.0	16.1
Per cent 75 and over	3.9	4.7	5.1	6.0	6.9
Per cent 20-64	54.5	57.7	58.1	56.1	56.5
Per cent 65-74	6.5	7.1	6.5	10.0	9.2
Ratio under 20/20-64	.64	.53	.52	.50	.49
Ratio 65 +/20-64	.19	.20	.20	.29	.28

Assumptions: Fertility rate at 2.11 (replacement level)
Immigration 400,000 per year
Slight increase in life expectancy before 2000

Source: US Bureau of the Census, *Current Population Reports*, Series P-25, no.
601, October 1975. Tables 8, 11.

living arrangements in the USA for 1971, and these are persisting
during this decade. Thirty-one per cent of aged women and 16 per
cent of aged men were living with someone other than a spouse, which
sometimes means that they live with adult children. Thirty-five per
cent of women and 14 per cent of elderly men were living alone,
and most of them were widowed. Those are the people most likely to
have a problem of loneliness. Many of them live in single rooms or in
small apartments in the larger cities. Havighurst secured data on numbers of older people living alone in Chicago, New York, Paris and
London, about 1970. He found that the proportions ranged from 26
(London) to 37 (Paris) per cent, with about twice as many women
as men living in this way.[2]

Table 6: Marital Status and Living Arrangements of the Aged, in the USA, 1971

| | Percentage distribution | | | | | |
| | Male | | | Female | | |
	65 – 74	75 +	Total	65 – 74	75 +	Total
Marital status:						
Single	8	6	7	8	7	7
Married	79	63	73	46	22	36
Spouse present	76	60	70	45	20	35
Spouse absent	3	3	3	2	2	2
Widowed	10	30	17	43	70	54
Divorced	3	2	3	3	1	2
Living arrangement:						
Living alone	12	18	14	33	38	35
Spouse present	76	60	70	45	20	35
Living with someone else	12	23	16	23	42	31

Source: US Bureau of the Census, *Current Population Reports*, Series P-23, no. 59, May 1976.

Physical Health and Disability

Poor health is mentioned by older people generally as one of their most serious problems. In the 1974 Harris poll, 28 per cent of the people aged 65-69 reported that 'poor health; or not enough medical care' was a 'very serious' personal problem for them. This percentage rose to 32 for those aged seventy or over. Although, in the USA, older people comprise 10 per cent of the total population, they account for 28 per cent of the national expenditures for personal health care. In contrast to the under-sixty-five population, senior citizens:

are admitted to hospitals about twice as often (in 1970, there were 220 admissions per 1,000 persons over sixty-five compared to 131 for younger persons); have hospital stays that are about twice as long (in 1970, 11.2 days per stay v. 6.2 days); visit a physician about 50 per cent more often (in 1972, 6.9 visits per year v. 4.8 visits); see a dentist about one half as often (in 1972,

0.9 visits per year v. 1.6 visits).

The medical profession has tended to neglect the elderly population, because medical practitioners like to work on acute rather than chronic diseases. The chronic diseases of arthritis, rheumatism and cardio-vascular diseases are not curable, and the doctor has little to offer his elderly patient except something to relieve the pain or relax the tension.

In their 1962 study, *Older People in Three Industrial Societies* (Great Britain, Denmark and the USA) Shanas and her associates found quite similar numbers of people living in old people's homes or nursing homes, and rather similar numbers who were living in their own homes but were bedfast or homebound. Four or five per cent of people over sixty-five are living in institutions (homes for the aged or nursing homes) and 2 or 3 per cent of those living in their own himes are bedfast, with another 6 or 7 per cent 'homebound' which means that they cannot go out of their home without assistance. Shanas repeated this survey in 1975 in the USA with very similar findings.

Economic Security Issues

In a modern industrial society, most older people are not employed, and they are not supported by their children. Hence they must have a retirement income, which may come from their savings, or from pensions which they have earned by a lifetime of work. Policies and practices with respect to retirement income vary from one country to another. All countries now have some form of government-administered programme of retirement income. A basic issue has to do with the question of paying uniform versus wage-related benefits to retired persons. The United States Social Security system pays benefits related to the past earnings of the retired person. If these are insufficient to support the person, he can apply for a Supplementary Security payment which is given to him if he can prove financial need. Most European government funds pay higher benefits, with less relation to past earnings. These benefits are generally high enough to place the recipient above the poverty level.

The United States government defines what it calls the 'poverty level' for elderly people which depends on whether they live together in couples or alone, and whether they live in large cities or smaller places. Taking account of increases in the cost of living, the poverty level for an urban elderly couple in 1977 is about $ 3,500 a year, and about $ 2,800 for a person living alone. Approximately 16 per cent of the elderly population are living below the official poverty level, even after some are aided by the federal government programme of Supplemental Security Income.

It is generally concluded by economists both in the USA and in Europe that the retirement income should be about 70 per cent of the last full-time income from employment, for an elderly couple in good health to live at a level close to the level they had attained while being employed. Old age pensions in the countries of northern and western Europe do reach approximately this level, but social security benefits in the USA do not. For instance, a working man earning the median wage for male workers just prior to retirement would receive as social security benefits only 45 per cent of that median wage. Many elderly people own their own homes and a good many have income from savings, or pensions from pension funds, and therefore are well off financially. But something like 20 per cent of people over sixty-five have total incomes below the official poverty level or only slightly above it.

A government policy of providing funds to raise this group at least to the poverty level is generally favoured by economists and is justified on ethical grounds. The ethical argument runs as follows: Every generation earns its living during its working life of forty or fifty years, and also contributes to the support of its children while they are growing up. To a lesser extent, the working generation contributes to the support of its elderly parents in various ways, directly and through taxes that pay for services and welfare payments which some elderly people receive. As this generation grows older and retires from employment, it receives help from the generation that follows it into the working force. Thus it gets back the equivalent of what it paid out when it was working and paying taxes.

Furthermore, in an economy which is growing in per capita income, as the American economy has done most of the time, some of this economic growth is saved for investment to expand the factories and farms and thus to increase the productive power of the economy, and not paid out in extra wages to the workers who produced the added wealth. Thus a generation of workers is really contributing to a growing 'capital fund' which increases the income of the society. Since they do not receive these earnings at the time they did the work, they build a moral claim on the society for payments after they retire – payments beyond what they get from Social Security as a result of the Social Security taxes they and their employers paid at the time they were working.

The Problem of Increasing Cost of Living. Clearly the effect of
persistent inflation on the purchasing power of the fixed income of
an elderly person must be dealt with in the United States where the
dollar has been losing purchasing power in nearly every year since
1950. The Congress has recognised this problem by adjusting social
security benefits to the changing cost of living – a process known as
'indexing'. Social security benefits are adjusted annually by raising
or lowering them in relation to the increase or decrease in the cost
of living index. But, since social security payments do not cover the
cost of living for most retired people, this device only partially meets
the need. People who have a fixed dollar income from annuities or
bonds or other investments find that inflation reduces the purchasing
power of this fixed income. For instance, if the cost of living increases
at an average rate of 5 per cent a year (it has increased more than this
in recent years), the purchasing power of a fixed dollar income is
cut in half in about seventeen years.

Dependency Ratios. The working population is producing the goods
and services used by the entire population of all ages. All of the young
people below working age are supported by the working population,
and most of the elderly people live on goods and services provided
by the working population, paying with money from their savings or
from pension or old age benefits. Thus the working population is
supporting those who are not working, mainly retired former workers,
and youth too young to be employed. To study this situation, the concept of a *dependency ratio* or *dependency index* has been developed.
This is simply the ratio of the dependent population to the working
age population. There are two aspects – the elderly population/working
age population, and the youth population/working age population.
Table 7 shows how this dependency ratio has varied from one country
to another, and from one date to another. The actual age limits of the
several groups depend on the more or less arbitrary age boundaries
that are chosen. In Table 7, the working age population is defined
as the 15-64 age group. It is more common to use 20 to 64 as the
defining boundaries.

The Retirement Transition

The period of time from full-time work in one's major occupation to
full-time retirement from the labour force has become an important
transition period in the lives of many people. It may span five to ten
years for some upper-middle-class professional people, who are able

Table 7: Old Age Dependency Ratio and Ratio of Population 65 Years of Age and Over to Younger Population Groups for Nine Selected Countries, 1900–1975

| | Old age dependency ratio (persons 65 years and over per 100 persons 15-64 years) | | | | | | |
	1900	1910	1920	1930	1940	1950	1971-5
France	12.5	12.7	13.3	13.8		17.7	22.6
United Kingdom	7.4	8.2	9.1	10.8	12.9	16.2	21.6
Sweden	14.1	14.1	13.5	13.9	13.4	15.6	21.8
Germany*	8.1	8.3	8.5	10.6		13.8	20.7
United States	6.6	6.8	7.4	8.3	10.1	12.5	16.5
Italy	10.3	10.9	10.9		12.0	12.1	16.5
Canada	8.4	7.5	7.9	8.9	10.2	12.5	11.4
Netherlands	10.2		9.6	9.8	10.8	12.3	16.5
Czechoslovakia				9.8		11.3	19.1

* West Germany after 1950.

Source: United Nations, *The Aging of Populations and Its Economic and Social Implications*, Population Studies, no. 26, New York: United Nations, 1956; United Nations, *Demographic Yearbook*, 1974.

to secure the kind of work they want, on a temporary or a part-time basis. The sharp discontinuity from full-time employment one week or year to complete withdrawal from employment the next week or year is still the most widespread experience, especially for wage workers in factories and offices and commerce. But even for this major body of workers, the phenomenon of flexible retirement is visible and regarded by a growing number as a possibility for them.

Two agencies of the United Nations have taken note of these facts, and have recommended flexible arrangements for the closing end of the working life. The International Labour Organisation has spoken in favour of making employment opportunities open to elderly people at their option, and the Organisation for Economic Co-operation and Development in 1970 published a report entitled *The Flexibility of Retirement Age*. In 1971 OECD published the following policy statement:

The Manpower and Social Affairs Committee believes that increased possibilities for individual choice should be available as between leisure and work, particularly for mature and older workers. Flexibility in this sense would also be in line with changes as to working capacity and energy associated with ageing and yet give recognition to the fact that older people are usually reluctant to make drastic changes in the style of life to which they have grown accustomed . . .

The Manpower and Social Affairs Committee recognises that the widening of choice may lead a significant proportion of workers to opt either for continued employment over the traditional retiring age or for an intermediate condition of partial retirement and part-time employment or for early retirement (definitive or temporary) with the appropriate actuarial consequences. At present, it is not possible to do more than speculate on how individuals would react to this increased freedom of choice . . .

The Manpower and Social Affairs Committee believes that if a higher participation rate of middle-aged and older workers can be combined with increased individual choice to enter or leave the labour market, there could be real benefits for all age groups of society . . .

The Manpower and Social Affairs Committee, therefore, proposes that Member countries should give consideration to ways of establishing the facts about individuals' behaviour over a period of time when retirement options are presented. Such fact-finding exercises might take the form of localised experiments where these are feasible within the existing social security system or a follow-up of individuals who already have an option under existing schemes.[3]

The facts of participation in the labour force by men and women during the age period of sixty and sixty-nine are presented for several countries in Table 3. These show a decrease between the 60-64 and the 65-69 age period for both sexes. This table does not present information about the underlying processes of retirement, but we know that some people retire voluntarily in their early sixties or in their late fifties; while others seek and obtain part-time work; and others take several different jobs for short periods during their sixties. A study by Jacobson in Great Britain was made in three corporations, asking workers aged 55-64 what kind of retirement experience they would prefer. They were asked to choose among four possibilities: continued full-time employment beyond pensionable age; regular parttime employment; occasional employment; and complete withdrawal from work. Their preferences were, in percentages: 12, 39, 24 and 21 respectively for these four alternatives.

The government of Sweden has moved positively toward a nation-wide programme of flexible retirement since the summer of 1975, in the form of the Partial Pension Scheme. The Swedish Parliament adopted this plan to facilitate the transition from active work life to full retirement during the decade from age sixty to age seventy. All Swedish people are eligible for the national old age pension at age sixty-five, this pension being approximately sixty per cent of the average annual earned income during the fifteen best years before retirement. The new Partial Pension plan permits a worker between sixty and sixty-five to take a job with seventeen to thirty-five hours of work a week, and to draw a partial pension which will bring him up to 85 or 90 per cent of his earlier full income. Furthermore, the part-time work can be continued until age seventy, with total income at about this same level, and with some credits that will increase his full pension at the age of seventy.

Favoured Life-Styles

A cross-national study of adjustment to retirement was made in the mid-1960s, by a team of European and American researchers, involving men aged 69-76 in the following cities: Vienna, Bonn and a community in the Ruhr Valley; Nijwegen (Netherlands); Milan; London; Warsaw; and Chicago. The men were either retired teachers or retired workers in heavy industry (usually steelworkers). Some of these men had continued to work, although all of them were formally retired from their careers, and were receiving pensions. Interviews with these men were analysed and each man was assigned to one of several *life-styles*. A life-style is a way of distributing one's time, energy, and ego-involvement among the various possible activities of life. The following life-styles were found, and the men were distributed among these life-styles as indicated in Table 8.

A. *Continued interest and involvement in the worker role* as the organising axis of life. The man may continue to teach, or may shift to another job. He may draw full salary or part salary, or no salary at all, but his work is the central part of his life. This style may be continued well past age sixty-five by some men, whose formal retire-ment age may be seventy or seventy-two, and who may continue with full vigour in their work until this age or beyond.

B. *Engagement in family roles.* More time spent with spouse, more time with grandchildren. Much time spent around the house as a

Table 8: Life-Styles of Retired Men: Frequency Distribution

Group	A	B	C	D	E	F	G	Number
Teachers:								
Bonn	4	2	3	6	5	5	0	25
Chicago	7	1	2	5	2	8	0	25
London	4	2	1	3	2	8	0	20
Milan	8	1	1	3	2	10	0	25
Nijwegen	5	6	3	3	1	6	1	25
Vienna	0	0	3	1	0	3	0	7
Warsaw	7	8	0	6	0	4	0	25
TOTAL	35	20	13	27	12	44	1	152
Steelworkers:								
Chicago	0	3	0	1	1	18	2	25
Milan	2	2	3	0	1	16	1	25
Vienna	0	0	0	0	1	4	1	6
Warsaw	5	8	0	4	0	6	2	25
TOTAL	7	13	3	5	3	44	6	81

Source: Havighurst and de Vries, *Life Styles and Free-Time Activities of Retired Men.*

homemaker.

C. *Engagement in personal-social activities.* More time and energy spent with friends, acquaintances and informal groups. This is not a pattern which increases in intensity for many men as they grow older. It may be a pattern of a widower or of a person who is exceptionally sociable.

D. *Engagement in clubs, church, civic-political activities.* An increase of church or religious activity is seen occasionally. More time and energy spent in clubs, perhaps including old people's clubs. This apparently does not happen often, but it may occur if a strong old people's club is organised in a community. It may also occur if there is an active political campaign that enlists the interest of old people, such as a campaign for old age pensions, or for medical care or housing for the elderly.

E. *New leisure-time role created for oneself.* The man makes a speciality of one or more hobbies or develops former minor leisure activities into a social role. He become known as an outstanding gardener, or stamp collector, or world traveller. He may develop an artistic skill as a painter.

F. *General slowing-down and reduction of tempo.* The day is kept full in spite of the loss of the work role, and without any great increase of activity in other roles. Life goes on much as before retirement, but at a slower tempo, so that more time is taken up with the non-work roles. Social interaction is decreased in all or nearly all areas.

G. *Solitary, role-less activity.* The interstices of the day are filled up with aimless activity such as passively watching television, or sitting by the window or in a park and watching the world go by.

The modal or most common life-style for both groups is F – a general slowing down and reduction of tempo. After the work role disappears from the man's life, he fills the time with things he had been doing earlier, but now he lives at a slower pace, takes a longer time to do things. At the same time he reduces his social interaction in some non-family areas. He does not report boredom with life. He creates a routine which is interesting and satisfactory to him, usually including more association with his wife than formerly.

More than half of the steelworkers adopt this way of life, but less than one third of the teachers. Many teachers either continue with a part-time worker's role on into their seventies (Style A), or they become more active in church, club or civic-political activity (Style D). Thus the teachers have a tendency either to refuse to disengage from the worker role, or to substitue for this loss by maintaining or increasing their activity in another role. Steelworkers who substitute for loss of the worker role generally do so by increasing their family role-activity.

The Place of the Elderly in the Society

The western societies are sometimes contrasted with the societies of Asia in their attitudes toward and treatment of the elderly. Asian societies are thought to respect, revere and care for their elders more than European and North American societies do. The United States is often said to be a 'youth-oriented' country, with the implication that Americans pay less attention to their elders and treat them less well than do Europeans. The fact is that the proportion of older people is less in North America than in Europe, and the older segment of the population has been less visible in North America than in Europe, though the elders have become much more visible in the USA in recent decades.

Table 9: The Best and Worst Things about being over 65 Years of Age

| | Age and per cent Mentioning: | |
	65 plus	18 – 64
Best Things		
More leisure and free time	43	52
Independence, freedom from responsibility	31	33
Don't have to work	18	31
Financial security, if you have it	27	35
Family: children and grandchildren	7	9
Worst Things		
Poor health	70	61
Loneliness	20	36
Financial problems	17	29
Dependency	15	16
Boredom	8	11

Source: *Myth and Reality of Aging*, pp. 9, 20.

The comparative study of older people in USA, Britain and Denmark, made by Shanas and associates in 1962, showed more similarity than difference among these countries with respect to the life experience of their elders. However, there was some economic advantage for the Danish elderly, while the British and American elders were approximately equal in the amount of their income compared with average incomes of employed people in each country. There were more elders in real poverty in the USA than in Britain at that time, though the proportion of American elders below the official 'poverty level' has been considerably decreased in recent years.

In order to examine the psychological 'position' of the elderly, it is useful to find out how the elders are perceived or evaluated by the general adult population who are below the old-age boundary, and to compare this with the self-perceptions of the elderly. This is·possible in the USA through a national opinion poll made in the autumn of 1974 by the Harris Poll organisation. This poll was supported by a grant from a philanthropic foundation, and was conducted with advice and criticism from a Research Advisory Committee appointed by the National Council on the Aging.

Table 10: Relation of Age to Perception of Problems; Problems Seen as 'Very Serious' Personally

Age	Percentage saying 'very serious'			
	18 – 54	55 – 64	65 – 69	70 plus
Fear of crime	10	18	21	26
Poor health; not enough medical care	18	30	28	32
Not enough money to live on	18	17	17	15
Loneliness; not enough friends	11	11	14	18

Source: *Myth and Reality of Aging,* p. 37

Among other questions in the course of the interview with the sample of several thousand men and women, they were asked 'What are the best things about being over 65 years of age?' and 'What are the worst things about being over 65 years of age?' Although they volunteered their answers, most of their answers could be grouped into a small number of general responses, which are shown in Table 9. It is interesting to note that the people aged 18-64 and those over 65 years of age gave answers in almost the same order of frequency, thus indicating rather similar perceptions of what it is like to grow old. But the 18-64 year group saw leisure time and 'don't have to work' somewhat more frequently as 'best things' than did the over-65 group.

Another part of the interview asked the respondents to look at a list of possible problems and to say which ones were 'very serious' for them personally, which ones were 'somewhat serious' and which were 'not at all serious'. Their responses are shown in Table 10, for the four categories which were most serious. Here there were some problems that grew 'more serious' with age; notably, 'fear of crime' and 'loneliness, not enough friends.'

Another question asked people how much time they personally spent in each of some twenty activities, and also how much time they thought 'most people over 65' spent in those same activities. The results are shown in Table 11. In this case the general public perception of how older people spend thier time was somewhat different from the self-perceptions. Even the respondents who were over 65 had somewhat different perceptions of 'most people over 65' from their own self-perceptions.

Table 11: Use of Time in Relation to Age Group

	Per cent who say they spend 'a lot of time':		Total Public who think most people over 65 spend 'a lot of time':
	18 – 64	65 and over	
Socialising with friends	55	47	52
Gardening or raising plants	34	39	45
Caring for younger or older members of family	53	27	23
Working part-time or full-time	51	10	5
Reading	38	36	43
Sitting and thinking	37	31	62
Participating in recreational activities and hobbies	34	26	28
Watching television	23	36	67
Going for walks	22	25	34
Participating in sports, like golf, tennis or swimming	22	3	5
Sleeping	15	16	39
Participating in fraternal or community organisations or clubs	13	17	26
Just doing nothing	9	15	35
Doing volunteer work	8	8	15
Participating in political activities	5	6	9

Source: *Myth and Reality of Aging,* pp. 57,59.

Membership in Organisations and Church Participation

The various organisations (trade unions, political organisations, social clubs, sports and recreation clubs, professional associations) lose some of their attractiveness to people as they move into their sixties. In their place come age-specific organisations that serve older people. Several national organisations in the USA exert a good deal of political influence on government agencies and at the same time have local chapters which bring members together socially. The largest of these is the American Association of Retired Persons (AARP) with over nine million members. There is also the National Council of Senior Citizens which has a trade union base, and the National Retired Teachers Association. The Gray Panthers are very active politically, with strong feminine leadership.

Local clubs of Seniors in the USA are sponsored often by churches and synagogues, and by local recreation agencies such as the Young Men's Christian Assocation, and the local city government recreation departments. A widespread and growing number of Senior Centres have been fostered by the National Council on the Aging, and have recently gained some financial support from the national government. The active members in these local associations tend to be well over 65 years of age — often in the 70- to 75-year range.

Churches and synagogues are especially important to elderly people. In the Harris Poll, in 1974, 79 per cent of the people aged 65 and over said they had attended a church or synagogue 'within the last week or two', and 71 per cent said religion was 'very important' in their lives. For many elderly people the church or synagogue is both a place of worship and a place of association with friends.

Senior Centres are less widespread, of course, but 51 per cent of the age-group 65 and over said there was a senior citizens' centre or golden age club convenient for them to attend. About one third of this group (18 per cent of the 65 and over group) reported that they had attended a golden age club or senior citizens' centre within the past year, and two thirds of this group (12 per cent of the 65 and over group) had attended within the last month.

These American associations are paralleled in Europe with variations that reflect differences in national culture. The Netherlands, with a strong social-political church culture, have old people's clubs in many churches, and the church is often a weekday social centre for seniors. In England the local government unit may provide space in public buildings for senior centres.

The Future of Ageing

Our discussion of ageing has indicated that the more developed western countries have arrived at a kind of plateau with respect to the social and economic and demographic status of the elderly. This period will extend until about 1990. After that, the average age of the population will gradually increase, and the proportion aged sixty-five and over will increase from 10 or 12 per cent to 16 or 18 per cent, reaching a stage of zero population growth in the more developed countries by the years 2030 to 2050.

The period after 1990 will find the economic structure of the developed societies dominated by the supply and the cost of energy. The twentieth century industrialisation of the 'affluent third' of the world's peoples has been based essentially on cheap petroleum, steel, aluminium, lumber, paper, plastics and fertilisers. These are now increasingly scarce and expensive. By the year 2000 the world's supply of petroleum and natural gas will be nearly used up, if the present rate of use continues. Coal will be available for at least a century but will cost more in human labour per unit of energy than petroleum has cost.

These changes will cause major changes in the material standard of living and in life-styles, especially, at first, of young and middle-aged adults. By 1990 these changes will probably affect the lives of elderly people as well, and in ways that will interrupt the stability which we have projected for the coming decade.

The situation with respect to employment, income and life-styles of any adult age group will depend, after 1990, upon the following:

The gross national product per capita, the distribution of this product among the various groups of people and its destribution in terms of consumption versus capital investment.
The demand of the economy for human labour.
The cost of energy.
The distribution of the working population between the sexes and among various age groups.

In order to look ahead into the intermediate future, we need data on these matters, or at least we need estimates that are based upon our best judgement concerning these matters. The probable age distribution in the United States is presented in Table 5, with special attention to the sizes and relative proportions of the age groups 20-64 and 65-74. The sizes of these two age groups are important because, while nearly all the work of the nation will be done by people aged 20-74, the sub-group 65-74 will probably be seen as marginal, a group with less moral claim to employment and less working capacity than the 20-64 group.

The Future Cost of Energy

The cost of energy during the first half of the twenty-first century is a matter which will depend not only upon research but also upon political action during the remainder of the present century. Because any serious attempt to plan ahead for a quality society must be based on knowledge about or estimates about the cost and consumption and sources of energy, it is essential to set forth what we know and what we can reasonably estimate. The United States in 1975 consumed about 30 per cent of the energy used in the entire world, for its 6 per cent of the world's population. The United States secured about 20 per cent of its energy supply from coal, about 40 per cent from petroleum, about 30 per cent from natural gas, about 4 per cent from hydro-electric plants and miscellaneous souces, and the remaining 6 per cent from nuclear or atomic energy. Nuclear reactors are now being built in increasing numbers by the major energy-selling companies and with very large capital costs. For instance, the Commonwealth Edison Company, which supplies energy to the Chicago area, in 1975 produced 35 per cent of its energy from nuclear reactors. This move has been expedited by the increase in the cost of Arabian petroleum which rose from $ 3 to $ 13 per barrel from 1973 to 1975.

Solar engery coming directly from the sun to the earth's surface has come into serious consideration as a commercially practicable source recently. The American Congress passed the Solar Energy Research, Development and Demonstration Act of 1974, and appropriated $ 80 million for research in 1975-6.

By the year 1990, it is likely that the new forms of energy-producing technology will be far enough developed to enable us to estimate the costs of energy over the ensuing thirty or forty years. Also, policies for developing energy resources and for controlling the consumption of energy will have been worked out in the political arena. Then, the American economy will be adjusting its production technology to the situation. This adjustment will go far toward determining the life-styles, incomes and activities of the elderly population.

Basically, the cost of energy will control the socio-economic structure of the twenty-first century. It will determine the numbers and age structure of the labour force. It will affect the distribution of the population between big cities and smaller cities. It will affect the structure and size of dwelling units. Related to this will be the cost of certain scarce and critically important metals including manganese, copper, lead, tin, tungsten and aluminium.

There is almost no expert on the problem of energy sources and energy uses who now believes that we will, in the next seventy-five years, have energy as cheap as it was between 1900 and 1970.

Alternatives for the Life of the Elderly After 1990

The most generally accepted prediction for the United States and the Western European countries is that the cost of a unit of energy in the year 2000 will be at least four times what it was in 1970. Making these assumptions, how will the life-styles and values of elderly people respond?

Alternative Energy Policies. If we assume the continuation of a democratic political structure probably moving toward somewhat greater government participation in the economy, and if we assume that there will be no major war, we may describe two contrasting futures both tolerable for a population which has achieved a zero population growth state and which has come to terms with the need to maintain an equilibrium between the use of energy and critical materials and the creation and restoration of the same.

The proper utilisation of human resources and the education and development of human beings will be essential for both alternatives. The success of the society will depend on the efficiency with which energy, capital and labour are used.

The alternative energy futures have been described recently in a major paper by Amory B. Lovins, a British physicist, and author of the book *World Energy Strategies: Facts, Issues, and Options.* Lovins describes two very different policies and programmes for meeting the world's energy needs over the next fifty years. They are:

A. *Energy from continuing replaceable sources.* This means energy from the sun, which consists of direct solar radiation, wind, tides, hydro-electric power, ocean thermal gradients, and which, through photosynthesis, produces the annual plant growth on the earth, called bio-mass. Major attention will be given to more efficient use of energy in the USA.

B. *Energy from non-replaceable sources.* From fossil fuels: coal, petroleum, natural gas; atomic energy, from atomic fission or nuclear fusion. Though the transformation of matter into energy in nuclear reactors does use up a certain amount of matter, the actual mass of matter turned into energy is small, and does not threaten the existence of the earth. But there are other dangers to human life and human society which must be considered.

At present the more or less official American policy is B — using fossil fuels, especially coal, increasingly for a couple of decades, while enormously expanding the atomic power industry at a very high cost in capital investment. By the year 2025, more than half the energy needs of the USA would be met by nuclear power plants. There would be a major problem of safe storage of poisonous radioactive waste materials which will be dangerous for thousands of years, and nuclear energy technology would be shared with many other countries, all of which would obtain the means of waging atomic warfare.

However, there is a growing public pressure for alternative A — turning to energy from continuing replaceable sources, mainly the sun.

This policy would be tied to a programme of more efficient use of energy in the United States, which now uses its energy resources only two thirds as efficiently as do the Western European nations, with their more efficient passenger and freight transportation systems. Lovins cites energy-use research studies which show that the USA can double the efficiency of its use of energy by the year 2000, and by the year 2040 can reduce the per capita use or consumption of primary energy to one third of today's performance. This would require no reduction of physical comfort by Americans, but they would use more efficient automobile engines, more bus service, more railroad passenger service, and more efficient heating methods for homes and commercial buildings.

By the year 2025, the USA would be using almost completely energy from replaceable sources – the sun. And the USA would be using less energy than it does today, though it would have a population approaching 300 million.

The European situation will move in the same direction, but with differences due to the facts that:

1. Europe uses energy more efficiently than does the USA.
2. Europe has less potential solar energy than the USA, because the climates are different, and there are no large sunny desert areas in Europe; but European countries might get access to solar energy from the Sahara Desert.
3. The B alternative, with heavy reliance on nuclear energy, may be adopted more fully in Europe than in the USA.

Effects on the Elderly Population

The two futures will differ most, from the point of view of the elderly, in the use the society makes of them as workers, and in the access they have to jobs and earned income. The A alternative will cause more employment of workers, with minimised expenditure of mechanical energy. The B alternative will present an energy intensive technology, with much capital invested in labour-saving machinery. Both alternatives will produce enough goods and services to raise the material standard of living above the present average level; but the B alternative will give people more leisure than the A energy alternative. It appears likely that the A alternative will produce a high degree of ego-involvement and of work-satisfaction on the part of the workers, with more attention to skilful use of tools and on easy human relations at the work-place. The B alternative will use more mass production and assembly line methods, with a somewhat higher average per capita income than will be true of alternative A.

Material Standard of Living. A major increase of costs of energy and certain scarce critical materials will tend to lower the material standard of living. People will probably respond by working more years or longer hours to increase the production of goods and services, and thus to maintain the present standard of living. Therefore it appears likely that elderly people will be encouraged to stay in the labour force as long as they are reasonably productive. One may even imagine that the notion of mandatory retirement at a fixed age will be forgotten, and the average age of retirement may go up to about age seventy. There may be a considerable development of part-time employment.

This would suggest that there will be more emphasis on research with the aim of fitting work assignments to persons with the skills and strength appropriate to these jobs. The work of Leon Koyl in matching persons and jobs after the age of fifty is likely to be developed, as well as the work on the training of older workers for new jobs, done in England by Belbin.

Personal Income: Earnings and Retirement Income. With a longer work life and therefore a shorter period of retirement, the social security programme and private pension programmes will be substantially modified, with lower social security tax and smaller pension trust funds. The goal of a 60 to 70 per cent replacement income after retirement will be easier to achieve, since the average duration of the period of retirement will be decreased by five to ten years.

Housing. The living quarters of people need energy for heat, for air conditioning, for lighting and cooking. The most of these facilities will rise, possibly enough to cause home builders to seek greater efficiency in the supply and use of energy. This will apply to all age groups, but especially to elderly couples and singles, whose space needs are not great. It is likely that multiple-unit housing will be designed for economic use of energy, and also for the collection and use of solar energy. Similar action will probably take place in the construction of subsidised public housing for low-income elderly.

Residential Arrangements for the Elderly. An interesting and possibly important response to rising costs of energy and of food (farming uses 14 per cent of the energy consumed in the USA) may be the creation of colonies of middle-class and upper-working-class elderly couples on the outskirts of big cities, with gardens, orchards and small dairies. People aged sixty to seventy five may be interested in living in such areas, where they might produce up to half of the food they need through a kind of producer-consumer co-operative. They could freeze vegetables and store fruit and root vegetables for year round use. Some could keep a few milk cows, and some might like to produce butter and cheese for their own consumption. Working two to four hours a day would keep them happily occupied. Bus services to the commercial and theatre centres, and to libraries and churches would keep them in touch with younger family members and old friends.

Less interesting but equally necessary will be a systematic programme designed to help older people who are living alone in the inner city, in small apartments and single rooms in low-cost residential hotels.

Civic-Political Action. We have noted earlier that there is no national political movement of the elderly, and neither political party appears to have the allegiance of a majority of older voters. However, older people exert influence on government in connection with specific government actions: such as linking social security benefits to the purchasing power of the dollar, and providing federal and state government support for state and local programmes for the elderly.

It seems probable that this kind of united action by older people will become more evident and more decisive as the cost of energy rises and as human labour is more in demand. For example, after 1980, when the current American crisis of unemployed youth has somewhat abated due to the decreasing numbers in the 15-25 age group, it is probable that senior citizens through such organisations as the AARP, NCSC and the Grey Panthers will push to amend the Age Discrimination in Employment Act so as to raise the age level covered by the Act up to seventy from the present sixty five. Thus the economic position of the elderly will become more and more a conscious concern of older poeple in their political and educational activity.[4]

Notes

1.   Ernest W. Burgess (ed.) *Aging in Western Societies,* pp. 17, 19.
2.   B.R. Bild and R.J. Havighurst, 'Senior citizens in Great Cities. The Case of

Chicago', p.8.
3.   Organisation for Economic Co-operation and Development: Manpower and Social Affairs Committee, 'Policy on Flexible Retirement', Paris, 1971.
4.   The introduction of a Bill in the US Congress in the autumn of 1977 has already moved in this direction.

Bibliography

B.R. Bild and R.J. Havighurst, 'Senior Citizens in Great Cities: The Case of Chicago'. *The Gerontologist*, vol. 16, no. 1, Part 2, February 1976

G.W. Burgess (ed.), *Aging in Western Societies: A Comparative Survey* (University of Chicago Press, Chicago, 1960)

J.C. Corman, 'Health Services for the Elderly', pp. 81-7 in *Social Policy, Social Ethics and the Aging Society,* ed. by B.L. Neugarten and R.J. Havighurst. (US Govt. Printing Office, Washington, D.C. 1976)

R.J. Havighurst (ed.), 'Research Designs and Proposals in Applied Social Gerontology: Flexible Careers; Perceptions of Aging', *The Gerontologist,* vol. 11, no. 4, Part II, Winter 1971.

R.J. Havighurst and A. De Vries, 'Life-Styles and Free-Time Activities of Retired Men', *Human Development,* 12:34-54, 1969

D. Jacobson, 'Planning for retirement and anticipatory attitudes towards withdrawal from work', *British Journal of Guidance and Counselling,* 2, 72-83, 1974

L.F. Koyl and P.M. Hansen, *Age, Physical Ability, and Work Potential* National Council on the Aging, Washington, D.C., 1969)

A.B. Lovins, 'Energy Strategy: The Road Not Taken?', *Foreign Affairs* 55: 65-96, October 1976

National Council on the Aging, *The Myth and Reality of Aging in America* (Harris Poll, Washington, D.C., 1975)

B.L. Neugarten (ed.), 'Ageing in the Year 2000: A Look at the Future', *The Gerontologist,* vol. 15, no. 1, Part 2, February 1975

E. Shanas, P. Townsend, D. Wedderburn, H. Friis, P. Milhoj, and J. Stehouwer, *Old People in Three Industrial Societies* (Atherton Press, New York, 1968)

2 AGEING IN EASTERN SOCIETY

Daisaku Maeda

A Japanese old person now in his seventies has lived through one of
the stormiest periods in his country's long history. When he was born,
Japan was only one of the underdeveloped countries of Asia. At that
time, Japanese people lived mainly on the agricultural and fishing
industries. As a nation, Japan was following the policy of centralisation
of power and strengthening of the military forces to catch up with
the advanced countries of the western world.

When he was in his twenties the old person of today experienced
the Great Depression, with both economic and psychological suffering.
Then came the war against China, and later the Second World War with
loss of friends and relatives. In the course of these long years, Japan
advanced gradually toward an ultranationalistic and totalitarian
society. This greatly influenced the way of thinking of Japanese old
people of today.

Then came defeat, and a totally opposite national policy was
established having marked features of a democracy with its emphasis
on decentralisation, liberalism and internationalism. Thus, it can be
said that a typical old person of today experienced a political and
cultural revolution in his middle to late forties.

During his life time, the Japanese economy made great progress.
Though it suffered seriously in the Great Depression, and later had
a fatal blow from the Second World War, between 1900 and 1970
Japanese manufacturing industry expanded 150 times, while during
the same period, that of the USA expanded 14 times, Italy 17 times,
Germany 9 times and France 6 times.[1] The change has been
especially conspicuous since 1955. During the fifteen years between
1955 and 1970, Japan's industrial production expanded 6.7 times.

Industrialisation inevitably brings about urbanisation. Thus the
speed of urbanisation has also been very fast in these twenty-five
years. This is illustrated in the rapid growth of the population in the
six large metropolitan areas of the country. Between 1950 and 1969
the proportion of the population of these areas increased from 13.5
per cent to 18.4 per cent.[2] If the decrease in the proportion of the
labour force engaged in the primary industries (though this is an

45

indirect variable) is taken into consideration, the change becomes even more significant.[3] In 1950, five years after the end of the Second World War, as much as 48 per cent of the labour force was engaged in the primary industries, but its proportion decreased to only 13 per cent by 1974.[4] These two factors, combining rapid industrialisation and urbanisation, caused a drastic social change in the life of the Japanese people; sometimes referred to as the 'westernisation of life'; it deeply affected both the social and economic life of the people of all classes in both rural and urban communities.

Thus, Japanese old people of today have lived under two completely different sets of national goals and ideologies. They have also been through very rapid changes in standards of living with the shift from an agricultural to an industrialised country. This unique experience that older persons have had should always be kept in mind when studying the problems of ageing in Japanese society.

Characteristics of the Problems of Ageing in Japan

Once the author of this chapter told a western social gerontologist that three out of four old people live with their children in Japan. She reacted by asking 'Why do you have to study our social services for the elderly then? You don't need them!' This seems to be a typical example of excess simplification a foreigner sometimes tends to make about other countries. An American anthropologist once rightly wrote, 'Ageing in Japan, as elsewhere, is a matter for deep human ambivalence.'[5] In fact, because of the very fast and drastic social changes, two contradictory factors coexist in the many aspects related to ageing in Japan. For example, while respect for the aged is still regarded as one of the essential virtues, social services for the aged, which are indispensable for their well-being, are much less developed compared with those in the advanced countries of the western world. To give another example, while there are many older persons sometimes over eighty years old at the head of large firms, the compulsory retirement age of most large firms is very low (55-57). In the same way, while the psychological tendency of INKYO still remains with its literal translation 'living in hiding in one's old age' (Having delivered the responsibility of daily-life and living a quiet and peaceful life); there are many very old politicians who never think of retirement. Thus it is very difficult to give a clear picture of ageing in Japanese society. In this aspect as in many others, it can be regarded as a society of contradiction.

Definition of Old Age

Japanese people used to define old age to mean people of sixty years of age and over, as in most of the societies under the influence of Chinese culture. In ancient China the calendar year was named with the combination of two sets of Chinese characters — one consisted of twelve characters and the other five characters. Therefore, on becoming sixty-one years old, the name of that year was the same as that of the year of birth. For this reason the sixty-first year after birth is called KANREKI (return of the calendar) and it used to have a special meaning in life. This custom is also observed in some of the Southeast Asian countries.[6]

KANREKI was often regarded as the beginning of second childhood. In Japan many people used to hold a passing rite to mark KANREKI. At the time of the ceremony of KANREKI, the person becoming sixty-one was presented by their children and relatives with a red vest designed to signify the coming of second childhood. Thus, in Japan people over sixty years of age and over were permitted to be dependent on others — mainly their adult sons. Generally speaking, people of sixty years of age and over were not obliged to work to earn money. In other words, KANREKI signified the social sanction permitting entry into INKYO — retired life, if this was desired. In reality, however, most Japanese old people continued to work, either for money or for the sake of the satisfaction in continuing to have a meaningful role in life.

But now the concept of old age is changing greatly. According to recent nation-wide research, three our of four middle-aged persons between thirty and forty-five think that 'old people' describes those aged sixty-five and over (there is no significant difference between men and women, or among the age categories).[7] Moreover, about 40 per cent of the interviewees answered that 'old people' meant those aged seventy and over. In common with most gerontologists in western countries, Japanese gerontologists also tend to use the age of sixty-five as a dividing line between middle age and old age, the main reason being that the proportion of the population aged sixty-five and over seems to be appropriate for considering social programmes for them. But in many actual programmes persons aged sixty and over are generally treated as old people. In fact, the pensionable age of the largest public pension programme, called KOSEINENKIN-HOKEN (Welfare Pension Insurance Programme) is sixty for men and fifty-five for women, five years younger than the average pensionable age of western countries.

Demographic Aspects

At the present time the total population of Japan is about 111.9 million (1975 national census). The number of old people aged 65 and over is 8.9 million, which constitutes 7.9 per cent of the total population. Although this percentage is the highest among the countries of Asia, it is the lowest among the industrialised countries of Europe and North America.

Table 1 indicates the age structure of Japan's population was quite stable from the beginning of the twentieth century to the mid century. This is because the very high birthrate (promoted by national policy) offset the gradual increase of the aged population resulting from the advancement of medicine and public health and the general improvement of the standard of living. Since 1950, five years after the end of the Second World War, the birthrate has decreased very sharply as it is shown in Table 2. Now Japan belongs to the second lowest birthrate group in the world (Table 3). This low birthrate, combined with the extension of life expectancy of old people (Table 4) which necessarily increased its number, especially that of *very old*, old people (Table 5) brought about a sharp increase in

Table 1: Population of the Aged — Past, Present and Future

Year	Total population (thousand)	65+ number (thousand)	65+ %
1920	55,391	2,917	5.3
1935	68,662	3,189	4.6
1950	83,200	4,109	4.9
1955	89,276	4,747	5.3
1960	93,419	5,350	5.7
1965	98,275	6,181	6.3
1970	104,665	7,393	7.1
1975	111,934	8,858	7.9
1980	118,012	10,327	8.8
1995	131,427	16,276	12.4
2005	138,397	20,757	15.0
2015	141,760	25,091	17.7
2025	142,963	24,853	17.4

Source: 1920–1975: National Censuses; 1980–2025: National Institute of Population Problems.

Table 2: Decrease of Birthrate in Japan

1935	31.6
1950	28.2
1955	19.5
1960	17.3
1965	18.7
1970	18.8
1974	18.6

Source: Health and Welfare Statistics Association.[8]

Table 3: International Comparison of Birthrate 1973

Japan (1974)	18.6
Hungary	15.0
Sweden	13.5
Finland	12.2
France	16.4
Great Britain	13.8
W. Germany	10.2
Italy	16.0
USA	15.0
USSR	17.7

Source: Health and Welfare Statistics Association.[9]

Table 4 (a): Extension of Life Expectancy at Age Sixty-Five

	Male	Female
1965	11.86	14.59
1974	13.38	16.18

Source: Ministry of Health and Welfare of Japan.

Table 4 (b): Life Expectancy at Age Sixty-Five: International
Comparison

		Male	Female
Japan	1974	13.38	16.18
Norway	1966-70	13.86	16.55
Sweden	1972	14.04	16.95
France	1971	13.0	16.8
Denmark	1970-71	13.7	16.7
USA	1972	13.1	17.2
Great Britain	1970-72	12.1	16.0
USSR (at age 60)	1970-71	18	

Source: 1973 UN *Demographic Yearbook*, and the Ministry of Health and
Welfare of Japan.

Table 5: Increase of Very Old People (unit: thousand)

Age	1950		1970	
60 – 69 (index)	4,075	(100)	6,718	(165)
70 – 79 (index)	1,967	(100)	3,381	(172)
80 +	371	(100)	949	(256)

Source: Ministry of Health and Welfare of Japan (the indexes were calculated
by the author).

the proportion of the aged population. This tendency of sharp increase
is expected to continue until the beginning of the next century (as was
shown in Table 1), when the proportion of the aged of Japan will
become one of the highest in the world.

The increase of the aged population itself lays a heavy burden on
society. In the case of Japan, the very fast rate of the increase makes
the situation much more difficult. Table 6 shows an international
comparison in the length of time which some western countries took to
increase the proportion of their aged population from 5 per cent to
12 per cent. The fastest rate ever recorded was that of Great Britain,
which took fifty-five years. On the other hand, France increased her

Table 6: International Comparison of the Speed of the Ageing of
Population

	Year when population 65 + was 5% and 12%		Length of time from 5% to 12%
	5%	12%	
Japan	1950	1995	45
France	1790	1960	170
West Germany	1890	1965	75
Sweden	1855	1960	105
Great Britain	1905	1965	55

Source: Ministry of Health and Welfare.[10]

aged population very gradually. Japan is expected to make the same
increase only within forty-five years, ten years less than Great Britain.

It is predicted that the Japanese tradition of family care for aged
parents cannot avoid a considerable degree of weakening if it is not
to be totally lost. Accordingly, in the near future Japan will be
confronted with two difficult problems at the same time. One is
the very fast increase in the number of old people, especially those
very old and needing special care: the other is weakened family
support and care. This means that Japan must make every effort to
achieve a fast expansion of public support and care services for its
rapidly increasing very old population.

Another important implication of the changing population
composition is the prospect of ageing in the labour force. According
to T. Kuroda, the age composition of the labour force will be changed
significantly in twenty-five years.[11] While the age group between
15 to 29 will grow by only 6 per cent and the age group between
30 to 44 will even decrease by 4 per cent, the age group between 45
to 59 will grow as much as by 54 per cent. This change will greatly
influence the future social and economic conditions of Japanese
society. For example, while an increasing number of younger workers
will be needed for growing manufacturing industries which are vital
to support a rapidly increasing older population, the number of such
workers will increase very slightly. On the other hand more people
will be needed to engage in the personal care services for expanding
numbers of very old people and other physically dependent persons.

Generally speaking, in other parts of Asia, ageing of the population has hardly started yet. This is mainly due to the birthrate which remains high and offsets the increase of the older population. The very fast ageing of Japan's population was a result of the sudden decrease in the birthrate in the 1950s.

A well-developed fundamental education enabled Japan to succeed in persuading people of the need for birth control within a very short period. In other countries of Asia, however, in spite of the tremendous efforts of the national governments, the decrease in the birthrate is much slower compared with that of Japan. This, of course, aggravates the problems of population expansion, but as a result of this slow decrease in the birthrate, these countries will not have to face the problems of an ageing population until much later than Japan. It should be noted, however, in other parts of Asia, too, the life expectancy of old people has already become much longer, though not so significantly as in industrialised countries. This means that these developing countries will also have to adopt some social measures for their increasing numbers of older persons. Although recognition has been slow, it is now possible to see growing concern about this problem.

Another important demographic factor of an ageing population lies in its geographical distribution. The proportion of the aged population is much greater in rural areas than in the large metropolitan areas. This is mainly due to the enormous migration of the younger population from the rural areas to the industrialised areas For example, in 1975, the proportions of old people aged sixty-five and over in Tokyo and Osaka, the two largest metropolitan areas of Japan, were 6.2 per cent and 5.9 per cent respectively. On the other hand, there were several rural prefectures where the proportion of old people aged sixty-five and over already exceeded 11 per cent. It is predicted that this discrepancy will continue to exist or even to grow in the future.[12] It is feared that it may make the development of services for the rural aged very difficult, because many more old people will be scattered over wide areas where the population of younger people who can work in the services for the aged will be limited.

Work and Retirement

Very Early Mandatory Retirement Age

One of the major problems related to ageing in Japanese society is the very early fixed mandatory retirement age applied in most large firms. As is shown in Table 7 over two-thirds of enterprises having more than thirty employees adopt a fixed mandatory retirement age, even though people argue that a fixed mandatory retirement age should be abolished because it is illogical and inhumane in the process of ageing which is quite different in each individual.

Table 7: Proportion of Enterprises Practising Fixed Mandatory Retirement Age

Size of enterprise (number of employees)	% of enterprises having fixed mandatory retirement age system 1973
Total	66.6
5,000 +	100.0
1,000 – 4,999	99.0
300 – 999	94.3
100 – 299	90.4
30 – 99	55.0

Source: Ministry of Labour.[13]

Table 8: Age of Fixed Mandatory Retirement (%)

Size of enterprise (No. of employees)	– 54	55	56 – 59	60 +
Total	0.3	52.0	12.3	35.4
5,000 +	–	38.0	51.0	11.0
1,000 – 4,999	–	42.7	37.4	19.9
300 – 999	–	49.5	27.7	22.8
100 – 299	0.2	53.6	16.7	29.5
30 – 99	0.3	52.3	6.4	41.0

Source: Ministry of Labour.[14]

In Japan the problem is aggravated because its fixed mandatory retirement age is very low as shown in Table 8. In over 70 per cent of enterprises having such a system, the age is between 55 and 59.

According to the same government survey, it is clear that among those whose fixed retirement age is sixty and over, more than nine-tenths set the age at sixty years old.[15] Most government employees retire before or at the age of sixty, although there are neither legislation nor orders on a mandatory retirement age. In most cases they are merely told by their supervisors on an informal basis that they had better retire soon.

For the majority of Japanese people, the fixed retirement age of 55 to 59 is premature, because, generally speaking, their children have not yet finished high school or college. Japanese men usually get married in their late twenties. Therefore, their last child may be born when they are around thirty-five or later. Thus, if they are forced to retire at the age of fifty-five, their last child will still be in high school or in college, and college education is generally expected for middle-class children. Even with retirement at sixty, the last child will just have started work and can hardly be independent from the parents. (Wages of young persons are rather low in Japan compared with other industrialised countries.)

In 1975, one year after the survey quoted above was carried out, 69 per cent of the total labour force was employed by someone. Among these employed persons, roughly 7 out of 10 persons were working in enterprises having more than thirty employees – exactly corresponding data are not available. As enterprises with less than twenty-nine employees sometimes have a fixed mandatory retirement age, it can safely be said that more than half of the total labour force of Japan is under a very early fixed mandatory retirement age.

As already stated in the early part of this chapter, Japan's public pension has not yet matured and the pensionable age is sixty for men and fifty-five for women except for the pensions of government employees. As a result, the majority will try to find another job when they first retire. With a few exceptions (very high government officials and senior executives), jobs after first retirement offer a much smaller income, with lower social status. In addition, they are often unstable and/or irregular. Thus, in spite of the early fixed mandatory retirement age, 81 per cent of old people aged between sixty and sixty-four are working (Table 9). The labour force partici- pation of old people over sixty-five is also much higher in comparison to other industrialised nations (Table 9).

The major cause of the higher labour force participation of Japanese old people seems to be lack of income. But it should be noted that most of them are willing to work in their later life. Table

Table 9: International Comparison of Labour Force: Participation of Men

	60 – 64	65 and over	
France (1968)	65.7	19.3	pensionable age is 60
Italy (1971)	40.6	13.4	"
Canada (1961)	75.8	28.5	pensionable age is 65
The Netherlands (1971)	74.8	13.1	"
Sweden (1970)	75.7	15.2	"
Great Britain (1971)	80.7	15.8	"
USA (1970)	73.0	24.8	"
W. Germany (1973)	67.1	15.1	"
Japan (1973)	81.0	46.7	

Source: Office of the Prime Minister.[16]

Table 10: Opinions about Work in Later Life (in percentages)

	40 – 49	50 – 54	55 – 59	60 – 64	65 – 69	70 +
Want to continue the job of younger days as long as they can	44	43	45	44	43	36
Want to enjoy a job suitable to old age after certain age	28	24	22	16	13	12
Want to enjoy retirement life after certain age	21	24	23	28	28	31
Others, don't know	7	10	9	12	16	21

Source: Office of the Prime Minister.[17]

10 clearly shows the work-orientated attitude of Japanese old people. That is, more than 40 per cent of old people aged between sixty to sixty-nine answered that they wanted to continue in the job they had

been engaged in from their younger days for as long as they could.
It should be noted that the percentage of middle-aged persons who
answered likewise was about the same as that of older persons. This
suggests that the labout force participation of older persons will not
decrease for twenty years to come, if other conditions are held
constant.

Table 11: Older Persons Engaged in the Primary Industries and
Working as Self-employed (%)

Age	Primary industries		Self-employed	
	Men	Women	Men	Women
45 – 54	14.7	25.7	28.8	19.4
			(0.8)*	(30.7)*
55 – 64	20.8	32.5	39.8	24.3
			(1.5)*	(37.8)*
65 –	33.3	40.0	50.3	29.3
			(7.9)*	(45.3)*

* The percentage of those who are working as family member of the self-
employed.
Source: Office of the Prime Minister.[18]

Another factor which influences the labour force participation of
older persons is the availability of jobs which are acceptable and
suitable. According to a 1974 Labour Force Survey, older persons
tend to be engaged in the primary industries or to be self-employed.
(Table 11). In the case of older women, nearly one half work as a
family member of the self-employed. However, these figures do not
necessarily mean that older people change their jobs, move into the
primary industries and become self-employed. According to the
national census of 1955, 41 per cent of the total labour force was
engaged in agriculture or the fishing industry. It is reasonable to
assume that most of those who were engaged in these industries have
continued in their jobs until the present time. This may well be the
reason why more old people are engaged in the primary industries
now.

What, then, will be the labour force participation of old people in
the future, when the primary industries have further declined and when

all old people have adequate incomes from public pensions? Most Japanese social gerontologists accept that the labour force participation will be decreased to a considerable degree.

Living Arrangements

One of the most conspicuous differences between the life of old people in western countries and Japan can be seen in their living arrangements. Table 12 clearly shows this difference. While four out of five old people live with their children in Japan only less than one third or even one fourth of them live with their children in western countries.

Table 12: Comparison of Living Arrangements in Western Societies and Japan

	Denmark 65 + (1965)	USA 65 + (1965)	Great Britain 65 + (1965)	Japan 60 + (1969)	Japan 60 + (1973)
Old people living with a child	18%	25%	33%	79.2%	74.2%
(married child)	(4%)	(8%)	(12%)	(61.0%)	
(unmarried child)	(14%)	(17%)	(21%)	(18.2%)	
Old people living with other relatives	3%	7%	8%	0.5%	
Old couples living alone	45%	43%	33%	13.1%	
Old individuals living alone	28%	22%	22%	5.2%	
Others	6%	3%	4%	2.0%	

Sources: Shanas *et al.*;[19] Office of the Prime Minister (1969);[20] Ministry of Health and Welfare (1973).[21]

The difference is especially startling when comparing the number of persons living with married children. It should be noted, however, that in western countries about a half of those living separately from their children live geographically very close to them.[22] If this type of living arrangement is taken into consideration, the difference becomes significantly smaller, although there still remains a considerable gap. It should be understood that two generations living together

in Japan in the same house very often have two economically
independent households. Moreover, the number of older persons
living close to their children in the same community seems to have
increased in recent years.

What are some of the factors that may be influencing the living
arrangements of older people? A hypothesis can be readily constructed
that Japanese old people live with their children because of the housing
shortage. It is certainly true that in large metropolitan areas there is
still a serious shortage of houses. However, more careful examination
discloses the fact that the proportion of old people living separately
is significantly larger in metropolitan areas than in smaller cities
and rural areas (Table 13). In other words, older people live together
with their children even in the localities where there are less housing
problems. The greater percentage of those living separately in large
cities probably results from the limited size of available homes. In
fact, 17 per cent of old people living separately in large metropolitan
areas said that their reason for living separately was the limited size
of their houses, while only 8 per cent of old people in smaller cities
and 5 per cent of old people of rural areas answered likewise.[23]

Table 13: Percentage of OP 60 + Living Together and Living
    Separately

	Together	Separately	Unknown
Large cities	67.7%	32.0%	0.3%
Small cities	70.6%	29.0%	0.4%
Rural areas	77.6%	21.9%	0.5%
Total	72.8%	26.8%	0.4%

Source: Ministry of Health and Welfare.[24]

Another possible hypothesis is that Japanese old people live with
their children because many jobs are available for the younger generation in the areas where their parents live. Recent social research showed
that the number of old people living with their children is somewhat
smaller in a medium-sized city where the opportunities for young
people to find attractive jobs are rather limited.[25] However, the above
figures are not high enough to explain fully the startling differences
in living arrangements between Japan and western countries. There

are also a number of other factors which seem to be statistically significant in influencing the living arrangements of old people. But none of them can provide a definitive explanation of the difference. In other words, the very high proportion of old people living with their children seems to be due to the unique attitude of Japanese people, both young and old, towards the living arrangements of older persons.

Generally speaking, Japanese culture expects the eldest son to live with his parents, to support them and to take care of them. If older persons and their children live separately, the situation is very often interpreted by others as though the parents are disliked by their children or there is something wrong on the part of the children. To the average older parents, living separately from their children will bring shame upon them. On the other hand, in western societies, most older parents want to live spearately and independently for as long as their health permits. In other words, independence, which is one of the most highly esteemed virtues of western societies, is not necessarily regarded so in Japanese society. It might not be too much to say that Japanese older persons are not only allowed but are also expected to be dependent on their adult children, rather than to be too independent or stubborn. In fact a very popular proverb runs, 'When old, obey your children'.

This attitude is clearly shown by a recent nation-wide survey (Table 14). Namely, 70 per cent of old people aged 60-69 think that 'it is natural to live together' or 'it is better to live together, if possible'. The percentage of middle-aged persons who answered in the same way is only slightly smaller than for older persons. According to similar research amongst younger generations, 46 per cent of those aged 30-34 answered that even if married one child should live with parents if possible. In addition, 21 per cent answered that married children may live separately from parents, if the two generations can visit each other very often.[26]

What emerged from the analysis of recent research results is that younger generations still hold a sense of strong filial duty to satisfy the parental expectation to live together or very close to each other, and to take care of them. The research results amongst younger generations show that, if other conditions are held constant, even twenty years from now, the proportion of older persons living with their children will not change very significantly. It will still be more than six out of ten as shown in Table 14.

In this connection, the Special Committee for the Study of the

Table 14: Opinions about Living Arrangements in Later Years (%)

Age	40 − 49	50 − 54	55 − 59	60 − 64	65 − 69	70 +
Opinions						
It is natural to live together	42	43	46	49	51	61
It is better to live together, if possible	22	23	20	21	19	17
While parents are healthy, it is better to live separately, but when they become weak, it is better to live together	23	23	24	18	18	12
It is better to live separately, if possible	7	6	5	6	6	4
Other opinions, or don't know	6	6	5	5	6	5

Source: Office of the Prime Minister.[27]

Future of Family Support and the Care of Aged Parents appointed by the Director of the Office of the Prime Minister predicted, applying three types of scientific method, that the number of old people living with their children will not decrease significantly at least for a decade to come, and the percentage in 1985 will be 70 per cent, only a 4 per cent decrease from that of 1973.[28]

Another interesting fact about the family life of Japanese old people is that unlike western societies, most of them live with their son, especially the eldest son, whenever possible. This is one of the characteristics of Japanese and Korean families. In most parts of China, also, old parents usually live with their son, but not necessarily the eldest son.[29] In other parts of the East and Southeast Asia, the custom is different from that of the Far East. For instance in Thailand, as in many western societies, most of the old parents live with their daughters, especially with the youngest one.[30] Thus, in Japan, one of the most serious family problems old people have to face is the conflict between an old mother and her daughter-in-law, instead of the son-in-law problem in western societies.

Institutional services are provided for those who cannot live with
their families for various reasons. There are homes for the aged,
nursing homes and others. At present, only 1.3 per cent of old
people aged sixty-five and over live in these homes. The proportion of
institutionalised old people is very small compared with that of western
countries.

The Economic Life of Old People

It is a difficult task to give a clear-cut picture of the economic life
of Japanese old people. This is mainly die to the fact that the
overwhelming majority of Japanese old people live with their adult
children and are partly dependent on them economically. So, in most
cases, it is impossible to separate the household of old people from
that of their children. The money the child earns is more or less shared
with his retired parents. Therefore, first of all we should examine
the economic life of households whose heads are aged sixty-five and
over (in the case of women, aged sixty and over) and all the other
members are younger than twenty. According to research done by
the Ministry of Health and Welfare[31] (Table 15), 80 per cent of
these households belong to the lowest quartile group in the distribution of income. According to research in the United States,[32] roughly
speaking three-fourths of the families whose head is aged sixty-five
and over belonged to the lower half group in the distribution of
income (1960), while in Japan nearly nine-tenths of such families
belonged to the lower half group (1973).

Table 15: Income Distribution of Households whose Head is Aged
Sixty-Five and Over (in the Case of Women, 60 +)

Yearly income quartile groups	Total households	Households whose head is aged 65 and over	Ordinary households
1st quartile group (lowest)	25.0	79.6	21.5
2nd quartile group (lower-middle)	25.0	7.9	26.0
3rd quartile group (higher-middle)	25.0	5.4	26.3
4th quartile group (highest)	25.0	7.1	26.2

Source: Ministry of Health and Welfare.

The difference between Japan and the United States seems to stem mainly from the fact that Japanese public pension programmes have not yet matured and that the number of old people who are receiving a substantial pension is very limited. According to recent research,[33] the proportion of old people aged sixty and over and receiving the benefit of the public contributory old age pension was only 22 per cent. Even if those older persons who are receiving non-contributory old age pensions and special war pensions are taken into account, the total percentage is 61 per cent. In other words, more than one third of the old people aged sixty and over are not covered by any public pension programme. Therefore, the numbers of old people who can live an economically independent life are very small in comparison with western industrialised countries.

Table 16: Middle-Aged People and Old People Who Can Live an Economically Independent Life in their Later Years (%)

	Total	Yes	No	Don't Know
Total	100	38	50	12
50 – 54	100	48	37	15
55 – 59	100	45	42	13
60 – 64	100	37	51	12
65 – 69	100	31	57	12
70 +	100	25	67	8
Sub-total of 60 +	100	31	58	11

Source: Office of the Prime Minister.[34]

As is shown in Table 16, only 31 per cent of the old people aged sixty and over answered that they can live an economically independent life. Of this group, 59 per cent have a sizeable earned income; 35 per cent have such amount of pension; and 27 per cent have such amount of income from their property. On the other hand, 57 per cent answered that they could not be independent economically. Among them, 90 per cent said that they had to be dependent on their children and/or relatives, and 17 per cent said that they had to be dependent on public measures.

How do middle-aged people predict the possibility of living an economically independent life? According to the nation-wide research

cited before (Table 16), nearly half of the people aged 50-59 answered
that they would be able to live on their own income in later life.
But it seems that this figure includes some wishful thinking. According
to the same research 59 per cent of the people who answered 'yes'
expected that they would earn money from work. But, ten years from
now, when industrialisation will have advanced much more, it is difficult
to visualise so many persons aged sixty and over having any sizeable
income from work. It is true, however, that at the present time even
in urban areas 60 per cent of old men (16 per cent of old women)
aged sixty-five and over are earning at least some money from work.[35]

Another important source of income for elderly people in Japan
is financial assistance from their children. According to a recent
nationwide survey,[36] 45 per cent of old people who have living
children (both living with and separately from them), are receiving
financial assistance from them. Even in the case of the elderly living
separately from their children 27 per cent are receiving some financial
assistance. Among the persons receiving financial assistance from their
children (100%), 59 per cent are receiving a substantial amount; 19
per cent are receiving some part of their living expenses, and the
remaining 21 per cent are receiving just pocket money. Then why are
some not receiving financial assistance? Seventy-six per cent of them
said that they did not need it; 16 per cent said their children could
not afford it; and 2 per cent said that their children did not have a
mind to do so. The same survey disclosed that about one-tenth
of old people (aged 60-74) having living children were helping them
financially either in cash or in the form of lending a house without
charge.

In short, it is true that most of Japanese old people cannot live
on their own income. In this sense they are poor, but because most
of the old people are receiving financial support from their children,
their actual life is not so miserable as is sometimes imagined by the
people of other countries. But it is also true that many old people
who have no children to rely on cannot help being dependent on
public assistance. In 1973, the percentage of old people aged sixty-
five and over who are members of families receiving public assistance
was 3.7 per cent, while the percentage of public assistance recipients
in the total Japanese population was only 1.2 per cent. The economic
distress of these old people can be seen more clearly through study
of the public assistance statistics of aged households. In 1974, 15 per
cent of aged households throughout Japan were receiving public
assistance, although in 1960 the percentage was as high as 25, much

higher than at present. Incidentally, the proportion of aged households in all the families receiving public assistance has been gradually increasing from 22 per cent in 1965 to 35 per cent in 1974. Now, in Japan the second most important cause of falling into poverty after illness and/or disability is old age.[37]

Daily Life of Retired Persons

Use of Time by the Elderly

In this section, the author will deal with the people over seventy years old. This is because in Japan many persons, especially men, are still working in their sixties (see Table 17).

Table 17: Hours Spent Daily on Various Activities by Japanese Old People

	Weekday			Sunday		
	Men 60 – 69	Women 60 – 69	M & W 70 +	Men 60 – 69	Women 60 – 69	M & W 70 +
	h m	h m	h m	h m	h m	h m
Sleep	8.18	8.19	9.32	8.51	8.45	9.35
Meals	1.37	1.40	1.41	1.39	1.45	1.38
Personal care	0.58	0.55	0.56	0.57	0.49	0.53
Work	6.36	2.51	2.23	4.05	2.38	2.17
Travelling	0.32	0.12	0.14	0.20	0.10	0.10
Household chores	0.56	5.20	2.10	1.07	4.17	2.35
Meeting friends and neighbours	0.38	0.51	0.51	1.04	1.13	1.04
Resting	0.50	0.54	1.35	1.02	0.43	1.24
Leisure	0.32	0.18	0.32	1.12	0.32	0.48
Reading	0.37	0.17	0.25	0.37	0.09	0.26
Radio	0.26	0.12	0.18	0.29	0.12	0.15
TV	3.39	4.25	4.11	4.00	4.37	4.07
Hours at home	16.41	20.16	20.45	18.08	20.09	20.27

Source: Japan Broadcasting Corporation.

According to recent nation-wide research on hours spent daily on various activities of Japanese people (Table 17),[38] old people aged seventy and over are in bed for about 9.5 hours a day on average. Work occupies about 2.5 hours. Unlike old people between the ages of sixty to sixty-nine, there is no significant difference in the length of working hours during weekdays and on Sunday. In addition to work, they are engaged in household chores and personal care for about three hours. They usually spend about an hour and 40 minutes in eating three meals and 50 minutes a day in meeting friends, neighbours and relatives.

For the rest of their time, old people aged seventy and over engage in free activities, among which watching television and listening to the radio involve the longest periods of time. On average, about 4.5 hours are spent on these activities. Other types of leisure pursuits use about half an hour. Reading occupies a little less than half an hour. Finally they usually spend half an hour resting. It should be noted that the above description still encompasses two types of old people, the first group comprising those who are more or less engaged in their work, the second, those who have almost completely stopped working. This research does not explain anything about the difference between these two groups of old people. However, by observing the daily activities of those who have completely retired from work, it can be assumed that those retired people spend more time with television and radio than resting in comparison with those who work, and little difference is seen in the length of time spent in other activities for both groups.

No comparable data about the daily life of the elderly in western societies is available to the author. But from observation and research, the characteristics of Japanese old people seem to be as follows: first, they spend more hours on work; second, they spend more hours watching television and listening to the radio; third, they spend less hours on active leisure activities such as visiting, reading and hobbies in general. It seems that, generally speaking, Japanese old people are less active, or more socially withdrawn than those in western countries. In fact, Japanese people tend to expect the elderly to be quiet and meditative rather than bustling and active. This is also true in Korea and other societies under the influence of Chinese culture.

To add one final observation: There is an interesting recent trend in the activities of old people, associated with a growth in the number of old people's clubs and welfare centres throughout the nation. Older people participate in activities and programmes promoted by such organisations and are showing an increasing interest in taking part in volunteer services for their communities as well as in political activities to promote social policies for their welfare.[39]

Roles of the Elderly

Although Japanese old people are socially less active than their counterparts in western societies, this does not necessarily mean that they have no meaningful roles in their later life. On the contrary, most of them have at least a few meaningful roles to play in their homes, because they usually live with their children and gand-children. Even in urban areas, most Japanese old people have some roles in their homes. According to recent research of urban old people aged sixty-five and over,[40] 33 per cent of them (both sexes) still take full responsibility for housekeeping; 12 per cent have more than four roles; and 35 per cent have between three and one roles. Only 20 per cent have 'no role'. In this respect, there seems to be a great similarity between Japan and other Far East Asian societies.[41]

Firstly, many old people help in the work of their children. This is especially true when the family is engaged in self-employed work; i.e. farmers, retail dealers, small restaurants, etc. Secondly, most of the old women help in taking care of their grandchildren. Sometimes they find real life satisfaction in this role. When the grandchildren are big enough and do not need their care any more, watching them grow up then becomes an important source of life satisfaction. This attitude of Japanese old people makes a sharp contrast with that of western people. An American friend of the author once wrote when his youngest child left home that he and his wife felt quite relieved that they had finished their duty and were able to enjoy themselves with whatever they wanted to do. A typical Japanese person having a similar experience, might feel 'deserted', 'lonely', or 'vacant' rather than 'relieved'.

Leisure Activities

On average, Japanese old people seem to spend a limited amount of time on leisure activities. But this does not necessarily mean that there are few leisure activities which old people can enjoy. On the contrary, there are a number of folk-arts and hobbies which are suitable for aged persons to take up. Generally speaking, those activities are easy to begin, and as people develop their skill, they find satisfac-tion and a sense of achievement. To name some, there are: *haiku* – a very short poem of 17 syllables; *senryu* – a humorous short poem of the same style as *haiku*; *waka* – a short lyric poem of thirty-one syllables; *shodo* – calligraphy; *ikebana* – flower arrangement; *sado* – tea ceremony; *shigin* – recitation of poems; *utai, nagauta* and many other Japanese styles of classic singing; *koto, shamisen* and other

Japanese classical musical instruments; *bonsai* — growing live miniature trees in small pots; *ueki* — growing small trees in a garden; Japanese classical dancing; Japanese folk dancing; *shogi* — Japanese chess; *go* — Chinese chess; various traditional and modern handicrafts, and so on. It should be noted that many of these Japanese arts and hobbies can be enjoyed alone. This may be one of the reasons why Japanese old people are less socially active.

In spite of the availability of various arts and hobbies suitable for older people, the actual number of persons enjoying them is rather limited. According to the nation-wide research of 1969,[42] less than a half (48 per cent) of Japanese old people had some kind of hobby. Among them the most popular was *bonsai* and gardening (18 per cent), the second most popular, travelling (11 per cent), the third and the fourth, reading and *go* (4 per cent respectively). Other arts and hobbies were enjoyed by only 3 per cent or less. If society would provide old people with more chances to pursue these arts and hobbies, the life of Japanese old people could become brighter and more meaningful.

Life Attitude in Middle and Old Age

According to recent nation-wide research,[43] over 80 per cent of Japanese old people aged sixty and over feel that their life and circumstances are more or less satisfactory (Table 18). No marked differences are to be found in different age groups although the proportion of those who are fully satisfied increases with age.

According to a research project on the happiness and worries of American adults by Gurin *et al.* in 1960,[44] 27 per cent of people aged fifty-five and over were classified as feeling 'very happy' and 55 per cent as feeling 'pretty happy'. That is 82 per cent were judged as feeling more or less 'happy'. There is a striking similarity between the feelings of American older persons and of Japanese. It is very interesting to note that in a society where most old people do not have any substantial income or cannot help but continue to work, or have to be dependent on their children, over 80 per cent of the old people are more or less satisfied with their life and circumstances.

The Japanese situation with its feeling of happiness amongst older people may seem to be contradictory. It can be interpreted in a number of ways. First, it may be due to the psychological need of mature persons to accept themselves and their life situations and be happy with them. This interpretation can explain the similar percentage of happy and satisfied persons of the two completely different societies.

Table 18: Satisfaction with the Present Life and Circumstances (%)

	40 − 49	50 − 54	55 − 59	60 − 64	65 − 69	70 +
Fully satisfied	15	20	23	24	30	37
Pretty satisfied	61	57	58	58	51	46
A little bit dis- satisfied	17	16	14	11	11	10
Totally dissatisfied	4	3	2	2	3	2
Cannot answer	4	3	4	5	4	5

Source: The Office of the Prime Minister.

The second possible interpretation is that the unique living arrangements of Japanese old people offset the lack or shortage of income in old age. That is, due to the life-style of living together with their children, Japanese old people rarely feel isolated or deserted, and more often feel that their life is meaningful.

Incidentally, most Japanese old people also feel happy about their past life. According to the research referred to above,[45] over 60 per cent of Japanese old people aged sixty and over feel that their past life was 'very fruitful' or 'pretty fruitful'. Only 20 per cent or less answered that their past life was not fruitful.

How do middle-aged persons feel about their life in old age? The same research project[46] disclosed that 60 per cent or more of middle-aged persons aged between forty and fifty-nine predict that their future life would be 'bright' or 'rather bright' (Table 19). Thus, it might be said that most of the middle-aged persons in Japan are psychologically well adjusted to old age. But in the light of social policy, attention should be placed on the fact that over 10 per cent of them are afraid that their future life will be more or less bleak, and about one fourth of them have uncertainties about the prospect of old age.

Summary

The improvement of living standards and the advancement of modern medicine, with the decreased birthrate in Japan, as in the countries of the western world, resulted in a growing proportion of old people, especially the very old, both in the relative and in the absolute numbers. Mainly due to the very rapid increase of the older population, the tradition of the very early mandatory retirement age has not been

Table 19: Views About Future Life

	40 – 49	50 – 54	55 – 59	60 – 64	65 – 69	70 +
Bright	19	20	24	24	27	28
Rather bright	41	43	40	40	35	35
Cannot tell	22	20	18	17	16	15
Rather dark	8	8	9	8	9	7
Dark	4	3	4	5	6	4
Don't know	6	6	5	7	8	11

Source: Office of the Prime Minister.

changed yet. Neither has the traditional high percentage of the labour force participation of older persons changed yet. It should be noted, however, that most of the working old people are very willing to be active in this way.

One of the most conspicuous differences between the life of the old people of western countries and that of Japan can be seen in their living arrangements. As many as 75 per cent of old people live with their children in Japan. It is predicted that this percentage will not decrease very much in the near future in spite of the fact that in many social and economic aspects Japan is becoming increasingly 'westernised'.

Because of the immaturity of the public pension programmes most Japanese old people are not economically independent. They cannot avoid being dependent upon their children. Nevertheless, the majority are more or less satisfied with their present life and circumstances. Thus may be partly due to the fact that they have meaningful roles to play in relation to their children and grandchildren living with them.

In short, in spite of the drastic social and economic changes of the twentieth century, the culture of Japan related to its older members; i.e. living arrangements, respect for the elderly, has seen little change. Thus, it appears that, in general, Japanese old people are leading a happy and satisfactory life. But, as Plath was right in pointing out,[47] the later life of Japanese old people naturally has many sorrows, pains and other sufferings. Social measures to alleviate these problems are not yet well developed. While the aged population in Japan is still comparatively younger and the family-oriented culture is dominant,

the Japanese must make every possible effort for the well-being of
their old people who made a major contribution to the development
of Japan. When we take into account the rapid increase of old people
in the near future, the efforts for the development of the social
programmes for them should be greatly accelerated.

Notes

1.   H. Oouchi, H. Arisawa, G. Wakimura, R. Minobe and M. Naito, *Illustrated
     Japanese Economy*, 5th ed. (Iwanami Publishing Co., Tokyo, 1971),
     p. 6.
2.   H. Oouchi, H. Arisawa, G. Wakimura, R. Minobe and M. Naito, *Illustrated
     Japanese Economy*, 3rd ed. (Iwanami Publishing Co., Tokyo, 1963),
     p. 36.
3.   Ibid., p. 35.
4.   Office of the Prime Minister, *National Survey of Labour Force Participa-
     tion* (Office of the Prime Minister, Tokyo, 1974).
5.   D. Plath, 'Japan: The After Years' in D. Cowgill and L. Holmes (eds.),
     Aging and Modernization (Appleton-Century-Crofts, New York, N.Y.,
     1972), p. 133.
6.   D. Cowgill, 'The Role and Status of the Aged in Thailand' in D. Cowgill
     and L. Homes (eds.), *Aging and Modernization* (Appleton-Century-
     Crofts, New York, N.Y., 1972), p. 93.
7.   Office of the Prime Minister, *Survey on the Planning for Later Life*
     (Office of the Prime Minister, Tokyo, 1975).
8.   Health and Welfare Statistics Association, *Trends of the Public Health
     of the People* (Health and Welfare Statistics Association, Tokyo, 1976),
     p. 58.
9.   Ibid., p. 57.
10. Ministry of Health and Welfare, *KOSEI HAKUSHO (Health and Welfare
     White Paper)* (Government Printing Office, Ministry of Finance, Tokyo,
     1974), p. 74.
11. T. Kuroda, 'Population Problems and the Aged' in K. Hasegawa and
     S. Nasu (eds.), *Handbook of Gerontology* (Iwasaki-Gakujutsu Publishing
     Co., Tokyo, 1975), p. 374.
12. Society for the Study of Population Problems, *Prediction of Population
     Distribution among Regions* (Society for the Study of Population
     Problems, Tokyo, 1972).
13. Ministry of Labour, *Survey on the Employment and Administration of
     Enterprises* (Ministry of Labour, Tokyo, 1973).
14. Ibid.
15. Ibid.
16. Office of the Prime Minister, *Statistical Information on the Problems of
     the Aged* (Office of the Prime Minister, Tokyo, 1975), p. 53.
17. Office of the Prime Minister, *Survey on the Life and Opinion in Later
     Years* (Office of the Prime Minister, Tokyo, 1974).
18. Office of the Prime Minister, *National Survey of Labour Force Participa-
     tion* (Office of the Prime Minister, Tokyo, 1974).
19. E. Shanas *et al.*, *Old People in Three Industrial Societies* (Atherton
     Press, New York, N.Y., 1968).

20.   Office of the Prime Minister, *Survey on the Opinion about the Life after Retirement* (Office of the Prime Minister, Tokyo, 1969).
21.   Ministry of Health and Welfare, *Survey on the Actual Living Conditions of the Elderly* (Ministry of Health and Welfare, Tokyo, 1973).
22.   E. Shanas *et al., Old People in Three Industrial Societies*, p. 265; D. Cowgill, 'Aging in American Society' in D. Cowgill and L. Holmes (eds.), p. 254.
23.   Office of the Prime Minister, *Survey on the Family Support and Care of Aged Parents* (Office of the Prime Minister, Tokyo, 1974).
24.   Ministry of Health and Welfare, *Survey on the Actual Living Conditions of the Elderly* (Ministry of Health and Welfare, Tokyo, 1973).
25.   Nihon Toshi Centre, *Life and Opinions of Middle-aged and Older Persons in Urban Areas* (Nihon Toshi Centre, Tokyo, 1975), pp. 34-5.
26.   Office of the Prime Minister, *Survey on the Family Support and Care of Aged Parents*.
27.   Office of the Prime Minister, *Survey on the Life and Opinion in Later Years* (Office of the Prime Minister, Tokyo, 1974).
28.   Y. Yuzawa, 'Prediction of the Relation between Aged Parents and Their Children', unpublished paper presented to the National Congress of Sociology, 1976.
29.   K. Aoi, 'Characteristics of the Japanese Family', *The Community*, no. 46 (Chiiki-shakai Kenkyujo, Tokyo, 1976), pp. 9-23.
30.   D. Cowgill, 'The Role and Status of the Aged in Thailand', p. 94; K. Aoi, 'Characteristics of the Japanese Family', pp. 9-23.
31.   Ministry of Health and Welfare, *Survey on the Actual Conditions of the Life of the People* (Ministry of Health and Welfare, Tokyo, 1973).
32.   M.W. Riley and A. Foner *et al., Aging and Society* (Russell Sage Foundation, New York, N.Y., 1968), p. 76.
33.   Office of the Prime Minister, *Survey on the Life and Opinion in Later Years* (Office of the Prime Minister, Tokyo, 1974).
34.   Office of the Prime Minister, *Public Opinion Survey about the Problems of Old Age* (Office of the Prime Minister, Tokyo, 1973).
35.   Nihon Toshi Centre, *Life and Opinions of Middle-aged and Older Persons in Urban Areas*, p. 10.
36.   Office of the Prime Minister, *Survey on the Family Support and Care of Aged Parents*.
37.   Health and Welfare Statistics Association (Health and Welfare Statistics Association, Tokyo, 1976), p. 103.
38.   Japan Broadcasting Corporation, *Research on Hours Spent on Various Activities* (Japan Broadcasting Corporation, Tokyo, 1970).
39.   D. Maeda, 'Growth of Old People's Clubs in Japan', *Gerontologist*, 1975, vol. 15, pp. 254-6; E. Palmore, *The Honorable Elders – a Cross-Cultural Analysis of Aging in Japan* (Duke University Press, Durham, North Carolina, 1975), p. 115.
40.   Tokyo Metropolitan Institute of Gerontology, Sociology Department, *Research on the Object and Functions of the Community Welfare Centre for the Aged (II) – a Comparative Study of Users and Non-users* (Tokyo Metropolitan Institute of Gerontology, Tokyo, 1974), p. 90.
41.   D. Cowgill, 'The Role and Status of the Aged in Thailand', p. 98.
42.   Office of the Prime Minister, *Survey on the Opinion about the Life after Retirement* (Office of the Prime Minister, Tokyo, 1969).
43.   Office of the Prime Minister, *Survey on the Life and Opinion in Later Years* (Office of the Prime Minister, Tokyo, 1974).
44.   M.W. Riley and A. Foner, *et al., Aging and Society*, p. 342.

45.   Office of the Prime Minister, *Survey on the Life and Opinion in Later Years* (Office of the Prime Minister, Tokyo, 1974).
46.   Ibid.
47.   D. Plath, 'Japan: The After Years', p. 150.

3 AGEING AND THE ENVIRONMENT

Robert J. Newcomer and Elizabeth Falor Bexton

While the natural process of ageing is associated with a decline in specific functional abilities, diminished ability need not lead to dependency if physical and social environments are matched for compatability with the individuals' abilities and needs. Like most adults who are given adequate information, older people are quite capable of choosing environments for themselves which seem to satisfy their needs and resources. Even when the environment does not meet their needs most people have shown remarkable ability to adapt. Yet not everyone can choose his living circumstances; suitable alternatives may not be available. What can or should be done to assist such a person? What information is being used and who is using it in creating these environments?

The concept of environment to be developed and elaborated in this chapter includes first, the physical environment created by designers and builders — that is our houses, offices, hospitals, furniture, even spatial placement of these structures in our cities; and secondly, the social environment that is created by service providers of all varieties as well as by friends and neighbours.

An understanding of what is meant by environment, and of the interactive influences of people and environments is important if we, as advocates, designers or policy-makers, are to create circumstances that are supportive of the needs of older people. Often we may not fully understand how our decisions or actions can ultimately influence the quality and suitability of a situation. As an illustration, consider US government programmes for construction of housing for the elderly — due to cost considerations these programmes have set limits on the size of dwelling units and on maximum cost per unit, delimited types of amenities and supportive services that may be offered, and defined acceptable project tenants by their physical capabilities. In combination these guidelines have produced facilities which are very similar and thus become targeted, apparently inadvertently, for a rather identifiable sub-population among older people. It takes no housing genius to realise that one bedroom or smaller units attract single-person households, or that units without kitchens are unacceptable to those

who wish to cook. Building, fire and safety codes, zoning licensure
requirements and financial considerations may decrease variety in
residents of particular buildings. As an example, they impose
restrictions on behaviour by defining which doors may be opened by
residents, or they limit neighbourhood housing variety, by restricting
an area to single family housing, and excluding multi-unit family
units and nursing homes. These examples point up the tremendous
interdependency between the processes of policy decision and
environmental solution. Environments are manipulated by our policies,
not always to the benefit of persons in need of support.

Two primary purposes of this chapter are to provide an introduction
to the theoretical models in man-environment[1] studies of older people
and to summarise major findings that have emerged from research
in this field. Through this process we hope to produce a sensitivity
to the importance of man-environment relationships and to highlight
issues and areas where conscious manipulation of the environment
is possible. The chapter concludes with a critique of the state-of-the-
art in man-environment research. As a final introductory note,
mention should be made of the recent lively discussion concerning
suggestions to reconsider the name of man-environment relations or
man-environment studies. Among the arguments are that while the
use of 'man' may follow strict grammatical rules, that is, man is a
generic term for all human beings, the implication of its use is variously:
that the male experience of life is more important than the female and
the fact of existence around which research is organised; that the use of
'man' not so subtly excludes more than half humankind; or that the
use of 'man' reinforces stereotypic behaviour and linguistic sexism.

'Person' has been suggested as an alternate (and is used by Kahana
in her work to be discussed in this chapter) but may be mistaken as a
reference to person-ality. 'Human' is another suggestion but *human-*
environment studies (as differentiated from animal environment
studies?) sounds a bit strange to one author (EFB) and seems a
laboured attempt to deal with the very real problem of sexism.

Thus, we will use man-environment throughout this chapter,
suggesting that the reader insert hu- before -man. Unless otherwise
stated, 'man' as we are using it is not a sexual reference. It seems all
too obvious to recall that in almost any study of older people the
subjects are predominately female. Thus, this 'man-environment' work
may actually discriminate against men.

A Brief History of Man-Environment Studies in Gerontology

Following the Second World War, growing out of and beyond operations research, evaluative concepts and studies developed in the social and behavioural sciences while rather major changes were being wrought in the man-made environment which would directly affect older people. This is not to say that people of other ages were not also affected. Yet it is intuitively obvious and easily documented that many older people are at risk in the environment, most commonly due to various combinations of physical problems especially affecting agility, grace, speed and strength, as well as movement, sensory perception-vision, hearing, balance, touch, taste and smell.

Over the last decade or so a new area of man-environment studies in ageing has come about, initially through adaptations of concepts and research designs from psychology and sociology. By the mid-1970s the area has generated its own theoretical frameworks for examining man-environment interactions and has begun to affect other disciplines.

A tracing of the brief history of this area may suggest the excitement that was generated in academic and research settings over the last decade (especially in schools of architecture and environmental design and within maverick university departments of psychology and sociology and innovative research centres) as developing theory was tested and refined. Rather than deal at length with the various applications, this section will suggest some of the major themes in man-environment studies with illustrative examples of theory, research or application. Examples have been chosen that will highlight those studies in which man-environment *interaction* is stressed. Studies in which the environment is treated coincidentally or in which people are only casually considered will not generally be included. Not surprisingly, most examples will be from the USA, a reflection not only of the location of the authors, but also of the location of the great majority of work in the area.

Two general streams of activity seem to have stimulated or directly influenced the subsequent development of the area of man-environment studies in gerontology. The general stream relating to issues of competence and adaptation, now the most vital area within man-environment studies in ageing and one of the most important areas within man-environment studies in general, may be traced within the field of psychology via Murray's need-press theory[2] and Helson's adaptation level theory[3] to Lawton and Nahemow's concepts of competence and adaptation.[4] Kahana's work on congruence between environment and individual behaviour shares similar roots.[5] Lawton's and Kahana's theoretical frameworks will be treated in some detail in subsequent sections of this chapter.

A second stream of development of man-environment studies in ageing was indirect, but without it, man-environment studies would probably have become a sub-speciality within psychology and would not have taken hold within the design professions.[6] This indirect influence was the publication of Alexander's *Notes on the Synthesis of Form.*[7] Developed from a mathematical and architectural background, laced with behavioural and social science notions, this work argued that it was not only desirable but also possible to create an environment which would systematically take into account the specific needs of the user of an environment — creating a fit between user and environment. The argument stated further that human needs could be specified methodically, so that a solution to the broad range of problems posed by environmental design might theoretically be solved together. For the subsequent decade, significant portions of architectural research have been organised about the solution to the insoluble — first, the specification of every one of the clients' needs and secondly, the development of computer assisted methods to solve difficult environmental design problems.

The importance of Alexander's work has been its lasting influence on designers, especially architects. While a brilliant and sensitive designer might intuitively understand a solution to major problems, how would the majority profitably use the notion of it in design? In looking beyond anthropometric data the architectural and environmental design researcher was challenged to evaluate the existing environment and to study the persons for whom he was designing: their present housing patterns, environmental use, environmental preferences as well as their personal characteristics (e.g. motor or perceptual differences, differences in social capabilities by age, etc.).

Roughly parallel to the conceptual division within Alexander's work, man-environment fit v. methods, two societies for architectural and environmental design researchers and practitioners as well as social and behavioural scientists have come about. The Design Methods Group[8] is concerned with systematic approaches to design and with evaluation of environments, while the Environmental Design Research Association (EDRA)[9] has focused on studies of man-environment interaction, often but not always emphasising research methods or replicability.[10] The former has produced a few applications directly relevant to man-environment work in ageing. However, at each of its annual meetings over the past few years EDRA has attracted several papers dealing with gerontological man-environment issues.

Examples of the focus on concern in design-oriented man-environment research in gerontology include: housing or institutional design,[11] urban design and site selection,[12] location of housing and services,[13] transportation,[14] and human characteristics which form the parameters of good design such as data on motor abilities,[15] information on perception.[16] Several books provide access to the results of man-environment studies of older people without requiring readers to wade through the research.[17] There are also several volumes on existing US and European elderly housing for which there may or may not be specific environmental research background.[18] In addition to the general streams of activity mentioned thus far, two research monographs by Frances M. Carp[19] and by Irving Rosow,[20] a conference, and a project sponsored by the Gerontological Society have helped to shape the development of man-environment studies in ageing. Carp's study examined adaptation, or adjustment, to a new environment in terms of expressed satisfaction and improved morale among the tenants of the first US public housing specially designed for older people. She recognised and documented that appropriately planned and designed living environments for older people could effect significant psychological and social changes for the residents. Rosow showed that for many older people sufficient numbers of peers living in close residential proximity could mitigate some losses associated with growing old. His results called into question the commonly held belief, firmly rooted in egalitarianism, that environments in which all ages are represented are somehow better for all concerned, particularly the elderly resident. His data suggests that quite the opposite is true for certain elderly people. Thus, there would be a new base for policy and application.[21]

In 1968 a conference on the spatial behaviour of older people was held at the University of Michigan.[22] The conference papers appeared in book form in 1970 thereby becoming accessible to social and behavioural scientists as well as to architectural and urban designers and planners whose interest was aroused not only by the topic but by the various approaches to work that should necessarily be (but not often was) interdisciplinary. Within a year another stimulus to the development of this gerontological interest group had occurred: US Federal funds were allocated to the Gerontological Society for a project on environment and ageing.[23] This project has sponsored a series of conferences and publications, the majority of which have specifically addressed man-environment issues (for example: theory development; hardware design for the elderly user). This project has nurtured the development of the area by raising the level of understanding about older people and their design and environmental needs, preferences, their behaviour, and environmental constraints on design.

To what extent do gerontological man-environment studies follow man-environment studies generally? Amos Rapoport has developed a typology of man-environment studies,[24] by which we may categorise related gerontological studies. The categories in his 'Major Theoretical Models in Man-Environment Studies' are:

Perception and complexity
Cognitive/image
Behaviour setting
Communication symbolism, non-verbal communication
Competence and adaptation
Information flow
Ecological models
Ethological models
Evolutionary models
Socio-cultural models
Preference in environmental quality = choice
Performance based

Among the areas above which have received some attention within gerontological man-environment studies are, for example: competence and adaptation; perception and complexity; preference in environmental quality or choice; cognitive/image; behaviour settings; and ethological models. It must be noted that it would be extremely rare to find a study in which only one of these categories would be evident. Without attempting a comprehensive literature review one may point to competence and adaptation as major foci for theory as well as practice. Both Lawton and Nahemow's[25] and Kahana's[26] work, which concern competence and adaptation, are examples and will be reviewed in detail in the chapter. Among others, Carp's study[27] of Victoria Plaza considers adaptations to and of a new environment.

Reflecting a background in psychology for many people involved in man-environment studies, perception is another category which has interested researchers and practitioners. Both groups raised questions about how environmental design might mitigate the losses of old age. One set of those losses is perceptual: especially visual, aural and tactile senses. Pastalan recognised that in order to be incorporated into physical design, data about perception would have to be translated into material understandable to policy-makers, designers and other professionals working with the elderly. Most adults experience change in their sensory capabilities and if one lives long enough, one's perception of and interaction with the physical environment may be reduced. These effects are interactive within the individual to the extent that one sense may to varying degrees take over from another, declining sense. Thus Pastalan developed an 'empathic model' of sensory decrement, mirroring an average person of advanced age.[28] The model allows a younger or unimpaired individual insight into the phenomenal world of an impaired person, this to suggest new areas for research on environmental problems of the elderly (e.g. Is what I see that which the elderly see? Have they formed an adaptive response to this impairment such that their functional impairment is minimal?), new design criteria (e.g. Is this sign readable? Can this warning sound be heard?), and new empathy with older people (e.g. Now that I have a better understanding of the world as you experience it, I can alter my behaviour to increase communication between us. Together we may be able to work on a more accessible environment for all.). Studies related to preferences in environments have been of several kinds. A number of these have concluded that choice in environment is significant in mediating the effects of environmental change.[29] Other studies have attempted to understand the mechanics of preference for different types of housing or for one location over another.[30] Yet, in housing for the elderly in the US the two greatest determinants of housing preference affecting range of available choice are first, the free market housing choices of older people, and second, in special government backed elderly housing, the specific requirements within housing legislation which can virtually predetermine functionally significant design relationships within a living unit. For upper-middle-income groups or higher, the housing industry responds fairly well to the desires of the user, and there is an interactive process toward better sense of fit between the needs and desires of the older person and the characteristics of the environment. Of course, the relationship is far less neat for moderate or low income people, of whom many are aged.[31]

Another general man-environment area which will receive acknowledgement in a later section of this chapter is the category of 'cognitive image'. The basis for several such studies in man-environment research was Kevin Lynch's work.[32] Currently, the most successful development of that approach in gerontology has been done by

Regnier and Eribes.[33]

Work on behaviour settings as developed by Roger Barker[34] has encouraged greater rigour in studies using naturalistic observation and behaviour mapping. Rather than adopting the strict form used by Barker, gerontological studies have used naturalistic observation and behaviour mapping to emphasie a variety of environmental components such as social milieu[35] or use of an environment and its meaning.[36] Some of this kind of work has also had an ethological orientation, such as Barbara Felton and Eva Kahana's work on locus of control.[37]

Man-environment studies in gerontology seems to have gained momentum and to have captured professional interest because it offers researchers and practitioners an unusual opportunity to hypothesise, examine and evaluate their notions of man-environment interactions. This chapter continues to examine two major theoretical frameworks for man-environment research and their relationship to the expanding body of literature in the area.

Classifying Environments

A major need in our ability to understand and research the environmental aspects of the behavioural system is a definition or taxonomy of environments. M. Powell Lawton has discussed several attempts to construct such a taxonomy[38] and has proposed what he terms a 'beginning gross classification'.[39]

We have, for purposes here, elected to use Lawton's Taxonomy.[40] It consists of five components:[41]

1. *The Individual* including perceptual and cognitive skills and life experience.
2. *Inter-Personal Environment* comprised of the significant others (primarily friends, relatives and work associates) constituting the major one-to-one social relationships of an individual.
3. *Supra-Personal Environment* identified as the modal characteristics (e.g. the predominating sex, marital status, race, age, socio-economic status and functional ability) of all the people in physical proximity to an individual.
4. *Social Environment* comprised of the norms, values and institutions operating in the individual's sub-group, society or culture.
5. *The Physical Environment* encompassing the non-personal non-social residue of physical features.

Lawton's classification is most useful in differentiating among several non-physical environmental dimensions. In a more recent work, Lawton[42] attempts to reconceptualise the physical environment in higher order abstractions. These he terms:

1. *The Phenomenal Physical Environment* – the unique, idiosyncratic experience of a physical object by one individual.
2. *The Consensual Physical Environment* – While the environmental quality must be experienced by the individual, enough individuals experience the quality in a similar way so as to suggest a convergence on the 'real object' (e.g. crowded v. sparse).
3. *The Explicit Physical Environment* – qualities that may be measured in centimeters, grams and seconds.

Lawton proposes that the further development of environmental typologies should include the definition of qualities in both explicitly and consensually physical terms.[43] Examples of the terms include qualities such as:

Natural v. man-made	complex v. simple
large v. small	rich v. impoverished
crowded v. sparse	supportive v. demanding
stable v. unstable	novel v. familiar
homogeneous v. heterogeneous	

Acknowledgement should be made at this point that not all researchers agree that environments can be conceptually differentiated from the person as has been done by Lawton. A typical counter argument would be that an individual's actions, cognitions and feelings at a given moment incorporate aspects of the environment and the environment is defined only through the use, cognitions and feelings of individuals and groups.

The presentation to follow is firm in its insistence upon the empirical necessity for separating the person from the environment, and differentiating sub-aspects of the environment.

Theories in Man-Environment Relations

In the field of gerontology there has been one prevalent approach to conceptualising the impact of environments on the older person. It has concentrated on specifying and measuring the relationship between the capacity of the individual and the demands of the environment, and inversely the capacity of the environment to meet the individual's needs and life-style.[44,45]

In spite of the unitary conceptual perspective, two different theoretical models have been advanced. These are the ecological model of ageing, and the congruence model of person-environment inter-action. Both of these are reviewed for their similarity, differences and applicability to practical design and policy issues.[46]

Ecological Model of Ageing

As shown in Figure 1, the M. Powell Lawton and Lucille Nahemow ecological model of ageing consists of four major elements:[47]

1. *Individual Competence* represents a diverse collection of abilities such as perception, physical health and life experiences. This component is shown on the vertical axis. Minimum ability is at the zero point. Ability increases as one moves up the scale.

2. *Environmental Press* is a summation of the influences of all environmental resources which arise due to one's social and physical environments. This term has an obvious similarity to the concept of stress. Press, however, may be positive, neutrally or negative. It is measured on the horizontal axis. Stress implies only a potentially negative environmental demand. In general, the major dimensions on which press is classified is their strength from high to low. Their positive or negative quality can only be determined by knowledge of the competence of the individual. Minimum press occurs at the zero point and increases as one moves to the right on the horizontal axis.

3. *Adaptive Behaviour* is the manifestation of individual competence resulting from the man-environment interaction. The adaptiveness of behaviour must be judged by the extent to which it meets both society's expectations and the individual's standards or requirements for goal fulfilment. Within the shadowed limits shown in Figure 1 the individual functions without an erosion or overstress on independence. Outside these limits the individual is unsuited for the environment and is by definition maladaptive in that situation.

4. *Adaptation Level* refers generally to the individual's state of balance between the level of external stimulation and the sensitivity of the individual's perceptual and cognitive state. In other words, the individual tends to adapt to any given level of stimulation in such a way that awareness of the stimulus recedes. A change in the stimulation intensity brings the stimulus into greater awareness. A warm bath illustrates this concept. The immediate experience

of the bath produces an awareness of the water's temperature and touch. After a time these sensations become less keen. As the water cools, or is reheated, the sensations are re-experienced, but will gradually move toward a zero or neutral point again. This point at which sensation is minimal is called adaption level (AL). The value of the AL stimulus is a function of the current stimulus intensity, as well as the individual's previous experience with similar stimuli. The bath-taker having a lifelong experience with 110 degree water, will probably find water of 100 degrees to be cool. The magnitude of stimulus intensity defining AL also varies with other contemporary environmental aspects. It may take less water temperature to reach AL when the air temperature is cool.

Stimuli that deviate in either direction from AL are believed to be experienced positively up to the limiting point set by adaptive behaviour. Beyond this point, the individual experiences negative effects on satisfaction. Adaptation outside these limits is difficult due to either the high stress or sensory depreciation created by this situation.

Figure 1 indicates that the lower the competence of the individual, the lower the strength of press must be in order to maintain this steady state of automatic, but adaptive behaviour and mental effect.

The area of high environmental press is shown in the far right-hand area of Figure 1. If the need for support is great the individual may experience many types of stress that overtax adaptive ability. Low levels of support occur in the left-hand area. If press does not exceed ability this too creates a coping problem which may erode adaptive ability, and in so doing, produce needless dependency.

The transactive relationship between competence and press is illustrated by the following example. Consider an environmental press of magnitude (Y) being received by an individual of competence (B). This individual would be operating at (S) which is in the range of satisfactory adaptation. High ability is matched by high press. The individual is able to maximise satisfaction. If ability declines to point (A) such as from illness or chronic physical decrements, environmental press must decrease to level (X) in order for the individual to remain functioning within his adaptive range.

Functioning at this new level would also maximise environmental competence. If environmental press were not correspondingly decreased for this individual, the individual would be overstressed by the demands made by his setting as shown by point (Q) which lies just outside the

Figure 1: Ecological Model of Ageing

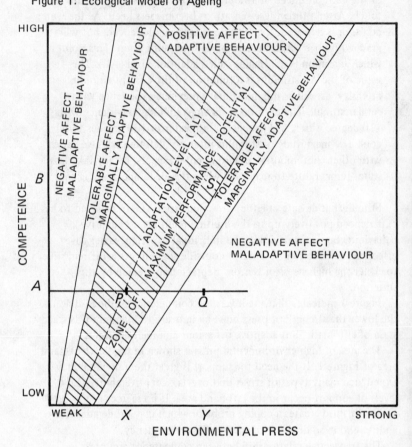

Source: Lawton and Nahemow, 1973.

zone of adaptive behaviour. This model is a dramatic illustration
of the increased vulnerability of persons with lowered capability.
More subtle within the model is the importance and potential of
environmental manipulation as a policy alternative. We have seen in
Figure 1 how the individual can be brought into a satisfactory
adaptation level through at least three interventions. These can be
applied either singly or in combination to meet a particular need at
the right time.

1. Resources within the setting can be altered (a shift in press) with
   the individual assuming a passive role. This might involve societal
   intervention in the form of special services or prosthetic design.
2. Active environmental changes by the individual might consist of
   trying to create a new household consistent with one's own needs
   (for example, renting a smaller unit, or living with a relative).
3. Increased individual competence can also take place either actively
   or passively. Passive approaches would again require the intervention of supportive services which compensate for individual
   incompetence (eyeglasses, hearing aids). Active increases in
   competence could occur through self-therapy and the realisation
   of new self-potential such as through acquisition of new friends,
   or new knowledge.

In principle, then, the process for matching an individual with an
appropriate setting becomes one of first assessing capability, and the
resources or barriers within the environment operating either to overtax or underestimate the individual: intervention overcoming the
mismatch can be directed either at changes in the individual or changes
in the setting.

Of course nothing is as simple as it seems. The competence and
press axes shown in Figure 1 are great simplifications of reality.
Neither press nor competence are made up of singular elements.
And the elements which comprise these characteristics are variable
over time.

The next man-environment theory to be discussed further elaborates
on the complexity of the man-environment relationship and proposes
an alternative method for relating these compretence-press dimensions.

Congruence Model of Interaction

The congruence model of environment-individual interaction developed
by Eva Kahana[48] also has its roots in Murray's[49] need-press model of
human behaviour. Rather than focusing on single environmental or
individual dimensions as major intervening variables, the Kahana model
attempts simultaneous consideration of a variety of environmental and
individual dimensions and measures them along parallel and commen-
surate dimensions. Simply stated, the model combines person[50] and
environment measures arithmetically producing a direct index of fit
along the given dimensions. This process is illustrated by Figure 2
which summarises what Kahana has described as seven dimensions of
necessary congruence between environmental settings and individual

Figure 2: Dimensions of Congruence

1. SEGREGATION DIMENSION

Environment

A. Homogeneity of composition of environment. Segregation based on similarity of resident characteristics (sex, age, physical functioning and mental status)

B. Change v. sameness. Presence of daily and other routines, frequency of changes in staff and other environmental characteristics.

C. Continuity of similarity with previous environment of residence.

Individual

A. Preference for homogeneity, i.e. for associating with like individuals. Being with people similar to yourself.

B. Preference for change v. sameness in daily routines, activities.

C. Need for continuity with the past.

2. CONGREGATE DIMENSION

A. Extent to which privacy is available in setting.

B. Collective v. individual treatment. The extent to which residents are treated alike. Availability of choices in food, clothing, etc. Opportunity to express unique individual characteristics.

C. The extent to which residents do things alone or with others.

A. Need for privacy.

B. Need for individual expression and idiosyncrasy. Choosing individualised treatment whether that treatment is socially defined as 'good' treatment or not.

C. Preference for doing things alone v. with others.

3. INSTITUTIONAL CONTROL

Environment

A. Control over behaviour and resources. The extent to which staff exercise control over resources.

B. Amounts of deviance tolerated. Sanction for deviance.

C. Degree to which dependency is encouraged and dependency needs are met.

Individual

A. Preference for (individual) autonomy v. being controlled.

B. Need to conform.

C. Dependence on others. Seek support, nurturance v. self-sufficient.

4. STRUCTURE

A. Ambiguity v. specification of expectations. Role ambiguity or role clarity, e.g. rules learned from others.

A. Tolerance of ambiguity v. need for structure.

/cont.

Figure 2: Cont.

B. Order v. disorder.	B. Need for order and organisation.

5. STIMULATION-ENGAGEMENT

A. Environmental input stimulus properties of physical and social environment (not only availability of stimulation, extent to which that is directed to resident).	A. Tolerance and preference for environmental stimulation.
B. The extent to which resident is actually stimulated and encouraged to be active.	B. Preference for activities v. disengagement.

6. EFFECT

Environment	*Individual*
A. Tolerance for, or encouragement of affective expression. Provision of ritualised show of emotions (e.g. funerals).	A. Need for emotional expression — display of feelings, whether positive or negative.
B. Amounts of affective stimulation. Excitement v. peacefulness in environment.	B. Intensity of affect, e.g. need for v. avoidance of conflicts and excitement.

7. IMPULSE CONTROL

A. Acceptance of impulse life v. sanctions against it. The extent to which the environment gratifies need immediately v. postponed need gratification. Gratification/deprivation ratio.	A. Ability to delay need gratification. Preference for immediate v. delayed reward. Degree of impulse needed.
B. Tolerance of motor expression — restlessness, walking around in activities or at night.	B. Motor control; psychomotor inhibition.
C. Premiums placed by environments on level-headedness and deliberation.	C. Impulsive closure v. deliberate closure.

Source: Kahana, 1975, pp. 190-92.

preferences.

The individual need in this figure is compared against the appropriate environmental condition. If this need is met, the individual-environment dimension would be characterised as congruent. If there is not a match, then there is incongruence.

Kahana's seven dimensions of congruence do not represent unitary aspects of needs or environment (she has for example further sub-divided them into eighteen subdimensions), but they do offer a comprehensive conceptualisation of these important relationships.

Kahana's work also highlights additional complexity in person-environment (PE) relationships. She asks: 'Does the environment have to fit the person's needs in every area? Can mismatch in one area be made up for by match in another area?'[51] To help answer these questions Kahana has described several possible models for person-environment relationships.

Cumulative Difference Model. The first of these assumes PE mismatch to be cumulative and continuous. In other words, the greater the differences between personal needs, preferences and environmental characteristics, the more negative would be the outcome. This model includes situations such as in the Lawton-Nahemow model, where either great positive or negative differences from preferences produce a negative outcome. A second conceptualisation of this model concerns only the effects of negative difference. A third conceptualisation assumes that the consequence of non-congruence differs depending upon whether the individual prefers more or less support than the environment provides. For instance, one may assume that the consequences of preferring more stimulation than is provided are different from preferring less.

The Critical Difference Approach. A second set of conceptual models considers the possibility of a critical mismatch. This approach assumes the effects of mismatch or non-congruence to be problematic only beyond a certain critical point or range. It should be noted that this model is still proposing a linear relationship which assumes that mismatch is consistently negative. This approach may be further sub-divided like the cumulative difference model in terms of non-directional, one-directional, or two-directional orientations.

Optimal Congruence Models. In both preceding sets non-congruence was assumed to have a negative effect while complete congruence resulted in a positive outcome. The optimal model proposes that complete congruence between an individual's needs and the environment may be harmful, just as extreme misfit would be harmful. The desired match would somehow optimise the variables which create congruence. This seems to be the mode Kahana prefers. This model, particularly in its non-directional form, relates to the adaption level modes.[52]

Morale and Other Man-Environmental Outcome Assessments

Having outlined two major theories for considering the fit between individuals and their environment, several conclusions are apparent.

First, the Lawton-Nahemow model focuses on psychological 'well-being' (e.g. morale) as the outcome of a compatible man-environment interaction. Such an approach assumes that competence and environmental variables are independent and have an additive relationship to each other. Kahana's notions of congruence imply an interactive, multiplicative relationship. For her, the level of congruence becomes a predisposition to satisfaction or well-being. The practical difference between these two models is seemingly slight. Lawton relates individual attributes to press. Kahana asks, 'Do these attributes match with the press?' If they do, she uses the congruence to predict outcome, i.e. morale. In other words, congruence has been achieved when an individual and an environmental match-up becomes possible. Thus, we might describe congruence as synonymous with Lawton's zone of adaptability. If we accept this interpretation, it becomes possible to merge these two models conceptually and to concentrate our critique on the practical variable definition and applications arising from their work.

A second conclusion results from the diversity of environmental and individual characteristics and needs. It appears unlikely that there will be a perfect fit in every area, or non-congruence in every area.

In fact, an individual would seemingly have to be in a situation where many compensatory resources were mismatched before low morale would be expected. Even in such a situation the influence of a single attribute would likely have little effect on moral scores. The generally high ratings for morale found among older persons regardless of their living environment support such an argument.

Morale is by its nature a cumulative outcome, a composite of one's total experience. Appropriately, morale typically has been measured either by a global question or scale.[53] The well-being thus produced has for the most part been evaluated in relation to other composite factors. An explicit appraisal of single individual attributes with single environmental attributes as these affect well-being have been infre-quently made.

A third conclusion is that the complexity and the apparent

necessity for optimising trade-offs between man-environment fit
raises a major challenge to existing applications of ME research. Given
the relatively few congruences that can be analysed at any one time,
is it reasonable to expect that situational congruence can account
for much variance in an individual's morale or well-being? In other
words, is it fruitful theoretically or practically to persist in explorations
of morale predictors? While morale is central to the Lawton-Nahemow
model, it is secondary to Kahana. We propose that we content ourselves with an achievable task of identifying elements of congruence,
particularly the critical difference dimensions, and the trade-off
behaviour occurring when congruence is established. Such an approach
in simple terms concentrates on the limits of adaptive ability and its
behavioural effects rather than on the affective outcome of adaptation.

To illustrate this difference in perspective consider the situation
in which we are concerned with defining neighbourhood suitability.
If we were concerned with morale as an outcome, we might ask how
selected service use or frequency of use predicted morale. However,
because we are now more concerned with examples of congruence,
the investigation might concentrate on the association between
distance, individual characteristics and service use patterns. The
identification of use-pattern correlates is more immediately useful for
designers and policy-makers than would be our ability to describe how
use patterns correlated with morale.

A final issue emerges from the theoretical models previously
discussed in the notion of environmental self-selection. According to
both models (and a variety of studies) individuals seek and are likely
to be found in environments which are at least substantially congruent
with their needs. ME research, in spite of this canon has studied and
continues to study persons who may well be congruent with their
setting rather than persons in a dissonant context. As a consequence
many biases may enter the research results. One of the most significant
is that we end up studying a relatively homogeneous population.
This problem in combination with the complexity of morale
assessments must be expected to mute the effect of environmental
test variables. To avoid this muting effect, greater attention must be
given to the measurement of the antecedent factors or conditions
which produce shifts in environment. In other words we must pick
subjects who are not congruent with their environment.

A Review of Man-Environment Relations
The provision of supportive services or prosthetic design to the older

person is an implicit attempt to aid that individual in matching his/her ability to the demands incumbent in daily living situations. Expressed in the environmental psychology terms presented in this section, this man-environment matching process is one which seeks to sustain the individual at a maximum level of functioning and satisfaction. Critical to the understanding of this process is a working definition of environment, knowledge of the tolerable limits of individual stress, and the interactive influence of a variety of physical and social conditions both on the individual and on each other.

Here we will continue to use the environmental taxonomy developed by Lawton[54] and the conceptual array of ME variables as presented in the two theoretical models of man-environment interaction. However, our attention will shift to an emphasis on behavioural outcomes, rather than on well-being. In keeping with the chapter's objective of linking ME research with guidelines for the conscious manipulation of environmental settings we have attempted to organise this section, which is a review of research findings, around a discussion of the influence of the major variables thus far identified. This has been done to highlight the germane contributions of each of these diverse environmental elements and to simplify the discussions of the multiple forces which simultaneously impinge on any situation. In response to the policy action emphasis of this whole book, we have given particular attention to how the ME relationships discussed influence invironmental preference, and hence selection. These influences can be either constraints or incentives. An awareness of these relationships can greatly aid policy efforts to widen or narrow the population base who could benefit from environmental manipulation.

Individual Attributes

The myriad of individual attributes could include physical functional ability, perceptual and cognitive skills, economic resources, educational training and personality type. The present discussion focuses on only one: previous life experience.[55] The others are dealt with in relation to specific environmental features. Previous life experience is singled out because it provides a pervasive influence across these other attributes.

Previous environmental experience and previous activity patterns reflect the ways in which people have used environments and thus their level of familiarity with and/or adaptability to new settings or changes in capability. The strength of these latter factors as needs is conditioned by perceptual and cognitive abilities. Reliance upon the familiar is also an adaptive response to lessened perceptual and cognitive skills. Familiarity and sense of orientation give a positive quality to an environment simply because they enhance a competence which is lost or diminished in a new environmental situation.[56]

Previous life experiences are an issue largely ignored in research into problems and issues in environment for the elderly. This is not to say people discount its importance, rather it frequently emerges an 'area for further study', or as an aspect of the research design which was inappropriately investigated and therefore not reported. For example, Frances Carp[57] in her study of the first US public housing project for older people questioned the potentially fallacious responses regarding housing satisfaction of the in-movers, as what they had left behind was far inferior to what they gained when entering public housing. More recently, two studies[58] have found that the middle-class older person, though living in objectively better housing than low-income counterparts, is nevertheless more likely to complain about it than would someone of lower income.

Illustrating a positive demonstration of the effects of familiarity, a study of room and floor preferences[59] found that older people preferred to inhabit rooms in the same general location on a floor, and rooms at least on the same floor as in their previous residence. Michael Caggiano when asking older people to model the room arrangement and room size they most preferred, found that they invariably used their current residence or an immediate past residence as a model of the 'ideal'.[60]

Neighbourhood familiarity has also been shown to be important to older people.[61] The perceived size of one's neighbourhood correlates with length of residence in a given location. Length of residence of less than one year has consistently produced a very small neighbourhood; length of residence of ten years or greater has consistently produced a large neighbourhood.[62] Further evidence of the importance of familiarity and rootedness in the lives of older people is found in mortality rates among relocated institutionalised populations and the commonly observed adjustment periods of other groups when relocated.[63]

Activity patterns represent another manifestation of past life experiences and are indicative of expected current propensities. Actual involvement though is affected by age, income and social class. With retirement from work, a period of at least eight hours in the average day becomes discretionary rather than obligated time. This by itself could permit a dramatic shift in behaviour. The breadth and range of alternatives is, however, constrained by reduced incomes.

For those relatively few older people who can afford extensive travel, expensive hobbies and recreation, the chances are that if they had not been involved in these activities prior to retirement, they are not likely to become so involved. For instance, a sample of in-movers to a leisure world retirement community were questioned as to their expected activity propensities and desires upon living in this recreationally oriented community.[64] A one-year follow-up established that residents had continued their previous life-styles although transferred to a new setting. Such behaviour patterns are consistent with the many findings reported in investigations of activity theory and disengagement theories of ageing.[65]

With increasing age, there is a decline in certain activities (as measured through cross-sectional studies). More time is devoted to personal maintenance, napping and reading. A little less time is devoted to entertaining and club and church participation. Visiting patterns do remain constant.[66] The geographic setting for many activities is related to functional ability, environmental opportunities and social class. Put briefly, the middle class tends to be much less spatially bounded than the working class, men less than women.[67,68]

The preceding paragraphs highlight the importance and constancy of activity patterns in the lives of older people. Anything which impedes the fulfilment of these needs can be considered detrimental to their well-being. The findings noted suggest that in choosing alternative living environments people tend to select those which offer as a minimum the resources which will assist them in maintaining their developed life-style.

This should not be interpreted to mean that older people cannot or will not adapt to new situations. Rather, it means that generally they will continue to live pretty much as they have in the years which preceded retirement given that opportunity, although the intensity of activity involvement may diminish.

Inter-Personal Environment

Friends, relatives and acquaintances are important influences in our lives. They form a major basis for social contact, emotional support in times of need, and perhaps direct assistance in emergencies. It is from others that the processes of acculturation and socialisation are transmitted. These interpersonal relationships, especially social contacts, have direct effects on activity patterns and morale. The importance of these relationships is dependent on individual competence and life-style.

Spatial proximity, length of residence, and age density are considered by many persons to be the most important variables explaining age-peer associations and friendships.[69] Together these variables produce the opportunity for social encounters. Social encounters in turn affect many other activities. Whether an individual chooses to avail himself of these opportunities has been found to be a function of personality type and social class. Satisfactory attainment of the individually desired level of social contacts results in high morale.[70] Figure 3 identifies the optimal match-ups between personality type and environmental context as proposed by Rosow. In this circumstance equal individual capability is assumed among all character types.

There are direct linkages between the desired or attained level of interpersonal contacts and an individual's activity patterns. Friends are frequent companions for shopping and various other recreations. Relatives are likely to be used for special occasion events like holidays or providing transportation to health services.[71] Both groups have been shown to be valuable emotional and emergency supports, but the family is expected to assume long-term care. The nature of these activities is in part attributable to the type of contacts made between individuals. Friends are seen frequently, most often several times a week. Relatives, although often within an hour's drive of the older person are seen less frequently.[72] Most contact with relatives occurs by telephone or mail.

Social class, sex, marital status and functional ability all directly bear on these patterns. The working classes, married women and persons with low functional ability tend to be greatly constrained in their perception and use of available facilities with respect to shopping and social participation. These sub-groups are more neighbourhood based than their middle-class, male and healthy counterparts.[73] This spatial orientation is a particularly strong influence on friendship formation. Proximity to relatives is less differentiated by social class or these other characteristics, as all groups are becoming widely dispersed with suburbanisation and employment mobility.[74] But regardless of the actual spatial distance to friends and relatives, generally older people state a desire to be located 'near' these individuals.[75]

Thus, it is evident that shopping, club participation and other activities typically occurring outside the home are frequently engaged

Figure 3: Neighbourhood Composition and Personality Types

Character Type and Description	Suggested Age Composition of Neighbourhood
Cosmopolitan: little contact with neighbours, no desire for more friends, most friends live outside this person's neighbourhood.	Might like to move closer to children or friends if mobility were restricted. At present age composition of neighbourhood not important.
Phlegmatic: socially inactive, prefers little outside contact.	Needs minimal social support from the environment. Can be satisfied in normally found age concentration.
Isolated: wishes for more contact with neighbours, presently has few friends.	Neighbourhoods with a predominance of elderly.
Sociable: satisfied with the present high level of contact.	Neighbourhoods with a predominance of elderly, although they might be satisfied anywhere.
Insatiable: high level of contact, but wishes for still more.	Neighbourhoods with a predominance of elderly.

Source: Abstracted from Rosow, 1967.

in with other people. Because of this, the life space of an individual seems to be somewhat influenced by the geographic distribution of one's social contacts. It has been shown that having lower socio-economic status and being a woman contribute to a small geographic neighbourhood orientation in the selection of friends. This combined with a propensity noted earlier, toward a familiar neighbourhood, leads to an expectation that, if they have to move, these persons will choose to remain in proximity to their social network, and by so doing, remain within a familiar neighbourhood. Persons who are dissonantly placed will, by supposition, have low morale, while those compatibly placed will have high morale.

Rosow's personality typology identifies those personality types who have so little need of satisfaction from social contacts that these other issues do not matter. However, the phlegmatic constitute a low percentage of the total population. In order for the vast majority of site residents to exhibit satisfaction, it is essential that they have a social network. Contact with relatives, although important for emotional and direct assistance, tends to be uniformly low among older people in spite of the spatial proximity. Therefore, the needed social network would appear to be comprised of friends.

Social Environment

Social norms offer perhaps the strongest evidence in support of the notion of environment 'self-selection'. In all societies and social settings, there are rules, either implicit or explicit, which prescribe appropriate behaviour for individuals and for groups. While the complexity of such norms, as linked to specific activities, is generally beyond the scope of this chapter, the authors recognise that administrative and other normative policies affect housing choice, and that these norms may directly influence individual morale.

The literature in this field suffers from the difficulties inherent in attempts to measure norms. Frequently surrogates have been employed rather than direct attitudinal studies.

Within retirement communities, homes for the aged and low income housing projects for the elderly, several distinct patterns have been observed relative to activity patterns and tenant characteristics. In those facilities which are designed for recreationally oriented groups, norms have been developed that highly value participation and status attainment in recreational activities.[76] On the other hand residents in group housing rich with supportive services exhibit activity patterns which are much less oriented to vigorous physical activities.

While these differences exist largely as a result of the resources supplied within the respective housing types, these populations may also be self-selected which would serve to heighten differences between the two examples. Healthier people choose recreationally oriented facilities, while the less competent select supportive settings. A study of retirement housing in California provides indirect support for this supposition by its findings that each housing type investigated had distinctly different tenant characteristics.[77] Younger elderly were more often found in mobile home parks, retirement communities and housing for the elderly. Older persons (median 75-85) tended to predominate in homes for the aged and retirement hotels. Obviously, the age distribution could be an artefact of building age as well as building characteristics, but as argued by Lawton's docility hypothesis,[78] part of the difference could also be attributed to failing competence. The Brody and Gumner study,[79] and Brody's follow-up[80]

of waiting list applicants to homes for the aged offers further
evidence in support of this hypothesis and the contention of self-
selection. She found that older people exercise considerable control
over their placement in specialised housing. They are not forced
into these facilities by their children, but choose residence only after
trying a variety of other housing alternatives.[81]

Of special importance in explaining the reality of self-selection are
decisions such as these regarding contextual compatibility. Early
experience with elderly housing facilities in the US has suggested
that healthy people do not like to live around the less healthy.
Administrators and staff do not like to mix individuals of varied
competence. Even the less competent themselves may often feel
happier separated from the competent.[82] Recent observations by
housing managers lends support to these conclusions. Among those
facilities offering high levels of supportive services, such as limited
personal care and meals, the tenants entering today are described as
being considerably older than those who entered the same project
ten years ago.[83]

Supra-Personal Environment

Closely related to the influences of social norms are the supra-personal
characteristics, i.e. the predominating modal characteristics of a social
setting. To date, the major behavioural effects attributable to supra-
personal characteristics have occurred when individuals are exposed to
what Rosenberg has called 'contextual dissonance'.[84] In other words,
behaviour is negatively modified because individuals deviating from
the predominating characteristics have tended to avoid such situations.
The possible self-selection of housing environments suggests such as
avoidance. In his study of age and poverty in San Francisco, Rosenberg
provides documentation of the influence of socio-economic status
and income on behaviour patterns. His initial interest was in the
relationship between poverty and social isolation. His findings are
important particularly with respect to neighbourhood use. The city
block was used as the basic geographic definition of neighbourhood.
Rosenberg's hypothesis predicted that those individuals in congruent
environments would be less isolated than those who were cut off from
'their own kind'. It was found that the poor and the solvent were
differentially sensitive to separate aspects of their neighbourhoods.
The solvent were more responsive in their social behaviour to the
socio-economic aspects of the neighbourhood context than were the
poor elderly. If the former were in an area which had people of

socio-economic backgrounds comparable to their own, they freely used the neighbourhood. If the congruence did not occur, they likely engaged in their social activities elsewhere.

Lower income groups were less sensitive to these issues in their activity patterns. For this population, social isolation was more often predictable when there was a disparity in the age and marital status of the neighbourhood residents.

In a further elaboration on neighbourhood activity propensities among low-income public housing residents Regnier's work suggests that racial disparity and population density (as reflected in land use patterns) also affect access, identification and use of an area as one's neighbourhood.[85] Neighbourhood in his study was defined as the area 'used' by respondents. One must recall the discussion of neighbourhood orientation of middle- and working-class populations raised previously. In the Regnier study the middle class avoided situations which were incongruent with their life-style. The working class stayed in their own neighbourhoods but they were inactive unless there were age peers with whom to associate.

Lawton examined possible effect on competent people when living in a milieu which was populated by many less competent people.[86] It was thought that competence in such a situation could be eroded. His findings were inconclusive because, as discussed in the preceding section, it appeared that most people were selective in choosing an environment matched to their needs. Other literature further suggests the absence of hard evidence about how the offering of services erodes a relatively independent person's adequacy. Generally, those who utilise a health service, for example, are those whose physical condition demands it.[87]

While the evidence for both social norms and supra-personal relationships is inferential rather than direct, it strongly suggests that people do self-select environments suited to their perceived physical and social competence. Selection in the process implies an avoidance of incompatible situations as much as it means a positive attraction to a particular setting. A further conclusion is that those persons living in a dissonant context will likely experience social isolation with negative consequences on life satisfaction.

Physical Environment

The last element of Lawton's environmental taxonomy is the physical environment. Physical features have their major effect on behaviour by spatially defining the social (behavioural) setting. In other words, physical resources in part predetermine the size or even type of social groups formed within a particular setting.

The major issues examined here concern the interactive influences of macro-settings[88] both on locational attractiveness and on the use of physical spaces within buildings (micro-settings).

These two issues demonstrate how the use of space within buildings and in neighbourhoods (and therefore activities) is influenced by the availability, location, quality and density of other on-site resources as well as neighbourhood resources. Elaborating these interactive influences is a necessary step in developing comprehensive site performance criteria. This process also helps operationalise concepts such as convenience and accessibility to desired goods and services. This is essential to the measurement of critical distances.

Building and neighbourhood interrelationships as observed by Lawton[89] and Nash[90] in their studies of the residents in twelve high rise housing projects, point to the salience of particular service features in the macro-environment for the individual. Relying principally on ecological observational data these studies derived occupancy and distribution percentages regarding the differential use of building spaces and facilities. Use of these spaces was found to be influenced by the building's location with respect to nearby competing space (e.g. boardwalks, central city locations). The accessibility of outside resources reduced use of in-building activities. Generally neighbourhoods were also found to be important in determining overall housing satisfaction. A 'convenient' and 'safe' location was typically found to define a good neighbourhood.

The importance of micro-macro linkages are further evidenced when considering the fluid nature of on-site activity patterns. From a social activity standpoint, many functional spaces in the building have been found to be systematically linked.[91] Tenants with limited physical capacity tend to sit in public places and watch on-going activity more than do the physically able. Entrance lobbies are particularly popular if congregating is allowed, and are much more heavily used than peripheral sitting rooms in the same buildings. Activity spaces correspondingly received their greatest use in buildings with only minimum lobbies. Hallways are similarly little used socially unless they are exterior, then they take on the function of a porch.

Apart from the neighbourhood or macro effects on micro spaces, is the influence of service rich settings on tenant characteristics and the consequent use of macro environments. Retirement hotels are one such highly supportive environment which have been found to produce distinct activity patterns in comparison to a neighbourhood sample of older people. The hotel, which served three meals a day and had no kitchens in the individual units, attracted a population which on average was over eighty years old. This, coupled with the supportive services, reduced the necessity for shopping and related trips. Further, the average perceived neighbourhood size for these tenants was only half that of community residents.[92] A one-year longitudinal study of eight low-rent government subsidised housing sites, and a matched community sample provided additional evidence of relative decline in extra-building activity by project residents.[93]

It is evident from the preceding material that there are important interactive effects between neighbourhood and building characteristics. These ultimately affect individual residents but many specific questions remain unanswered about neighbourhoods. Particularly important from the standpoint of site selection are issues of neighbourhood size, composition, service convenience.

The recently revived interest in neighbourhood studies provides suggestive answers to some of these questions. An initial study attempted to determine convenient distances to various services.[94] This information was, however, obtained from project managers, not older people themselves. The critical distances recommended from that study have been reassessed and elaborated in recent survey data from 575 residents living in 154 government-subsidised housing facilities.[95]

Figure 4 summarises the critical service distance recommended by Newcomer's study. In all, twenty-three services and facilities are listed. They are ranked by the percentage of persons who use them when they are provided within the central distance. Location within this distance was positively associated with the frequency of service use. Use patterns were much lower among persons having a service radius outside these limits.

A number of transportation and cognitive mapping studies have verified the relatively circumscribed area defined as neighbourhood and documented as well that older people spend most of their time in their neighbourhood.[96] Studies of retirement community in-movers have found that site location criteria such as being close to shopping and to friends were highly valued.[97] Using three neighbourhood environmental factors — distance to facilities, judged convenience of location, and accessibility to supportive services, Kermit Schooler shows a positive (although low correlation) relationship with morale.[98]

Other variables affecting the utility of these factors or the dimension of the critical distance have been suggested by recent research on

Figure 4: Neighbourhood Service Critical Distance Recommendations

Service	Critical Distance	Maximum Recommended Distance
Bus stop	on-site to 3 blocks	1 block
Outdoor area	on-site to 3 blocks	3 blocks
Laundromat	on-site	on-site
Grocery store	1-10 blocks	6 blocks
Supermarket	1-10 blocks	6 blocks
Bank	1-10 blocks	6 blocks
Post office	1-3 blocks	3 blocks
Department store	1-3 blocks	3 blocks
Cleaners	1-11 blocks	6 blocks
Senior centre	on-site	on-site
Beauty/barber	on-site to 10 blocks	10 blocks
Physician	1-10 blocks	10 blocks
Butcher shop	1-10 blocks	6 blocks
Snack bar	1-10 blocks	10 blocks
Public library	on-site to 10 blocks	10 blocks
Dentist	1-10 blocks	10 blocks
Eye doctor	1-10 blocks	10 blocks
Foot doctor	indeterminate	10 blocks
Centre (for all ages)	used as a senior centre	on-site
Movie	indeterminate	10 blocks
Church/synagogue	indeterminate	indeterminate*
Bar	no importance	no importance

* Indeterminate critical distance due to high percentage of persons who do not use, and only small number who do use.

Source: Newcomer, 1976.

functional neighbourhoods. The intention of most of this work has been first to establish the existence of cognitive neighbourhoods by having individuals draw the boundaries of their neighbourhood on a block map. Analysis was then conducted to determine the influence on boundary location. Steep slopes and heavy vehicular street traffic were found to be instrumental in shaping the borders.[99] Changes in racial characteristics and socio-economic status between city blocks were also important.[100] The size of the functional area was dependent on length of area residence, access to public transportation, and car ownership.[101]

The service types (such as grocery stores, doctors' offices, department stores) which may form the core functions in neighbourhood areas have not yet been clearly determined. Convenience shopping, more than any other service, has consistently emerged as an element in the consensus neighbourhood area.[102]

Service richness as an indicator of service availability has been previously introduced in the section on supra-personal influences. It was alleged there that on-site and neighbourhood service density have an important bearing on a project's perceptual image which is instrumental in resident's self-selection.

Studies of retirement community[103] in-movers present information that these middle-income retirees are younger, healthier, better educated, more likely to be married, still working, to have fewer children, and to see them less frequently than the older population at large.[104] Housing environments which are less recreational activity oriented and more service oriented tend to attract patrons who are older, in poorer health, and more often not married.[105] Studies of institution waiting list applicants, a comparably aged sample of community residents, and institutional residents similarly confirm these findings. Those persons who consider themselves to have the greatest need for highly supportive services are the most likely to accept admission to supportive facilities.[106] In short, service richness qualities may help predetermine such substantial population traits as functional ability, socio-economic status, sex and marital status. Tenant characteristics also seemingly have important influences on service use and other activities. Newcomer's study of 154 housing projects found on-site service richness to be, next to distance, the most consistent correlate with service use patterns.[107]

An added reason for considering resource or service richness comes from work done by Regnier.[108] He observed that elderly public housing residents living near a major commercial street had substantially higher daily service use rates than a similar sample of residents living in a less resource rich area. This is suggestive of the notion that service richness had trip generative effects independent of the preceding tenant related activity patterns.

Conclusion

The process of matching people to environment in a manner which sustains the individual at a maximum level of functioning and satisfaction is complex. Using the environmental taxonomy postulated by Lawton as a basis for selecting and relating variables this chapter has attempted to highlight major known relationships. We have also attempted to support an argument advanced by M. Powell Lawton that man-environment interactions have an ecological relationship. In other words one can influence individual behaviour by manipulating any one of a number of factors in a setting – not simply by influencing the individual directly.

A remaining task is to link theoretical models and research results into policy relevant information. The vehicle we have chosen for this linkage combines Eva Kahana's congruence model, Lawton's environmental taxonomy and our own preference for behavioural outcome variables rather than psychological outcome. In summary, this approach takes the form of the following equation:

$$B = P + I + N + S + PE$$

where

B = behaviour
P = personal competence or capabilities
I = interpersonal environment characteristics
N = social norms and other cultural environmental characteristics
S = suprapersonal environmental characteristics
PE = physical environmental characteristics

As is apparent from the preceding sections, each variable in this equation represents a vector of attributes. These vectors can be represented in the form of a matrix:

	B	P	I	N	S	PE
1						
2						
3						
4						
n						

In the simplest of terms, this expression directs us, in any man-environment decision, to progress through at least four steps:

1. Designate the behavioural (B) outcome desired (e.g. frequency of service use);
2. Inventory the capabilities (P) of the intended target group or actual clients;
3. Compare these with an inventory of relevant inter-personal (I), social norms (N), supra-personal (S) and physical environment (PE) characteristics;
4. Compare the expected effects of the intended policy or decision with the inventory of characteristics.

In progressing through these steps, a variety of questions will have to be answered: Where will be the *direct* impact of the action? Are there any secondary consequences (such as changes in the supra-personal characteristics)? Could an alternative intervention produce the same desired outcome with fewer secondary effects?

This array of attributes and the comparisons of compatibility is essentially the intent of Kahana's congruence model, as illustrated in Figure 2. Our literature review provided many other examples of inter-actions of various personal attributes with environmental conditions.

Kahana[109] has proposed a methodology for relating the 'whole person and the whole environment'. This involves counting the number of dimensions of congruence or incongruence. Her suggested variation on this approach includes counting the number of areas of critical mismatch. Within these approaches one could either count total congruences separately among each of her seven congruence dimensions ot count across all dimensions.

Conceptually, we find her approach to be exceedingly useful. The limitation is in the assignment of relative value to the congruences, because values vary among elements in the comparison. While this limits the rigour with which we can translate research into decision, it need not prevent the systematic use of what we do know. The balance of this paper outlines a decision-making process which requires the incorporation of information from each of the five environmental elements. To illustrate the simplicity and practicality of this procedure, we have elected to discuss a policy issue. The issue chosen concerns the population served by government-subsidised elderly housing in the United States. The principal variables to be considered in this example are shown in Figure 5. Each column in this table corresponds to Lawton's environmental characteristics. The terms shown within the columns represent important variables defining these characteristics.

Figure 5: Illustrative Variables in a Study of Public Housing:
Housing Selection Influences

Housing selection (i.e. behaviour)	Personal attributes	Inter-personal	Social norms	Supra-personal	Physical
	Sex	Marital status	Income limits		Unit size
	Race				
	Income	No. of friends	Functional ability require-ments	% aged men	Unit amenities
	Functional ability			% aged women	Neighbour-hood character-istics
				Age density on site	
			Residential independence		

Personal Attributes. The 1971 National Survey of Housing for the Elderly[110] found that females predominated in this housing. Whites accounted for 71 per cent of the elderly tenants. Females comprised 78 per cent. All had income at or near the poverty levels. In addition, all had functional ability at a level high enough to accomplish daily self-maintenance.

Inter-Personal. Most residents lived alone (82 per cent). Almost an equal number of persons had three or more friends on site. Over half the residents had lived within a two mile radius of the project site prior to moving into the project. This further facilitated familiarity with neighbourhood and on-site social networks.

Social Norms. Allowable annual income ranged from $ 2,400 to $ 7,000 for single older persons and from $ 4,000 to $ 10,000 for elderly couples. In all projects three quarters of the residents have incomes of less than $ 6,000.

A specific level of tenant functional ability was required for daily self-maintenance. Minority populations expressed a greater preference and propensity to reside in households of their children or relatives than was true of whites.

The Bureau of Census publication *Housing of Senior Citizens*[111] which is a special tabulation of persons aged sixty and over, provides additional information about the housing choices made by the total elderly population. Non-institutionalised older persons appear to prefer residence in their own homes (either owned or rented) as evidenced by the fact that 88.4 per cent of them reside in such accommodation. Men (97 per cent) are most likely to be housed in this fashion because most men (77 per cent) live with a spouse. On the other hand, only 40 per cent of the women reside with a spouse. Among those persons who do not have a spouse present, the residence pattern shows little sex difference. Forty-four per cent of single women live with relatives or other non-relatives. For single men, the figure is 45 per cent. Forty-eight per cent of single women live in single person households, compared to 43 per cent of the men. The balance for both sexes reside in group quarters.

Breaking these percentages down to their relative proportion in the total single elderly population, it is found that 75 per cent of the single person households are composed of women. This distribution closely approximates the 80:20 sex split now residing in elderly housing. Thus, it appears that sex itself has little influence on the preference for elderly housing. Rather, it is the reality of living *alone.*

Supra-personal. The mean concentration of elderly on all the sites sampled was 78 per cent. This high level has been shown by Rosow[112] to be strongly associated with friendship formation. The male/female ratio was consistent with the sex split among the elderly living alone. (Neighbourhood supra-personal attributes, particularly tenant congruity with neighbourhood demographic profiles present additional variables of possible importance, but will not be considered in our present example.)

Physical. The unit mix, particularly an emphasis on efficiency units, was one feature found to be contributing to the household size of the tenant populations. The services on-site, and within the neighbourhood were consistent with the expectations of self-maintenance. Tenants had kitchenettes, and minimal on-site supportive services and common areas. Neighbourhoods were generally accessible for convenience goods.

Housing Selection. Housing selection as shown in Figure 5 is the outcome we are attempting to predict. Measured in relation to the satisfaction of current housing tenants, the housing programme must be judged a success. Virtually all tenants reportedly were happy. However, if we begin asking behaviourally based evaluative questions such as 'who is benefiting from residence in these projects', compared with 'who should benefit', the data arrayed in our matrix have expanded usefulness.

For example, what if these programmes were thought to be capable of serving the functionally impaired? A brief review of just the data discussed here provides a strong suggestion that these facilities do not serve the functionally impaired. Without modifications in at least two environmental vectors – the admissions criteria (social norms) and on-site amenities (physical) – these projects could not serve functional impaired. Even with changes in these areas it could be seen that there would be an additional problem of transitioning in newer client groups given the supra-personal age, sex and functional ability densities of current tenants.

As another example, could this housing be used to house elderly couples, if it became necessary to free their housing for larger and younger families? The small units and housing preferences of couples to remain in their own homes, as discussed under the social norms variables, seemingly mitigates against this.

The array of variables in Figure 5 has expedited our ability to answer questions such as these. But does it have usefulness in directing us to future design and other policy decisions? Yes, it does, although not always directly. Consider again the example of couples v. single person households and unit mix.

If it is truly our desire to expand the beneficiaries of government housing programmes to more couples, we need a policy and action applied to the area(s) that will most likely produce the desired result. At least two variables have been shown to impede access to this target group. Of these two, the unit size is something most easily altered by policy. Having made that determination, the next step becomes one of understanding and influencing how we might alter the unit size and mix in these housing programmes. The current analysis, though not providing the answer to the appropriate intervention, has helped isolate the locus for the action.[113]

In closing this chapter, it is well to reflect on the vast uncertainty within the field of environmental psychology and in the crudeness of our applications of knowledge. From its inception man-environment research has been policy oriented. Improved morale has been the major outcome tested. This focus has come from several sources, but psychology more than any other discipline has been involved in this research.

This orientation was functional because the initial questions asked were also global. However, as attempts are made to incorporate man-environment research into specific design recommendations, greater outcome specification is needed. Assessments of the limits of adaptive capability (e.g. service distances) measured in behavioural terms becomes germane.

Another lesson learned is that every action we take which alters either the physical or social environment is essentially an experiment into dynamic relationships. Enough variety now exists for us to have begun a systematic evaluation and prescription for intervention. We have learned from our experience. Incremental changes are needed to further test and refine our effectiveness. We have attempted to provide enough background to raise your sensitivity to key issues and to develop a practical framework for decision-making. In so doing, we hope we have helped reinforce the usefulness of experimentation. We only learn by doing. The concept of man-environment relations, we believe, open up many more avenues for fruitful intervention. As one further aid in this process, we have provided references to recent handbooks on environmental design in the 'Selected Bibliography' accompanying this chapter. These offer specific guidance for such issues as site selection and building design criteria.

Notes

1. For example see the *Journal of Man-Environment Studies,* vol. 6, no. 4 (1976), pp. 228-9.
2. H.A. Murray, *Explorations in Personality* (Oxford, New York, 1938).
3. H. Helson, *Adaptation Level Theory* (Harper and Row, New York, 1964).
4. M.P. Lawton and L. Nahemow, 'Ecology and the Aging Process' in C. Eisdorfer and M.P. Lawton (eds.), *The Psychology of Adult Development,* (American Psychological Association, Washington, D.C., 1973).
5. E. Kahana, 'A Congruence Model of Person-Environment Interaction', in P. Windley, T. Byerts and E. Ernst, *Theory Development in Environment and Aging,* (Gerontological Society, Washington, D.C., 1975).
6. Indeed, architectural research might still be focused on strengths of materials and architectural monuments; landscape architectural research focused on ornamental horticulture; and city and urban planning split between table top planning and economic models.
7. C. Alexander, *Notes on the Synthesis of Form* (Harvard Press, Cambridge, Mass., 1964).
8. The Design Methods Group is associated with the Design Research Society in Great Britain through the DMG/DRS Journal published through

the Department of Architecture, University of California, Berkeley.

9. EDRA annual proceedings have been published for several years by Dowden, Hutchinson and Ross, Inc., Stroudsberg, Pennsylvania.

10 In addition to these societies, there are two major journals. The first of these, *Environment and Behavior,* is published quarterly. It tends to emphasise those man-environment studies that fall within 'environmental psychology' (rather than social ecology) and have a clear methodological base. This journal is published by Sage Publications, Inc., Beverly Hills, California. The second journal is *Man-Environment Systems,* published by the Association for the Study of Man-Environment Relations, Inc., Orangeburg, New York. It appears bi-monthly as a forum for communications among researchers and practitioners in man-environment work. Its content is fairly broad and without disciplinary focus.

11. M.P. Lawton, *Planning and Managing Housing for the Elderly* (John Wiley and Sons, Inc., New York, 1975); J.A. Koncelik, *Designing the Open Nursing Home* (Dowden, Hutchinson and Ross, Inc. Stroudsberg, Pennsylvania, 1976).

12. M.P. Lawton, R.J. Newcomer and T.O. Byerts, *Community Planning for an Aging Society* (Dowden, Hutchinson and Ross, Inc., Stroudsberg, Pennsylvania, 1976); S.C. Howell, 'Site Selection and the Elderly' in Lawton, Newcomer and Byerts, *Community Planning,* pp. 181-94.

13. Lawton, *Planning and Managing Housing for the Elderly;* R.J. Newcomer, 'An Evaluation of Neighborhood Service Conveniences for Elderly Housing Project Residents' in P. Suedfeld and J. Russell (eds.), *The Behavioral Basis of Design* (Dowden, Hutchinson and Ross, Stroudsberg, Pa. 1976); F.M. Carp, 'User Evaluation of Housing for the Elderly', *Gerontologist,* vol. 16, no. 2 (1976), pp. 102-11.

14. F.M. Carp, 'Public transit and retired people' and 'The mobility of retired people', in E.J. Cantilli and J.L. Shmelzer (eds.), *Transportation and Aging* (Government Printing Office, Washington, D.C., 1971); S.M. Golant, 'Intraurban Transportation Needs and Problems of the Elderly' in Lawton, Newcomer and Byerts, *Community Planning,* pp. 282-308.

15. S. Goldsmith, *Designing for the Disabled* (McGraw-Hill Book Co., New York, 1968).

16. L.A. Pastalan, 'How the Elderly Negotiate their Environment', T. Byerts (ed.), *Housing and Environment for the Elderly,* (Gerontological Society, Washintgon, D.C., 1972).

17. Lawton, *Planning and Managing Housing for the Elderly;* Lawton, Newcomer and Byerts, *Community Planning;* L. Gelwicks and R.J. Newcomer, *Planning Housing Environments for the Elderly* (National Council on the Aging, Washington, D.C., 1974); I. Green, B.E. Fedewa, C.A. Johnston, W.M. Jackson and H.L. Deardorff, *Housing for the Elderly: The Development and Design Process* (Van Nostrand Reinhold Company, New York, 1975); Koncelik, *Designing for the Open Nursing Home;* M. Ernst and H. Shore, *Sensitizing People to the Processes of Aging: The In-Service Educator's Guide* (Center for Studies in Aging, North Texas State University, Denton, Texas, 1975).

18. G.G. Beyer and F.H.J. Nierstrasz, *Housing the Aged in Western Countries* (Elsevier, New York, 1967); N. Musson and H. Heusinkveld, *Buildings for the Elderly* (Reinhold, New York, 1963); J.D. Weiss, *Better Buildings for the Aged* (Hopkinson and Blake, New York, 1969); R.B. Rutherford and A.J. Holst, *Architechtural Designs: Homes for the Aged, the European Approach*

(Howard Company, Peoria, Illinois, 1963).

19. F.M. Carp, *A Future for the Aged* (University of Texas Press, Austin, Texas, 1966).

20. I. Rosow, *Social Integration of the Aged* (The Free Press, New York, 1967).

21. Among the many applications which support these findings is A.R. Hochschild, *The Unexpected Community* (Prentice-Hall, Englewood Cliffs, New Jersey, 1973).

22. L.A. Pastalan and D. Carson, *Spatial Behavior of Older People* (University of Michigan Press, Ann Arbor, Michigan, 1970).

23. Principal investigators were Carl Eisdorfer, a psychologist-psychiatrist, and Roslyn Lindheim, an architect. The project committee included such additional people as M. Powell Lawton and Sandra C. Howell, both psychologists, and Leon A. Pastalan, a sociologist. Project Director was Thomas O. Byerts, an architect and gerontologist.

24. A. Rapoport, 'An Approach to the Contruction of Man-Environment Theory' in W.F. Preiser (ed.), *Environmental Design Research* (Volume 2 by Dowden, Hutchinson and Ross, Stroudsberg, Pennsylvania, 1973), pp. 124-35.

25. Lawton and Nahemow, 'Ecology and the Aging Process'.

26. Kahana, 'A Congruence Model of Person-Environment Interaction'.

27. Carp, *A Future for the Aged.*

28. L. Pastalan, 'How the Elderly Negotiate their Environments', in Preiser, *Environmental Design Research*; L. Pastalan, R. Mautz, II, and J. Merrill, 'The Simulation of Age-Related Sensory Losses: A New Approach to the Study of Environmental Barriers', in Preiser, *Environmental Design Research;* Pastalan contributed to the development of a simulation package entitled *Age Related Vision and Hearing Changes* (Institute of Gerontology, University of Michigan, Ann Arbor, Michigan, 1976); M. Ernst and H. Shore, *Sensitizing People to the Process of Aging,* shows ways in which to develop one's own sensory sumulation.

29. Among these are N.C. Bourestrom and L.A. Pastalan, *Preparation for Relocation: Relocation Report no. 3* (Institute of Gerontology, *University of Michigan, Ann Arbor, Michigan, 1973); Carp,* A Future for the Aged.

30. J.T. Mathieu, 'Housing Preferences and Satisfactions', in Lawton, Newcomer and Byerts, *Community Planning,* pp. 154-72.

31. F.M. Carp, 'Housing and Minority Group Elderly', *The Gerontologist,* vol. 9, no. 1 (1969), pp. 20-24; Newcomer, 'Evaluation of Neighborhood Convenience'; L. Gelwicks and A. Larson, 'Housing Choice as a Determinant of Environmental Needs of the Aged', paper presented to the 25th Annual Meeting of the Gerontological Society, 1972; In *Idle Haven* (University of California Press, Berkeley, California, 1971), S.K. Johnson explores mobile home retirement living.

32. K. Lynch, *The Image of the City* (MIT Press, Cambridge, Massachusetts, 1960).

33. The various publications and papers produced by these individuals are discussed and appropriated by references throughout this chapter and are not repeated here.

34. R.G. Barker, *Ecological Psychology* (Stanford University Press, Stanford, Calif., 1968).

35. Hochschild, *The Unexpected Community.*

36. T.O. Byerts, 'Reflecting User Requirements in Designing City Parks', in Lawton, Newcomer and Byerts, *Community Planning,* pp. 317-29.

37. B. Felton and E. Kahana, 'Adjustment and Situationally-Bound Locus of Control Among Institutionalized Aged', *Journal of Gerontology,*

vol. 29, no. 3 (1974), pp. 295-301.

38. Lawton and Nahemow, 'Ecology and the Aging Process'.

39. M.P. Lawton, 'Competence, Environmental Press and the Adaptation of Older People' in Windley, T. Byerts and F. Ernest (eds.), *Theory Development in Environment and Aging,* (Gerontological Society, Washington, D.C., 1975).

40. M.P. Lawton, 'Ecology and Aging' in L. Pastalan and D. Carson (eds.), *Spatial Behavior of Older People* (University of Michigan Press, Ann Arbor, Michigan, 1970).

41. There are a variety of other taxonomies, but they are largely social in nature. S.B. Sells (ed.), *Stimulus Determinants of Behavior* (Ronald Press, New York, 1963) for example, has developed a listing of 'basic aspects of the total stimulus situation' which is highly detailed in terms of personal and social stimuli (a total of somewhat under 250 entries.), but this treatment of physical environment is dissatisfying. One major category, 'Natural Aspects of the Environment', with a total of 25 subentries is concerned with gravity, weather, terrain and natural resources. A sub-aspect of another major category 'Description of Task Problem, situation and setting' presents little clarification on man-made physical environment with three entries. B.P. Indik, 'The Scope of the Problem and Some Suggestions Toward a Solution' in B.P. Indik, and F.K. Berrien (eds.), *People, Groups , and Organizations* (Teachers College Press, Columbia University, New York, 1968).

42. Lawton, 'Competence, Environmental Press and the Adaptation of Older People', p. 24.

43. Ibid.

44. Lawton and Nahemow, 'Ecology and the Aging Process'.

45. E. Kahana, 'A Congruence Model of Person-Environment Interaction'.

46. A full discussion of a variety of proposed alternative theoretical models is presented in a 1975 conference proceedings by P. Windley, T. Byerts, E.G. Ernst (eds.), *Theory Development in Environment and Aging* (Gerontological Society, Washington, D.C., 1975).

47. Their work is principally based on an elaboration of H. Nelson, *Adaptation Level Theory;* J.F. Wohlwill, 'The Physical Environment: A Problem for a Psychology of Stimulation', *Journal of Social Issues,* vol. 22 (1966), pp. 29-33; and H. Murray, *Explorations in Personality.* The description of this model is adapted from Lawton, 'Competence, Environmental Press and the Adaptation of Older People'.

48. Kahana, 'A Congruence Model of Person-Environment Interaction'.

49. H. Murray, *Explorations in Personality.*

50. 'Person' rather than 'man' is used throughout this presentation of Kahana's model in reference to the conventions she employed.

51. Kahana, 'A Congruence Model of Person-Environment Interaction'.

52. Lawton and Nahemow, 'Ecology and the Aging Process', and Helson, *Adaptation Level Theory.*

53. Global in this context refers to a single question which asks about a person's level of happiness: 'Overall, would you say that you are happy living here?' Morale scales, on the other hand, consist of several questions which measure both positive and negative affect. Affect is well being. Generally the level of high well-being found varies between 60 per cent and 80 per cent. Scales commonly in use have been developed by R. Havighurst, 'Successful Aging', *The Gerontologist,* vol. 1 (1964), pp. 8-13; N.M. Bradburn, *The Strucutre of Psychological Well-Being* (Aldine, Chicago, Ill., 1969); M.P. Lawton, 'The Dimensions of Morale',

in D. Kent, R. Kastenbaum and S. Sherwood (eds.), *Research, Planning and Action for the Elderly* (Behavioral Publications, New York, 1972); M.P. Lawton, 'The Philadelphia Geriatric Center Morale Scale: A Revision', *Journal of Gerontology*, vol. 29 (1974), pp. 194-204. Many other studies have asked global questions about well-being rather than using a scale. The number of people reporting high satisfaction are comparable to those found by studies using scales.

The measurement of housing satisfaction has a similar history, although assessment techniques are less standardised. Virtually all studies have relied upon global questions.

Studies of housing satisfaction have found that 60 per cent to 93 per cent of older people tend to be satisfied with their current housing. For example, see M. Hamovitch, J. Peterson, A. Larson, *Housing Needs and Satisfactions*, unpublished final report, University of Southern California, 1974; S. Sherman, W. Mangum, S. Dodds, R. Walkley and D. Wilner, 'Psychological Effects of Retirement Housing', *The Gerontologist*, vol. 21 (1966), pp. 103-8; M. Langford, *Community Aspects of Housing for the Aged* (Cornell University, Ithaca, New York, 1962). This has been true regardless of housing type — single family, garden apartment. Except in the Hamovitch *et al.* study, little attempt has been made within a single study to consider relative happiness across a variety of housing types.

Low satisfaction has been reported because of such global factors as safety, housing costs and upkeep. See for example Hamovitch *et al.*, 'Housing Needs and Satisfactions'; M.P. Lawton, M. Kleban, M. Singer 'The Aged Jewish Person and the Slum Environment', *Journal of Gerontology*, vol. 26 (1971), pp. 231-9; M.W. Riley and A. Foner, *Aging and Society, Volume One: An Inventory of Research Findings* (Russell Sage Foundation, New York, 1968).

54.   Lawton, 'Ecology and Aging'.
55.   For a full yet succinct discussion of these other dimensions, see Lawton, 'Competence, Environmental Press and the Adaptation of Older People'; and P. Windley, 'Environmental Dispositions: A Theoretical and Methodological Alternative' in P. Windley, T. Byerts and F.G. Ernst (eds.), *Theory Development in Environment and Aging* (Gerontological Society, Washington, D.C., 1975).
56.   C. Eisdorfer, 'Arousal and Performance and Intellectual Functioning in the Aged', *Journal of Gerontology*, vol. 18 (1963), pp. 358-63; Lawton and Nahemow, 'Ecology and the Aging Process'.
57.   F. Carp, *A Future for the Aged*.
58.   R. Newcomer and M. Riesenfeld, 'A Study of the Relationships Between Housing and Life Satisfaction in Two Elderly Populations', mimeo, University of Southern California, 1970; Hamovitch *et al.*, 'Housing Needs and Satisfaction'.
59.   L. Gelwicks and A. Larson, 'Housing Choice as a Determinant of Environmental Needs of the Aged'.
60.   M. Caggiano. 'The Application of Models to Apartment Design and Furniture Selection', mimeo, University of Southern California, Los Angeles, 1970.
61.   Neighbourhood familiarity is important to people of all ages. Three among many examples are: H.J. Gans, *The Urban Villagers* (The Free Press of Glencoe, New York, 1962); M. Young and P. Willmott, *Family and Kinship in East London* (Penguin Books, Baltimore, Maryland, 1957); and E. Liebow, *Tally's Corner* (Little, Brown

and Co., Boston, 1967).

62. R. Eribes and V. Regnier, 'Neighborhood Cognition of Retirement Hotel Residents: Cognitive Mapping as a Methodology in the Study of the Urban Elderly', paper presented at the 25th Annual Meeting of the Gerontological Society, San Juan, Puerto Rico, 1972.

63. S. Tobin and M. Lieberman, *Last Home for the Aged* (Jossey-Bass, San Francisco, 1976).

64. J. Peterson, M. Hamovitch and A. Larson, 'A Time for Work, A Time for Leisure', final report, University of Southern California, 1966.

65. For a discussion of this literature, see R. Atchley, *The Social Forces in Later Life,* Second Edition (Wadsworth, Belmont, California, 1977); B. Neugarten (ed.), Middle Age and Aging (University of Chicago Press, Chicago, 1968).

66. G. Beyer and M. Wood, *Living and Activity Patterns of the Aged* (Center for Housing and Environmental Studies, Cornell University, Ithaca, New York, 1964).

67. I. Rosow, *Social Integration of the Aged.*

68. Most of the studies on class linked activity behaviour have been done in large, old, urban areas such as Chicago, Boston or Cleveland. Each of these cities have traditions of ethnic districts. Newer urban centres may exhibit much less ridigity along these lines and may be less spatially bounded for all residents.

69. Rosow, *Social Integration of the Aged;* Carp, *A Future for the Aged;* Hochschild, *The Unexpected Community.*

70. Rosow, *Social Integration of the Aged.*

71. Beyer and Wood, *Living and Activity Patterns;* L. Gelwicks, A. Feldman and R. Newcomer, *Report on Older Population needs, Resources and Services* (Los Angeles County Model Neighborhood Program, Los Angeles, 1971).

72. D. Black, 'The Older Person and the Family' in R. Davis (ed.), *Aging: Prospects and Issues* (University of Southern California Press, Los Angeles, 1973). Approximately 80 per cent of all older people in the US have at least one relative within a one hour's driving radius.

73. Rosow, *Social Integration of the Aged.*

74. L. Nahemow and L. Kogan, *Reduced Fare for the Elderly* (Mayor's Office for the Aging, New York, 1971).

75. G. Bultena and V. Wood, 'The American Retirement Community: Bane or Blessing?', *Journal of Gerontology,* vol. 23 (1969), pp. 209-17; Hamovitch, Peterson and Larson, 'Housing Needs'.

76. Hamovitch *et al.,* 'Housing Needs'.

77. D. Wilner, S. Sherman, R. Walkley, S. Dodds and W. Mangum, 'Demographic Characteristics of Residents of Planned Retirement Housing Sites', *The Gerontologist,* vol. 8 (1968), pp. 164-9.

78. Lawton, 'Ecology and Aging'.

79. E. Brody and B. Gumner, 'Aged Applicants and Non-Applicants to a Voluntary Home: An Exploratory Comparison', *The Gerontologist,* vol. 7 (1967), pp. 234-43.

80. E. Brody, 'Follow-up Study of Applicants and Non-Applicants to a Voluntary Home', *The Gerontologist,* vol. 9 (1969), pp. 187-96.

81. The factors leading to the decision to relocate may be linked to class and ethnic cultural backgrounds. As shown by M. Lowenthal and P. Berkman, *Aging and Mental Disorder in San Francisco: A Social Psychological Study* (Jossey-Bass, San Francisco, 1967), working classes generally have a higher tolerance for deviance in their elderly

parents and may be more willing to keep them at home than the middle classes. Minority groups are under-represented in specialised housing relative to their proportion in the general population. This under-representation may be the result of minority groups' willingness to house their parents in their homes, a lack of sufficient income to place them in alternative housing, or perception of special housing as inappropriately located, e.g. in the wrong part of town. Carp, 'Housing and Minority-Group Elderly'.

82.   L. Rosenmayer and E. Köckeis, 'Housing Conditions and Family Relations of the Elderly', in F. Carp (ed.), *Patterns of Living and Housing of Middle-Aged and Older People* (US Dept. of Health, Education and Labor, Washington, D.C., 1965).

83.   T. Koff, 'Service Needs and Delivery', in R. Davis (ed.), *Housing for the Elderly* (University of Southern California Press, Los Angeles, 1973). There are several factors which also may be contributing to these tenant patterns. The relative importance of all or any of these is essentially an unanswered question. For one, there are now more alternative housing types and community support services available giving healthier people wider housing options while also reducing the necessity of relocation due to reduced capability. Contributing to the ageing of facility populations is a reluctance by both managers and tenants to relocate residents as competence declines. Thus, supportive services are added to help maintain them. Finally, if a facility has a long waiting list, it is likely that this list is ageing at the same rate as the tenant group. Therefore, older residents are replaced by elderly waiting list applicants.

84.   G. Rosenberg, *The Worker Grows Old* (Jossey-Bass, San Francisco, 1970).

85.   V. Regnier, 'Neighbourhood Cognition and Older People: A Comparison of Public Housing Environments in San Francisco', unpublished Master of Architecture Thesis, University of Southern California, 1973.

86.   M. Lawton, 'Supportive Services in the Context of the Housing Environment', *The Gerontologist*, vol. 9 (1969), pp. 15-19.

87.   N.H. Kuo, 'Queensbridge Health Maintenance Service for the Elderly', mimeo, New York City Department of Health, New York (1963); M.P. Lawton, 'Social and Medical Services in Housing for the Elderly', mimeo, Philadelphia Geriatric Center, Philadelphia (1968).

88.   Macro-settings refer to larger spatial entities such as the housing project itself, or to a city block or combination of blocks perceived as a neighbourhood, rather than to individual rooms.

89.   M.P. Lawton, 'Public Behavior of Older People in Congregate Housing', In Proceedings of the Environmental Design Research Association, Pittsburg, October 1970.

90.   G. Nash and P. Nash, 'The Style of Life in Urban, High Rise, Low Rent Buildings for the Independent Elderly', mimeo, Philadelphia Geriatric Center, Philadelphia (1968).

91.   Lawton, 'Public Behavior of Older People'; Lawton, 'Ecology and Aging'.

92.   Eribes and Regnier, 'Neighbourhood Cognition'.

93.   M.P. Lawton and J. Cohen, 'The Generality of Housing Impact on the Elderly', *Journal of Gerontology*, vol. 29 (1974), pp. 194-204.

94.   P. Niebanck and J. Pope, *The Elderly in Older Urban Areas* (Institute for Environmental Studies, University of Pennsylvania, Philadelphia, 1965).

95.   R. Newcomer, 'An Evaluation of Neighborhood Service Convenience for Elderly Housing Project Residents'.

96.   T. Lee, 'Urban Neighborhood as Socio-Spatial Schema', in H. Proshansky,

W. Ittelson, and L. Rivlin (eds.), *Environmental Psychology* (Holt, Rinehart, Winston, New York, 1970); Nahemow and Kogan, 'Reduced Fare'; Eribes and Regnier, 'Neighborhood Cognition'; R. Eribes, 'The Spatio-temporal Aspects of Service Delivery: A Case Study', unpublished Master of Architecture Thesis, University of Southern California, 1973; Regnier, 'Neighborhood Cognition and Older People'.

97. Hamovitch, Peterson and Larson, 'Housing Needs'.

98. K. Schooler, 'The Relationship Between Social Interaction and Morale of the Elderly as a Function of Environmental Characteristics', *The Gerontologist*, vol. 9 (1969), pp. 25-9.

99. Regnier, 'Neighborhood Cognition and Older People'; Eribes, 'Spatio-Temporal Aspects'.

100. Regnier, 'Neighborhood Cognition and Older People'; Rosenberg, *The Worker Grows Old*.

101. Newcomer, 'Evaluation of Neighborhood Convenience'; Eribes and Regnier, 'Neighborhood Cognition'; Nahemow and Kogan, 'Reduced Fare'.

102. Regnier, 'Neighborhood Cognition and Older People'; Eribes, 'Spatio-Temporal Aspects'.

103. A retirement community refers to large private apartment, condominium or single family housing developments designed and marketed for an age fifty-five or older population. Such developments feature many recreational activities.

104. M. Hamovitch, 'Social and Psychological Factors in Adjustment in a Retirement Village', in F. Carp (ed.), *The Retirement Process* (National Institute of Child Health and Human Developments, Bethesda, Maryland, 1968); S. Sherman, W. Mangum, S. Dodds, R. Walkley and D. Wilner, 'Psychological Affects of Retirement Housing', *The Gerontologist*, vol. 8 (1968), pp. 170-75; Bultena and Wood, 'American Retirement Community'; W. Mangum, 'Adjustment in Special Residential Settings for the Aged: An Inquiry Based on the Kleemier Conceptualization', unpublished PhD dissertation, University of Southern California, 1971.

105. Sherman *et al.*, 'Psychological Affects'.

106. M.P. Lawton, P. Nash and J. Bader, 'Statement on Housing Institutions and Older People's Relationships to their Environment', mimeo, Philadelphia (1969); Brody and Gumner, 'Aged Applicants'; Brody, 'Follow-Up Study of Applicants'; M. Lieberman, V. Prock and S. Tobin, 'Psychological Effects of Institutionalization', *Journal of Gerontology*, vol. 23 (1968), pp. 343-53; Lawton, 'Supportive Services'.

107. Newcomer, 'Evaluation of Neighborhood Convenience'.

108. Regnier, 'Neighborhood Cognition and Older People'.

109. Kahana, 'A Congruence Model of Person-Environment', p. 209.

110. M. Grimes, 'Who The Tenants Are', Second Report, National Survey of Housing for the Elderly, Philadelphia Geriatric Center, Philadelphia (1972).

111. US Bureau of the Census, *Census of Housing: 1970 Subject Reports, Final Report Housing of Senior Citizens* (US Government Printing Office, Washington, D.C., 1973).

112. Rosow, *Social Integration of the Aged*.

113. For a discussion of the factors impeding housing project decisions, see R. Newcomer, 'Meeting the Housing Needs of Older People', in M.P. Lawton, R. Newcomer and T. Byerts (eds.), *Community Planning for an Aging Society* (Dowden, Hutchinson and Ross, Stroudsberg, Pennsylvania, 1976).

Selected Bibliography

F.M. Carp, 'Housing and Minority-Group Elderly', *The Gerontologist*, vol. 9, no. 1 (1969), pp. 20-24

M. Ernst and H. Shore, *Sensitizing People to the Processes of Aging: The In-Service Educator's Guide* (Center for Studies in Aging, North Texas State University, Denton, Texas, 1976)

L. Gelwicks and R. Newcomer, *Planning Housing Environments for the Elderly* (National Council on the Aging, Washington, D.C., 1974)

I. Green, B.E. Fedewa, C.A. Johnston, M.W. Jackson and H.L. Deardorff, *Housing for the Elderly: The Development and Design Process* (Van Nostrand Reinhold Company, New York, 1975)

A. Hochschild, *The Unexpected Community*, Prentice-Hall, Inc., Englewood Cliffs, N.J., 1973)

J. Jacobs, *Older Persons and Retirement Communities* (Charles C. Thomas, Publisher, Springfield, Illinois, 1975)

S.K. Johnson, *Idle Haven* (University of California Press, Berkeley, California, 1971)

J.A. Koncelik, *Designing the Open Nursing Home* (Dowden, Hutchinson and Ross, Inc., Stroudsberg, Pa., 1976)

M.P. Lawton, *Planning and Managing Housing for the Elderly* (John Wiley and Sons, New York, 1975)

M.P. Lawton, R. Newcomer, T. Byerts (eds.), *Community Planning for an Aging Society* (Dowden, Hutchinson and Ross, Stroudsberg, Pa., 1976)

R. Newcomer, S. Newcomer and L. Gelwicks, 'Assessing the Need for Semi-Dependent Housing for the Elderly', *The Gerontologist*, vol. 16, no. 2 (1976), pp. 112-17

L.A. Pastalan and D.H. Carson, *Spatial Behavior of Older People* (University of Michigan, Ann Arbor, Michigan, 1970)

V. Regnier, 'Neighborhood Planning for the Urban Elderly' in D. Woodruff and J.E. Birren (eds.), *Aging Scientific Perspectives and Social Issues* (Van Nostrand, New York, 1975), pp. 295-312

S. Tobin, M.A. Lieberman, *Last Home for the Aged* (Jossey-Bass Publishers, San Francisco, California, 1976)

P. Windley, T.O. Byerts and F.G. Ernst, *Theory Development in Environment and Aging* (Gerontological Society, Washington, D.C., 1975)

4 AGEING AND EDUCATION

Lotte Marcus

This chapter is divided into two parts. Education for ageing conveys
the notion that the ageing process goes on throughout a person's
life, and adaptation to it can be influenced by education — by teaching and learning which is aimed at the prevention of crisis situations
arising at different stages in a person's life and the achievement of
a satisfying old age through the ability to deal with events and problems
of daily life in a satisfying and effective manner. Education 'about'
ageing, on the other hand, is used by the writer to describe the
transmission of knowledge, values and skills relevant to the ageing
process and the ageing individual, which is directed at the professional,
para-professional or lay person working in the field of gerontology.
The two thrusts overlap. Professionals may benefit from the learning
'about' ageing 'for' their own personal lives. The education 'for'
ageing can stimulate the development of helpers whose work resembles
that of the professional. The definition of education in the *Dictionary
of Social Science* which speaks of 'the transmission of knowledge
for the purpose of stimulating people to think for themselves, to apply
what they learn, and to gain competence in seeking and evaluating
new knowledge'[1] would certainly include both education 'for' and
'about' ageing. The term educational gerontology is of recent origin
and comprises both aspects of education of the professional, para-
professional and volunteer, and of the elderly and middle aged and
the general public.

Education About Ageing

The interest in raising the educational level of the practitioner in the
field of ageing is of relatively recent origin. The 1971 White House
Conference on Ageing presented evidence that only 10 to 20 per cent
of the one-third of a million people working with the aged had any
formal preparation. The projection was made that one million
professional/technical workers will be needed in this field in the USA
by 1980.[2] Most academic disciplines and professional programmes
could be criticised for their lack of serious attention to the training
of students in the area of gerontology.

117

Medical Education

When one examines medical education in North America, one finds
that the time allocated to classroom and clinical instruction in geriatrics by most medical schools is far less than the health problems
of elderly people would warrant. There is no specialty of geriatric
medicine, or geropsychiatry in North American medical schools,
quite unlike the situation in their British and some European counterparts. (There are ten Chairs of Geriatric Medicine in England.) The
curriculum content on ageing is often confined to a behavioural
science course at the beginning of the student's university career,
a practicum and a few electives in geriatrics (among a multitude of
others). Only two or three of the 640 US medical schools organise
geriatric internships. It is generally left to the family practice
specialisation to place a heavier emphasis in their training period on
the medical care of the elderly (personal communication). This
trend undoubtedly results in a greater number of family physicians
knowledgeable about the health and illnesses of older people attending
family clinics. But, until community services generally become more
plentiful and readily available, the elderly will still be institutionalised
in large numbers and cared for by physicians whose training gives
scant attention to this section of the population.

Education in Mental Health

A recent American report[3] about manpower and training needs in
mental health and illness of the ageing speaks of the inadequate
numbers of qualified professionals in this field — a mere 1 per cent of
those required. This is based on the estimate that 10 per cent of those
over sixty-five years need mental health services. This would mean
that 2.4 million Americans will require some kind of mental health
service by 1980. The report quotes as a conservative goal, over a ten-
year period, the increase in the number of psychiatrists needed
from the present 20 to 1,000, of psychiatric nurses from about 50
to 4,000, of clinical psychologists from approximately 100 to 2,000,
with similar increases in the number of psychiatric social workers,
nurses' aides, technicians and para-professionals. Thus training is
urgently needed for all these professionals, as well as a wide spectrum
of other personnel and volunteers to meet the needs of the growing
population of elderly persons. A very important recommendation of
the report is an emphasis on prevention in the training of mental
health personnel, to avoid problems of dependency and institutionalisation of phsyically and mentally disabled persons whose life

expectancy has been raised by modern medicine.

Social Work Education

Manpower needs are just as urgent in the field of social work where
a lack of motivation to specialise in the field of ageing on the part of
students has been the pattern until recently. Furthermore, in many
schools of social work the curriculum offerings in this area have
been rather restricted. In the teaching of 'Growth and Development'
the later stages of adult life are frequently dealt with rather perfunc-
torily, the learning of social work skills in work with the elderly
is often denigrated as 'merely supportive' and not requiring the same
sophistication as work with children or marriage counselling. The
report of the Andrus Gerontology Center[4] describes seven models of
gerontological teaching in social work.

In *model 1* content of ageing is integrated into most social work
courses. This involves careful planning on the part of the staff, to
fit knowledge about ageing processes and services to the elderly
into each course, including examples from practice with this
population.

In *model 2* ageing becomes a specialisation. Students with a
particular interest and some prior knowledge and/or practice
experience in this field are admitted into a Master's programme.
Its purpose is to broaden and deepen this knowledge by means of
specialised course work, varied field placements offering experience
in direct service to the ageing (preferably in an institutional as well as
a community setting) and in programmes on their behalf. A research
study closely related to the students' practice is an important requirement of such a specialisation.

In *model 3* a sequence of electives is available to students in the
school of social work.

In *model 4* there is collaboration between a Gerontology Institute
of the university and the school of social work in which the students
are enrolled in basic social work courses as well as in special seminars
on ageing.

Model 5 offers dual programmes between social gerontology and
social work, or social work and public administration and other
combinations.

In *model 6* students take electives in ageing in other departments
of the university in addition to their regular social work courses.

In *model 7* there is a multi-disciplinary, multi-professional approach
where courses in ageing are designed and shared by students and staff

from a variety of educational programmes, e.g. psychology, sociology, political science, economics, law, architecture, education, nursing, medicine, psychiatry, etc., as well as social work.

Different models, and combinations of these models, would fit the needs of different schools. It is to be expected that the multi-disciplinary, inter-disciplinary and multi-professional approach to teaching in this field, whether in individual courses or total programmes will become more widespread when the interest in ageing makes itself felt in educational institutions. The participation of older persons in these programmes, either as students or consultants, increases the value of the teaching and adds the benefits of inter-generational contacts. Of great importance are the offerings under the aegis of Continuing Education Departments available to social workers in practice, to agents in the community and to students of all ages.

The situation in Canada is interesting. With the introduction of the Bachelor of Social Work programme as the first professional degree, in 1969 (prior to this all North American schools trained students for a Master of Social Work degree, which was the requirement for entry into the professional organisation in social work), the emphasis was placed on generic teaching both in the classroom and the practicum. The focus was on elements of analysis and intervention which were common to all social problems and was intended to facilitate a perception of the social system in which problems had arisen. The more specialised knowledge and skills required to deal with specific problems (i.e. delinquency, rehabilitation, ageing, etc.) were thought to be more appropriate for the curriculum of the second professional degree (the MSW). This policy resulted in a decrease of courses on ageing in the early years of the students' university education. In recent years, however, more electives have appeared in the calendars of schools of social work, among them courses in ageing. The professional programmes of the community colleges have always included some content on ageing and field training in this area.

If publications and student research can be taken as indicators of the level of interest in a particular field, the funding of an extensive bibliographic search for the period 1964-72, carried out in Canada, should be noted. It revealed a strong current of value-oriented as opposed to fact-oriented articles about ageing and only 40 per cent of these articles contained new data.[5] This finding could be said to reflect the 'state of the art' during that period — strong on feelings and weak on knowledge.

An interesting controversy was raised by two American social work

educators concerning the approach to teaching about ageing.
Pincus[6] deplores the negative view on ageing and the elderly,
commonly held by social workers and frequently gained from working
with socially and economically disadvantaged clients. While he does
not deny the need for social workers to deal with the immediate
problems of inadequate social welfare provisions, he proposes that
greater emphasis be placed on social work education on a developmental view of ageing and the potential for well-being and successful
ageing which might offset the general pessimism. He quotes Peck's
three stages of psychological development in the second half of life[7]
which include a development of self-worth derived from activities
other than the work role, satisfaction in the mastery over physical
discomfort, rather than preoccupation with one's body, and finally
the active effort to make life more secure and meaningful for those
who go on after one dies, rather than passive resignation to one's
demise. Pincus' emphasis on this view of human growth and
development in ageing and teaching of it in social work programmes
was criticised by Kosberg[8] for its ineffectiveness in creating interested,
knowledgeable and concerned social work professionals. He believes
that students, as future practitioners, administrators and educators,
should be taught a social problem approach which would highlight
the neglect and discrimination against the old, the inequalities and
inadequacies of social provisions for them, and their effects on a
vulnerable population. Kosberg suggests that it is inconsistent to
discuss successful ageing with students without first presenting to them
the attitudes and practices of the society within which this ageing
process occurs. He proposes, furthermore, that all social work students
be required, rather than given the option, to take an introductory
course on the problems of the aged, so that they become enlightened
future professionals, conscious of their social responsibility toward
this group.

This writer is in sympathy with the sentiments expressed by
Kosberg, but is not convinced that an educational programme which
emphasises successful ageing necessarily fails to produce concerned
professionals. As advocates for the elderly we must emphasise their
problems, as their allies in a struggle for a better life, we must
recognise their strengths.

Psychology and Sociology

One could argue that the teaching of human growth and development
could best be done in courses in psychology. However, until recently,

little attention was paid to the area of adulthood and ageing in life-span, developmental psychology, nor to the clinical issues of mental health in later life. In a survey of ninety-six American Universities carried out in 1971,[9] only 10 per cent were found to offer training in developmental psychology. Likewise, a mere 13 per cent of books and 4 per cent of articles published between 1960 and 1970 dealt with the psychology of adulthood and ageing. A similar finding was reported by Blake[10] who located only eight articles dealing with middle aged and older people in the *Journal of Personnel and Guidance Counselling* between 1968 and 1974. In a special issue of that journal on 'Women and Counsellors', older women were not mentioned at all.

In recent years there has been an upswing in interest in ageing, as seen by the marked increase in courses on the psychology of ageing in American educational institutions. This development might also account for the fact that, among the 250 odd American and Canadian graduate departments of sociology, over fifty list ageing as a specialisation and many list other concentrations which relate to this area.[11] Of great interest also is the mushrooming of courses on death and dying in universities, high schools and even elementary schools throughout the USA.

Education in Nursing

Gerontological nursing is a new branch of nursing, offered by few nursing schools, and nurses with such training are therefore rare in the USA. This shortage of adequately trained nurses and nursing inspectors has led to shortages in acute care hospitals, in extended care facilities and particularly in nursing homes, and a lowering of nursing care for older people. The new geriatric nurse practitioner programme, as well as the emergence of gero-psychiatric nursing, are welcome additions to the education of nurses in this field in which there is a great need for trained and interested nursing personnel.

Gerontology Centres

Frequently is has been the enthusiasm and dedication of one or a few educators at a particular institution which has sparked the increase of teaching content in the area of ageing. Tobin defines his role as 'educator-advocate' who must 'simultaneously develop core training in aging; induce other faculty members to add gerontological content; build inter-disciplinary bridges with other academic units and influence other educational institutions'[12] — a heavy task if left to one person. Thus, in order to succeed, the educator-advocate must have interested colleagues, supportive administrators and sufficient academic freedom to experiment with different approaches to teaching and to stimulating the development of programmes. It may be necessary to 'open up' the curriculum and introduce innovations in the classroom, in field training and a creative combination of the two.

The 1971 White House Conference on Ageing, conscious of the need for a diversity of training programmes, recommended the establishment of regional training centres. These were later initiated by the Older American Act to serve the function, among other things, of training and supporting educators in smaller and less diversified institutions. Various model programmes emerged around the USA. They combine research and training in differing proportions, and for the most part involve several disciplines and professional schools. Some of these programmes constitute a centre, form a distinct entity within an educational setting and are housed in their own physical structure (e.g. Ethel Percy Andrus Gerontology Center, University of Southern California). Some award degrees in gerontology (e.g. Leonard Davis School, University of Southern California), others emphasise working across traditional boundaries of departments, colleges and schools through inter-disciplinary programmes, and functioning as catalysts and co-ordinators of scholarship and service, but do not offer a degree. Their concentration in gerontology will in some centres lead to the award of a certificate (e.g. All-University Gerontology Center, Syracuse University). Some centres are a consortium of several colleges, supported by the same authority (State) and sometimes distributed over several campuses (e.g. University of Michigan — Wayne State University). Others are more diffuse, with flexible inter-disciplinary linkages (e.g. University of Chicago). There are as yet no major training centres of gerontology in Canada.

The establishment of six Comprehensive Centres for Mental Health and Ageing were recommended in the report on Manpower and Training Needs in Mental Health and Illness of the Ageing.[13] These centres should conduct training, research, service and public education on problems of mental health and ageing. They can also encourage special training programmes for key persons in the community who are concerned with the living conditions of older people, e.g. policy-makers, town planners, architects, transportation experts and others. Furthermore, these centres could give an impetus to the formation of new careers such as (1) 'the patient advocate' who assists older persons to cope with bureaucratic complexities and the ambivalence of families; (2) 'the total care manager' who would maintain communication links between institutions, professionals and the elderly; (3) 'the gerontological specialist', a person variably trained with knowledge in many fields which interface with gerontology; and (4) 'legal workers' who could protect the rights of the elderly in situations of guardianship, commitment to institutions, etc. It is possible that innovative approaches of this kind may attract trainees to the field of ageing where established disciplines have failed in the past.

The Association for Gerontology in Higher Education began in 1972 in the USA and is now affiliated with the American Gerontological Society. Its stated purpose is to unite all educational institutions and services in gerontology, to provide a network of communications between them, to promote education and training of individuals preparing for careers in gerontology, to increase the awareness of the general public of the need for such education, to provide a forum for its members to exchange ideas, and to serve as a base for co-operation with public officials, voluntary organisations and other groups.[14] The Association for Gerontology in Higher Education holds annual meetings where some of the issues confronting education in this field can be discussed and information about new developments in the field and future directions is exchanged.

Issues in Educational Gerontology

This rather shetchy review of educational undertakings in the field of generontology has revealed many gaps and inadequacies, as well as promising efforts and plans. No one would dispute that more extensive and intensive training is needed for all persons working in the field. A variety of educational models have developed in response to local needs and opportunities of the teaching institutions and their societal context, and as the product of the ingenuity, ambition and effectiveness of their leaders and supporters. Greater opportunities, more leaders and supporters must be found for education about ageing to make an impact on society.

In a field as new as gerontology one may assume that beliefs are still flexible and few positions are firmly entrenched. Few persons would dispute that gerontology is related in varying degrees to most disciplines, scientific and humanistic, and to all professions serving people and that students of different disciplines should learn together so that they can begin to appreciate different perspectives on ageing and prepare themselves for productive team work in their later careers. It would also be readily accepted that education could help dispel the stereotypes about the ageing as a sick, sad, poor, passive, unproductive, isolated and predominantly dependent section of the population, a view which misleads the public, isolates the elderly and, worst of all, still permeates the work of professionals, physicians, nurses, social workers and others with an attitude of hopelessness and helplessness. The need for older adults to have access to educational resources, and the desirability for some to be involved as consultants and advisers to teachers and students in gerontology programmes, is not likely to be highly controversial. Further, it could hardly be negated that teaching institutions have a role to play in the well-being of older people by offering their expertise to service agencies, through policy development and other efforts to reach out to the larger community.

The agreement among educators may break down over the priorities between research and teaching when human and fiscal resources are scarce, or the balance between courses in the basic sciences, as core courses — the search for a theoretcial base — and courses where knowledge is applied very quickly to practice issues and service delivery — the 'training for now'. Another point of friction could arise over the quantity and quality of inter-disciplinary linkages and the potential danger of 'watering down' knowledge and losing disciplinary depth. Mention has been made of the controversy between a focus on ageing as a 'social problem' as against the developmental view of ageing and of the elderly as a 'population at risk', possibly more vulnerable, but with many strengths, and the consequences of these different perceptions on the learner. A further difference of opinion has arisen between educators who lean towards the creation of 'gerontologists' and aim for control of their educational programme and those who believe instead in the need for 'gerontologising' other disciplines and professions by encouraging and helping them to include content on ageing in their respective curricula.

A debate could arise between those in the educational world who look with favour on young students who are goal oriented and who pass through the educational channels quickly and purposefully and those educators who believe that the field of ageing would benefit from the older student who may have chosen this field because of personal experiences or even to prepare for his own ageing. Many educators believe that the training of non-professionals should have high priority, while others prefer to start by educating the trainers. Lastly, there are those who believe that too much support is given for laboratory research by some educational institutions at the expense of social research in gerontology.

The writer is of the opinion that these different points of view and controversies are useful and productive in a field as new and complex as gerontology. In order to be well prepared for work in the pluralistic world of ageing, a wide range of educational opportunities should be available for a great diversity of students. There should be ample room for studies emphasising disciplinary depth, inter-disciplinary linkages of knowledge of different kinds and the co-operation of many disciplines and professions. The pursuit of knowledge and skills and the transmission of values and beliefs may well take widely differing routes. If our future societies will comprise a much larger proportion of older citizens a great variety of teachers and learning centres will be needed. Most important of all will be well functioning and continuing communcational links among these centres and between them and the community at large, so that new knowledge and understanding can be translated into action.

Education For Ageing

This section deals with education for ageing in the broadest sense, a lifelong process which aims at helping individuals cope throughout their lives. Before discussing the various aspects of such education, the abilities, preparation and motivation of older learners and the methods of reaching them will be considered. Then the more formal, focused educational efforts, sometimes referred to as lifespan education, i.e. pre-retirement and retirement training, regular course work for older adults, and the different topics and approaches, will be described, followed by a section dealing with the elderly as teachers in a variety of formal projects. Lastly, attention will be focused on informal, lifelong learning which deals with the changing attitudes towards oneself and one's environment and the formation and transformation of values throughout a life time.

The Elderly as Consumers of Education

It is a well known fact that in today's world the old, as a group, have had less formal education than the young. Even though old people of the future will be bettr educated than those living now, they will still be perennially behind the young whose formal education has to keep pace with all the new developments. In 1971, in Canada, the population over sixty-five contained 64 per cent of persons whose schooling ended at grade eight or earlier, 32 per cent who completed secondary school, 5 per cent who passed through university though only 2 per cent graduated.[15] Interestingly enough, these figures are not basically different from those obtained in the 1961 census, except that among the 64 per cent of persons with some elementary education, in 1961, 17 per cent had not reached grade five and 5 per cent had no formal education, thus 23 per cent were functionally illiterate.[16] (The 1971 census did not report on those with no formal education – perhaps none existed.)

Possibly more important than these figures is the finding from a recent US survey[17] which compared serious problems experienced by persons over sixty-five with public expectations of the seriousness of these problems for the older people. Among a list of twelve major problems, the elderly ranked 'not enough education', fifth behind 'poor health', 'fear of crime', 'not enough money' and 'loneliness'. The general public, on the other hand, assigned 'not enough education' to eleventh place. Furthermore, while all other problems of the elderly were exaggerated by the general public, lack of education was minimised.

This belief that lack of education does not present a major problem for the elderly may go hand in hand with a widespread stereotype of older people as uneducable. This stereotype is false. Older learners differ from young learners in that they tend to respond more slowly, are more sensitive to interference while engaged in a learning task and often show a decline in immediate and short-term memory but they are by no means uneducable. In fact, they surpass young learners in verbal and integrating ability. When deficits, other than those mentioned above appear, they are usually caused by psychopathology, not by the normal ageing process.[18]

An apparent decline in learning ability is often caused by a number of extraneous factors, such as disuse of the powers of concentration, lack of opportunity to engage in structured learning and most importantly, lack of motivation, sometimes reinforced by past experiences with failures or rejection, other times created by a sense of futility and depression. Success in learning would seem to depend on the interest and motivation of the older learner, and the attitudes and understanding of his teachers. Educators of older adults may want to put into practice some of Rogers' views on 'learning through doing', learning which 'significantly changed behaviour' and which, furthermore, is self-discovered and self-appropriated which 'does away with teaching, but brings people together who want to learn'.[19] This

concept of enabling adults to learn through interaction with one
another is similar to Illich's idea of a 'transparent society' which
offers opportunities for 'meaningful participation in mutual
education'.[20]

Another activist who has made an important contribution to
adult education is Paulo Freire. His work with poor, illiterate and
powerless farm workers in South America, brought him to the awareness that education for these people had to take the form of what
he calls 'conscientisation', 'a process in which the person is helped
and encouraged to examine the reality which shapes his life and be
made aware of his potential to rransform it . . . an approach which
assists the person to perceive his world more adequately, to pose
questions and take the first step towards increased personal
freedom'.[21] Freire's idea of 'pedagogy of the oppressed', as it is
called, is often compared to education for the elderly by those who
believe strongly in the oppressed state of this segment of our population. The elderly who have been known to accept, or at least to
pay lip service, to the negative stereotypes held by the general public
about them, may well benefit from an educational approach which
helps them to question these stereotypes and to work for changes in
attitudes and actions of those with whom they come into contact.

Lifespan Education

This term is used when adult education becomes a planned series of
activities, undertaken by a person in a focused manner and aimed to
prepare him for personal and societal changes and to help him acquire
knowledge, skills and attitudes conducive to dealing with events such
as job changes, retirement, illness, bereavement, etc. Lifelong learning,
on the other hand, refers to learning which occurs throughout life,
often imperceptibly, and is all-encompassing. Sometimes it is sparked
by personal experiences and may be part of the intrinsic value of
acquiring knowledge for its own sake.[22] The end result in both types
of learning may be the same — the optimum functioning of the
individual — the processes differ. It could be argued that lifespan
education, as described above, has become necessary because of life in
our urbanised, industrialised societies where human values are often
subordinated to market values, where redundancy of skills and unem-
ployment force workers to retrain and recycle, where retirement is
often rigidly enforced wihtout regard for a person's competency,
making it necessary to prepare people for this event, rather than
adjust the event to the individual's capacity and needs.

The writer is in full support of flexible retirement, people-oriented work and the need for many other changes in society, but also believes that in a rapidly changing world, no matter how justly planned, there will always be people who need help to keep abreast and to function adequately. Various types of lifespan education, even though they may have been designed for a remedial purpose, i.e. to counteract the feelings of uselessness created by an unwarranted sudden disappearance of the work role, may go beyond the easing of the wounded feelings to a realisation of hitherto neglected potentials within the individual.

Pre-Retirement Training

Since retirement is a phenomenon of relatively recent origin, preparation for it has been developed only in the past two or three decades. It is of interest to note that the need for such training is rarely questioned by authors in this field. It is assumed that the loss of the work role, the lack of clarity and the ambiguity of the retirement role, the difficulties of the transition from one role to the other, the wavering between two worlds creates fears and anxieties in many individuals. Even though several studies have shown that many workers look forward to retirement and are able to enjoy it, the transition period is often hazardous.[23] With increasing numbers of retirees many more role models evolve and the newly retired may look to this group of already retired for advice and guidance. It could also be stated that the ambiguity of the retired role may be in the individual's favour, allowing him to experiment with different choices, rather than adjust to a prescribed role.

A pre-retirement programme thus could serve a useful function for many individuals. Many studies have indicated that this has happened, that fears of growing old and of retirement have been reduced, life satisfactions have increased and generally positive attitudes were found in persons who had taken such courses. However, the problem with some of these studies is the sample selection. Those who chose a pre-retirement course may already have been more amenable to change and thus have benefited from it.

In a recent small-scale research study of pre-retirement education, the overall positive evaluation of the participants was submitted to a detailed analysis and it was found that behaviour (i.e. attention to health, housing, finances, volunteer activities) had been more significantly affected by the training than attitudes towards the self (i.e. feelings of worth, zest, optimism, personal adjustments).[24] This finding may merely confirm the fact that behaviour tends to be altered more easily than attitudes. It could also point to the trend in pre-retirement programmes toward an emphasis on practical issues, with the expectation that a change in attitudes will follow an increase in knowledge and skills.

Pre-retirement programmes vary in scope and comprehensiveness. Some programmes focus mainly on the financial aspects of retirement — insurance, pensions, hospital benefits — others include health, leisure, housing, family life, etc. Programmes are sponsored by government agencies, industries, private consulting firms, trade unions, educational institutions, community organisations and others. The timing of programmes is important. If offered too soon, there may be few incentives for involvement; if offered too late, the individual may not have time to absorb the teaching. An interesting compromise was found by an American steel company where employees were invited to discuss retirement at ages fifty-five, sixty and sixty-four, followed by an interview two months before retirement and a continuing contact with the firm after it. A significant shift in the direction of more positive attitudes towards retirement was observed among these workers at the point of their exit from the company.[25]

Most pre-retirement programmes end when the person retires. Retirees may be invited to return, but rarely do so except as a gesture towards their fellow workers. If pre-retirement courses had a built-in feature not only to prepare participants by advising them of changes and adjustments that may be necessary, but to help them cope with the changes at the time when they are experiencing them, both pre-retirees and retirees would benefit.[26]

Little research has been done into membership in such programmes. Spouses are frequently included, but the advantages and disadvantages of heterogeneous versus homogeneous membership in relation to socio-economic levels have not been seriously explored. Programming differs greatly. The most frequently used method is sessions with a series of invited experts, sometimes interspersed by group discussions led by the co-ordinator of the programme and the presentation of written and audio-visual material. A rather different approach is described by Bolton[27] who applies principles of the humanistic school of education, as well as Freire's 'pedagogy of the oppressed'.[28] The teacher takes on the role of facilitator, rather than director of the learning experience, the method is student centered rather than content-centered. A differentiation is made between students' concerns and student interests, the former signifying unease and disequilibrium.

The latter may give a superficial clue to concerns, but can also be separate from them. Learning is thought to be affected by the structured group experience which leads to personal growth and to a desire for helping others. In this context, Freire's conscientisation would imply a raising of consciousness in the retiree, making him aware of his 'oppressed' status in society and providing him with practice in self-guided learning, promoting in him self-confidence and a will to effect change in his position and that of older persons generally. This may seem an ambitious aim. It also introduces an element which is not usually included in pre-retirement education, reaching beyond the hoped for benefit to the individual to that of the elderly as a group.

Education for the Older Adult

Another large area of education for ageing comprises courses aimed at providing the older person with alternative modes of thinking and living during the retired or later years. These courses can be very focused, offering vocational preparation for second careers and, employment after retirement, by unlearning old and learning various newer skills. Their educational offerings are less systematic, providing a wide variety of courses from which the older person can choose cafeteria style.

Three broad groupings can be distinguished; those directed very specifically toward learning about ageing, include courses such as 'Problems of the Aged', 'Legal Rights of Older Adults', 'Health Needs of Older Adults', 'Biology of Ageing', 'Sex and Old Age', 'Mature Characters in Literature', and others. Another grouping concerns education in the Social Sciences and Liberal Arts. Courses in psychology, sociology, history, communication, current events, literature and others are often designed to impart new learning to older adults who may not have had the opportunity of an involvement with such knowledge in their younger years. One often hears the view that persons with very little formal education and possibly monotonous jobs develop an apathy which makes it impossible for them to accept educational offerings. The success of most of the above mentioned courses in attracting large numbers of poorly educated persons, would belie this.[29] A third and perhaps the largest area is that of skill training, sometimes referred to as 'leisure time preparation'. This would include instruction in arts and crafts, courses in gymnastics, yoga, folk dancing, public speaking, leadership training and others.

The sponsorship for such educational programmes lies mostly with institutions of learning, frequently continuing education and

extension services, with gerontological centres and institutes, major
organisations for the retired, such as the National Retired Teachers
Association and the American Association of Retired Persons (the
latter two having sponsored the Institute of Lifetime Learning with
approximately fifty branches around the USA) and, on a smaller
scale, by senior citizens' clubs, retirement villages and homes for the
aged.

A controversy exists between those who are committed to an age-
integrated, inter-generational approach in educational offerings for
older persons and those who believe that age-segregated arrangements
are preferable. Among the former is Dr Pierre Vellas who started the
first Université du Troisième Age at the University of Toulouse in
1973, creating a model which has since been adopted by over
thirty European universities. The aims of these universities are three-
fold: (1) to improve the lives of the elderly by raising their level of
health, by making them aware of their cultural heritage and by preparing them for service to the community, (2) to contribute to an
improvement of the living conditions of older persons, through multi-
disciplinary research in the areas of legislation, economics, social
action and public health and (3) to co-operate with the public and
private sector in their efforts to provide information, education,
animation and to engage in applied research.[30]

The inter-generational aspect of these universities consists of
a free and natural intermingling of young and old students in special
lectures and seminars, libraries, cafeterias, etc. Young professors and
students are teachers, discussion leaders and guides for visits of observation and, as at the University of Toulouse, are very active in the
operation of their summer school. It is the general opinion of the
staff and students of these universities that the morale, attitudes and
even physical appearance of the older persons changes markedly,
with the inter-generational contacts as the major contributing factor.

A similar finding is reported from the All-University Gerontology
Center of Syracuse University, NY, where its staff is equally committed to the inter-generational approach in the training of students for
the field of ageing, as well as to offering the opportunity for the
elderly to benfit from the University atmosphere. A high-rise apartment building, Toomey Abbott Towers, for older persons was built
on the University campus, creating a variety of opportunities for
young and old to mix freely. An educational programme, greared to
the interests of the residents at Toomey Abbott Towers was designed
by staff and students from the gerontology centre, no registration

fee was charged and certificates of attendance were awarded. The first course, called 'Tower Topics', consisted of a medley of individual lectures about very concrete subjects, such as home economics, current events, the social services, etc. It is interesting that the second course, entitled 'Creative Ideas: Renaissance to Modern Times', was arranged at the request of the residents who wanted a more cohesive content and apparently also a much more abstract subject matter than that chosen by the Gerontology Centre.[31] Similar projects of housing for the elderly on campuses of universities have been reported from other parts of the world, offering similar inter-generational opportunities.

Those who espouse age-segregated educational programmes for older adults believe that the unique characteristics of the older learner, such as a generally limited prior education, long periods with no formal education, a varied age range, physical and psycho-social handicaps, status and identity diffusion, economic instability and diverse educational and cultural backgrounds, necessitate special consideration in the implementation of educational programmes for them.[32] An educational philosophy and methodology which enables older learners to move from a generally negative attitude to their intellectual and functional capacities to a more positive, independent and self-assured view of themselves, also emphasises the importance of a group consciousness and group solidarity, which is thought to be achieved by age-segregated learning environments, as also in age-segregated living arrangements. In view of the great need for educational opportunities for older adults and their diversity, both models, age-integrated and age-segregated, could profitably co-exist.

A creative programme of residential courses at several New England colleges and universities was described by Knowlton, named 'Elder hostels'. For the past two years short-term liberal arts courses were offered at low cost to the elderly who live in dormitories during the period of instruction. The expressed philosophy of this programme is to offer high quality courses, 'not designed to teach the elderly how to be old . . .'. The mean age of their students was seventy years in 1975; most had some prior college education.[33]

It has often been said that the care of the elderly is very rewarding for the care giver because so much can be learned from their maturity, experience and philosophy of life. Likewise, in the education of older adults, the teacher often learns a great deal from his students and, in many instances, the educational experience becomes a mutual give and take between teacher and learner.

The Elderly as Teachers

In pre-industrialised societies the old did not, as is sometimes believed, invariably enjoy high status and official authority. However, they were frequently revered for their wisdom, became the storytellers who passed on traditions and ancient skills and were also the teachers of the young. In modern societies the knowledge and skills of the old are less often utilised. The spread of formal education and the mass media made oral tradition and story telling less popular. As a consequence the role of the elders, including the grandparent role, became less active than it had formerly been. Grandparents of today rarely have authority over their grandchildren which, many writers have pointed out, has led to easier and less conflictful relationships between old and young.[34] The potential of the elderly as resource persons, advisers and teachers has been rediscovered in recent years and has led to a number of community projects which have proved beneficial to both old and young.

The Foster Grandparent Programme This was started in 1965 in the USA and was originally funded by the Office of Economic Opportunity and administered by the Department of Health and Welfare. It is now under the umbrella of the Federal Agency for Voluntary Services and is designed for persons sixty years and older, in good health and with limited income. The only stated requirements for such service are a concern for children and an ability to read and write and accept supervision. The work of the foster grandparents consists of giving one-to-one support and companionship to developmentally (physically and mentally) disabled children in hospitals, day-care centres and institutions, teaching them simple tasks and skills and offering them tender loving care. Those accepted as foster grandparents receive an orientation course, in-service training and often other educational classes. They work five days a week, four hours per day and are paid at an hourly rate (below the minimum wage rate), but are entitled to sick leave, holidays, physical examinations and other benefits. Since the inception of this programme, projects have sprung up all over the USA, employing over 13,000 foster grandparents, the majority of whom are in the sixty to seventy year age range and are widows, living alone.[35] The programme has been evaluated very positively, with benefits to the foster grandparents and their charges as well as to the staff of the institutions.[36] The physical and mental health of the elderly was found to have improved and their level of independence and self-esteem to have risen. Progress with severely damaged children is slow, but the older person's pace may also be slow. The persistence and patience of the latter in teaching simple skills often bears fruit where the busy staff of younger people has failed.

The foster grandparents derive much satisfaction from their work and their commitment to it is high (personal observation). It would seem that the structure of the programme and the precise job description provide the elderly with a clearly delineated role, contrasting sharply with the frequently ill-defined roles society sets for them. They are able to utilise their life experience and ingenuity and the usefulness of their contribution is constantly before their eyes. Even the monetary recompense for their work would seem to confirm this to them. They do not have ambivalent feelings about their value, as do many old people who believe that the work is more appreciated if it is paid for, but who are not sure that their contribution is worth it. It thus appears that the grandparent role of earlier times, of teaching and taking charge of young children, is reproduced in the relationship of these foster grandparents to their charges and to the staff.

A very interesting offshoot of this programme is the 'Foster Grandparent Home-Visitor Project', begun in Pittsburgh in 1975. A few foster grandparents who had worked for several years in an institution for retarded children were placed in the homes of families who wanted to keep their children at home and avoid institutionalisation. The tasks of these home visitors were to assist and instruct the parents in stimulating the child, to help the brothers and sisters of the exceptional child to establish relationships with one another and to give respite to the mother. A very careful matching by socio-economic level, race and personality of the home visitor and parents and a great deal of support and supervision for the foster grandparent was needed. Many of these home visitors worked with multi-problem families and, in such situations, the old person's role invariably expanded beyond the teaching and caring function for the child to that of family life educator, mediator and counsellor.

Adopted Grandparents. Much less structured and less demanding projects are those initiated by volunteer agencies or school teachers who encourage children to 'adopt a grandparent', usually an old person living alone or in an institution. The purpose is to establish a relationship in which the old person can impart some knowledge or skill to a child who wants to listen and learn. Many such projects have been very successful in bringing new life and stimulation to the old person and teaching a child at first hand about old age and older people. One can assume that a good match between child and old person could build up in the child a positive attitude toward older people generally, as well as to their own ageing.

The Elderly in the School System. Many elementary and secondary schools use volunteers to assist in teaching, to tutor slow learners, to read to children and to help them in choosing books and with other school activities. Only in recent years have older persons been sought out and actively recruited for this kind of work. In many of these projects orientation and training is offered, but sometimes the insecurity and anxiety of the older volunteers in this situation is not fully recognised and more persons are trained than finally volunteer for service in the schools. In an attempt to avoid such attrition, Master of Social Work students at McGill University have acted as group leaders, system managers and advisers to a group of senior volunteers who had recently graduated from such a course. This intervention resulted in the lowest drop-out rate of trainees from any volunteer course offered to date by the local school board.[37]

A research project to determine the concepts and feelings toward ageing held by students and the effectiveness of a variety of instructional activities in changing these feelings was conducted in the Dallas Public School system.[38] Among these activities were workshops for teachers, specially designed mini-lessons for children and the involvement of older people in the classrooms. The findings revealed that both children and teachers knew very little about the process and problems associated with ageing, but the children showed more positive attitudes toward older citizens than did their teachers. Considering the generally negative image of old persons held by children, one can surmise that in the Dallas study the teachers must have been rather pessimistic, but that their feelings had not been transferred to their pupils. The planned learning activities helped to improve the children's attitudes towards greater acceptance of and interest in older people for whom, likewise, the experience in the classroom was a rewarding one.

In the writer's study of the attitudes of the elderly toward the exchange of knowledge, skills and life experiences between old and young people,[39] it was found that the most frequently mentioned item in response to the open-ended questions 'What do you believe children could learn from the old?' and 'What do you believe the old could teach children?' were 'values and appreciations'. This finding

can be interpreted as a lack of confidence by the subjects in their
ability to teach more concrete knowledge and skills, or as a belief
that values and appreciations were areas where their teaching would
be particularly useful. Mead's observation, that roughly twenty years
ago the central problem people experienced was 'identity' and today
it is 'commitment', may point to a similar belief, i.e. that adults
cannot teach the young what to learn, or even to what they should be
committed, but that they can and should impart to them the value
of commitment as such.[40]

The Elderly Teaching Each Other. The teaching and helping to teach
in pre-retirement courses by retirees has already been mentioned
and the value of modelling a role as the aim for such teaching has been
emphasised. Based on a similar idea is the programme initiated by the
Institute of Study for Older Adults in New York City, in collaboration
with the United Neighbourhood Houses.[41] The latter was running a
Senior Companions Programme which involved a daily visit by a
'senior companion' to an elderly 'shut-in'. The Institute then started
courses for these Senior Companions who were expected to pass on to
their 'client' what they had learned and to report on the client's
viewpoint in the following class. This project yielded many benefits
for both parties concerned. The learning of the Senior Companions
was enhanced by their teaching, the homebound took a new interest
in their environment, the visits became more meaningful to both,
and without increasing the class size, twice the audience was reached.
This project is one example of the well elderly extending help to their
less able contemporaries and the value of such an enterprise. The
potential of these groups of 'young-old' and 'well elderly' in giving
service to those in need, has not been fully explored in our society.
Given the rapid growth in numbers of the very old, often sick and
dependent persons, a great need of helpers will arise in the near
future. Furthermore, it has been said that one of the most prevalent
needs of the elderly is to be needed. The project described above is
teaching one group of older persons, the Senior Companions, how to
earn the right to be needed.[42]

The Elderly as Teachers in Developing Countries. An area where the
teaching of older persons, and more specifically the passing on of their
work and life experiences is greatly appreciated is in developing
countries. Volunteers under the auspices of the International Service
Corps of Retired Executives (SCORE), in the USA, and the Canadian

Executive Service Overseas (CESO), in Canada, as well as similar organisations in other parts of the world, have as their objectives (1) to assist developing countries to achieve economic growth, by helping them to strengthen the effectiveness of their own organisations and institutions, (2) to provide opportunities for retirees to place their experience at the service of enterprises in developing countries and (3) to increase friendly relations between their own countrymen and those of other countries.[43] One might add that such efforts would also help to spread positive attitudes toward ageing in countries which will be facing demographic imbalances, similar to those in the more developed countries where the population of those over sixty-five years has reached 12 per cent, or is rapidly approaching this point which marks them as 'ageing' countries.

The example of a developing country which is making deliberate efforts to make full use of her own elderly potential, is the People's Republic of China.[44] There men can retire at fifty-five years of age and women at fifty and those who wish can continue to work full-time, sometimes switching to less demanding tasks. The elderly in rural areas can serve as teachers to students learning agricultural skills and, in the cities, help the police maintain order or guide tourists around shrines, etc. In addition, the elderly often teach each other in political re-education classes which are held in all parts of the country.

The writer has expanded on projects where the elderly act as teachers not only to point to the social value of such undertakings for both teachers and learners, but also in the conviction that people learn best when placed in the teacher role which is both humbling and enriching.

Education for Living

This phrase refers to 'lifelong learning' in which the aims resemble those set for positive mental health by Jahoda,[45] i.e. a sense of identity and self-acceptance, the growth, development and self-actualisation, the integration of one's experiences into a unifying outlook on life, a certain amount of autonomy in decision-making and independent action, the realistic perception of one's world, a social sensitivity and a sense of mastery over one's environment, with the capacity to 'love, work and play'. All the factors referred to by Jahoda are means to an end — a satisfying life — not an end in itself and are optimal in so far as the ultimate in degree is concerned. Thus the positiveness of mental health does not lie in the state, but in the

struggle to reach a goal. This reaching for a goal is important at all
stages of life, but particularly so in the later years when the goals are
often no longer defined by society, as they are during childhood,
schooling and worklife, but depend to a large extent on the individual's
capacity to choose and define them and his motivation to reach for
them. This implies a forward looking stance when the older person
may wish to evaluate the events of his past life and integrate them
into some meaning for himself and others.[46] Thus an emphasis on
'being', rather than 'becoming' may be the attitude for the later years
and the task one of consolidating rather than adding for some older
persons. 'Good' mental health in youth is 'a matter of preparing well
for the race', in ageing it can be 'an evaluation of how well the race
was run'.[47] This necessitates a shift in goals and a shift in time
perspective.

Conceptions of time are variable from one culture to another and
within the same culture at different stages of development. It has been
said that time in North America is 'handled' like a material; it can be
earned, spent, saved or wasted.[48] The concepts of time and leisure
are closely related and, like time, leisure can be perceived as a
commodity, to be earned or spent or wasted. This view differs very
widely from the meaning given to leisure by the ancient Greeks who
took leisure very seriously, saw it as an ideal, a state of being in which
activities would be performed for their own sake, with contemplation
as the most desirable activity.[49] The Greeks also spoke about
'education for leisure' which has become a concern in contemporary
society, especially in relation to retirement.

An interesting division of leisure into residual and discretionary
time was made by Moore.[50] Residual time can be defined as non-work
time, time 'left-over' after work, filled with activities which are meant
to supply satisfactions which work fails to provide. Discretionary
time, on the other hand, is perceived as similar to the Greek ideal,
offering opportunities to do the things we want to do for their own
sake and those we do for the sake of others. Moore argues that the
residual concept of leisure as a compensation for the alienation from
work, is ill conceived, that a constructive use of leisure depends on
the perception of the work situation as constructive. Satisfactions
and dissatisfactions, he believes, are mutually reinforcing and the
person who is fully involved in his work, will frequently also be
involved in leisure, and conversely, when work is a problem, leisure
will be a problem. This supposition would seem to apply to workers
who have no autonomy at work and do not exercise it during leisure

hours and those who make little use of their intellectual faculties on the job, who have no opportunity for self-expression and consequently escape into substitute gratifications and over-compensation through meaningless 'entertainment'.[51] On the other hand, there are occupations which do not afford a clear distinction between work and leisure.

A dichotomy similar to that between residual time and discretionary time presents itself in the definition of 'residual welfare' versus 'institutional welfare'.[52] The former refers to those welfare measures, such as supplementary pensions, which become necessary when the existing structures of family and local supports break down, whereas institutional welfare, such as hospital insurance, is directed to those needs which are normal and universal. A comparable dichotomy might be found in relation to educational programmes, between those with 'remedial' and those with 'preventive' aims. The retraining of workers whose jobs have become obsolete or the counselling of retirees who have never known true leisure, could be described as remedial, helping them to make the best of a bad job, whereas a more radical change in educational practices, i.e. Freire's 'pedagogy of the oppressed', or courses such as 'Legal Rights of Older Adults' could be described as preventive, as they aim at strengthening the learner in asserting himself and promoting change in his life situation.

When one examines the first two of the dichotomies, i.e. residual versus discretionary time and residual versus institutional welfare, it becomes obvious that the occurrence of residual time as well as residual welfare is undesirable, that both are merely compensating for the inadequacies of a social system where neither work nor social provisions are fulfilling human needs in many instances. In writing a blueprint for a model society, one might affirm that all time — work and leisure — should be discretionary and all welfare measures institutional.

The question then arises whether the third dichotomy, that between educational programmes described as 'remedial' and those seen as 'preventive' should be judged in the same manner. Could one say that retraining and pre-retirement courses should not be necessary, that they appease and distract people when they should help them assert themselves and work for changes in their lives? There is undoubtedly merit to this argument. It could, however, be said that even in the most humane society, there will always be those who need extra help and many of the elderly will be among them. As has been mentioned earlier, the education of the old will always lag behind that of the young, there will always be some who are unprepared

for retirement, even if retirement policies become more flexible
and the losses in the lives of the ageing, even if anticipated, will always
need palliation. Thus, in the education for ageing, remedial teaching
will always be necessary. At the same time efforts should be directed
towards the prevention of crises and dysfunctional conditions by
working towards changes in society, in attitudes toward ageing and
in the values of people of all ages.

Learning about Values

It has been said that the old, when well adapted, espouse the
'secondary values' of modern society.[53] They often become more
interested in conservation than in acquisition, in self-acceptance than
in self-advancement, in being than in doing, in co-operation than in
competition and in concern for others than in control over others. If
it is true that these secondary values are congenial to the elderly and,
when they are encouraged to put them into action, they could be in
the forefront of movements which predict dire consequences for
mankind, unless our values change in the direction of 'small is
beautiful' and 'economics as if people mattered'.[54]

Another list of values has been suggested by Birren and Renner as
being pertinent to the aged in preventing feelings of alienation, despair,
fear of death and suicide.[55] Labelled as the 5 Rs, the authors speak of
'review' of one's life, 'reconciliation', an acceptance of it, 'relevance'
of a set of values, 'reverence' to a set of ideals for one's life without
which there is regret, and 'release' or feeling that the mind can rest if
reconciliation has taken place between reality and the ideals for one's
life. The concept of the Life Review, the attention given to the focusing of a person's reminiscences, has been used in the therapy of the
elderly.[56] It can also serve a useful educational purpose, both for the
reviewer and the listener. In the 'Experimental Life History' class at
the University of Southern California led by a professor of English
and a professor of Anthropology, students and old people joined in
constructing a living history from the reminiscences and memorabilia
offered by the elderly.[57] The value for the old of being heard and
for the young of having models to identify with was accomplished
by this educational project.

A set of values such as the ones described by Birren and Renner,
could be the result of some process of self-education, as recommended
by Butler, when 'students of all ages extract from within themselves
what they have already learned from life . . . a new kind of education
which prepares people for survival and leisure'.[58] In the pursuit of

goals, essential at all stages of life, but crucial for the elderly, the cultivation of flexibility is perhaps the most important. This may involve the ability to enjoy company, but to be able to live alone, to adapt to a changing family and to expand one's solidarity beyond it, to be vitally concerned with one's society, but to be prepared to let others run it. Another very important goal, particularly in middle age, is to learn new behaviour patterns which may go counter to the sense of time-urgency, competitiveness and striving of the earlier years which are said to characterise the 'type A personality'.[59] This learning would involve relaxation, as well as exercise, the ability to read for enjoyment, to listen and to hear, to 'waste time' and not to feel guilty and other characteristics of what the ancient Greeks might have described as 'leisure with dignity'.

A better distribution of leisure and work throughout life has been advocated by many who believe that most people's lives are too compartmentalised. The practice of sabbatical leave, widespread in academic life, could become more common in other occupations. Among other things, a sabbatical is an excellent preparation for retirement. A Swedish economist has proposed plans in which the financing of educational leave, vacations and pensions would be consolidated into one programme into which payments would be made by the employers on behalf of workers.[60] In Canada a group of large companies have set up an employee exchange programme, called 'Interchange' which permits a civil servant to spend up to two years working in industry and vice versa, while his job, or an equivalent one, is held for his return. Sabbatical leaves allow people to experience, sometimes for the first time in their lives, how to organise their time meaningfully without the routine of a job or the guidance of a set educational programme.

Lastly, if the industrialised world is moving closer toward a 'service society' because this has a potential for unlimited growth in the environment of scarcity,[61] the value of involved citizenship will become more important. The education for service to the community has to proceed throughout life and could culminate in an age-integrated society where people are characterised by their personal attributes and needs, rather than their age.

Conclusion

This chapter started with a rather gloomy picture of shortages of trained personnel in all professions and disciplines dealing with ageing and the elderly and a lack of educational facilities for the dissemination of knowledge about ageing. A ray of hope was seen in the growing recognition that this situation is critical and in the measures which are beginning to be taken to remedy it.

In the second part of this chapter some interesting and innovative programmes were described where, in many instances, the elderly themselves are acting as teachers or trainers of their contemporaries or of children and younger persons. The writer is conscious of the fact that her examples are by no means exhaustive and are predominantly North American in origin. Undoubtedly other important and creative projects have been designed in other parts of the world.

Many interesting ideas are conceived, frequently executed on a small scale, sometimes reported on locally, occasionally evaluated and rarely published. 'Ageing International', the information bulletin of the International Federation on Ageing, offers a forum for brief reports on new developments in the field of ageing in different countries. National gerontological journals welcome articles on all aspects of ageing. The Association for Gerontology in Higher Education in the USA deals with the education of professionals and para-professionals and communication among them. National and international meetings offer opportunities for their participants to exchange knowledge and experiences. Local newspapers print stories of popular interest. All these communications are important. Nevertheless, the writer wonders whether a clearing-house may be needed for information specifically about projects where the elderly are teachers and/or learners. An easily accessible pool of information on such projects might stimulate educators to engage in similar efforts and communicate these to others; it might enable professionals to help their clients to become involved in a variety of projects which utilise their skills and, most importantly, convey to the elderly that their knowledge and experience can be and is being utilised in educating and helping others.

Notes

1.   J.T. Zadrozny, *Dictionary of Social Science* (Public Affairs Press, Washington, D.C., 1959), p. 104.
2.   W. Cohen, 'Report on the Demand for Personnel and Training in the Field of Aging', *Congressional Record*, vol. 65, no. 4 (1969), pp. 4465-8.
3.   J.E. Birren and B.R. Sloane, *Manpower and Training Needs in Mental Health and Illness of the Aging* (Ethel Percy Andrus Gerontology Center, Los Angeles, 1977).
4.   Ibid.

5.   Environics Research Group, *State of the Art: Research on the Elderly 1964–1972* (Central Mortgage and Housing Corporation, Ottawa, 1972).
6.   Allen Pincus, 'Toward a Developmental View of Aging for Social Work', *Social Work*, vol. 12, no. 3 (1967), pp. 33-41.
7.   Robert Peck, 'Psychological Development in the Second Half of Life' in J.E. Anderson (ed.), *Psychological Aspects of Aging* (American Psychological Association, Washington, D.C., 1956), pp. 42-53.
8.   Jordan I. Kosberg, 'A Social Problem Approach to Gerontology in Social Work Education', *Social Work*, vol. 12, no. 1 (1976), pp. 78-87.
9.   J.E. Birren and D.S. Woodruff, 'Academic and Professional Training in the Psychology of Aging' in C. Eisdorfer and M.P. Lawton (eds.), *The Psychology of Adult Development and Aging* (American Psychological Association, Washington, D.C., 1973), pp. 11-36.
10.   Richard Blake, 'Counselling in Gerontology', *Personnel and Guidance Journal*, vol. 53, no. 10 (1975), pp. 733-7.
11.   American Sociological Association, *Guide to Graduate Departments of Sociology* (American Sociological Association, Washington, D.C., 1976).
12.   Sheldon S. Tobin, 'The Educator as Advocate: The Gerontologist in an Academic Setting', *Journal of Education for Social Work*, vol. 9, no. 2 (1973), pp. 94-8.
13.   Birren and Sloane, *Manpower and Training Needs*.
14.   The Association for Gerontology in Higher Education, *Membership Application Form* (The Association for Gerontology in Higher Education, Washington, D.C., 1972).
15.   Statistics Canada, *Census of Canada*, 1971, vol, 1, part 5.
16.   Statistics Canada, *Census of Canada*, 1961, vol. 1, part 2.
17.   Louis Harris and Associates, *Myth and Reality of Aging in America* (National Council on the Aging, Washington, D.C., 1975), p. 32.
18.   L.F. Jarvik and D. Cohen, 'A Biobehavioural Approach to Intellectual Changes with Aging', in C. Eisdorfer and M.P. Lawton (eds.), *The Psychology of Adult Development and Aging*, pp. 223-4.
19.   Carl R. Rogers, *Freedom to Learn* (Charles E. Merrill Publishing Co., Columbus, Ohio, 1969), p. 153.
20.   Ivan Illich, 'Alternatives in Education', lecture delivered at the Ontario Institute for Studies in Education, Toronto, 1970.
21.   Paulo Freire, 'Cultural Action and Conscientization', *Harvard Educational Review*, vol. 15, no. 2 (1970), pp. 452-77.
22.   David A. Peterson, 'Life-Span Education and Gerontology', *The Gerontologist*, vol. 15, no. 5, part I (1975), pp. 436-41.
23.   Gordon F. Streib and Clement J. Schneider, *Retirement in American Society* (Cornell University Press, Ithaca, N.Y., 1971).
24.   D.M. Tibari and V.L. Boyack, 'The Effects of Pre-Retirement Education: an Evaluation', paper presented at the annual meeting of the American Gerontological Society, New York, October 1976.
25.   Philip Ash, 'Pre-Retirement Counselling', *The Gerontologist*, vol. 6, no. 2 (1966), pp. 97-9, 127-8.
26.   Nancy Campbell, 'Pre-Retirement Programs', unpublished paper, McGill University, Montreal, 1975.
27.   Christopher R. Bolton, 'Humanistic Instructional Strategies and Retirement Education Programming', *The Gerontologist*, vol. 16, no. 6 (1976), pp. 550-5.
28.   Freire, 'Cultural Action'.
29.   Lorraine Altmann and Peter W. Oppenheimer, 'Education and the Older Adult', unpublished paper delivered at the annual meeting of the American

Gerontological Society, Louisville, Kentucky, 1975.

30. Pierre Vellas, 'L'Université du Troisième Age de Toulouse', *Annales de l'Université des Sciences Sociales de Toulouse*, vol. 22, no. 1 and 2 (1974), pp. 322-72.

31. Jacques and Maureen Lebel, 'A Continuing Education Program: A Case Study in Potential Relationships Between an Institution of Higher Education and an Elderly Community', unpublished paper presented at the annual meeting of the American Gerontological Society, Houston, Texas, October, 1971.

32. Altmann and Oppenheimer, 'Education and the Older Adult'.

33. Martin P. Knowlton, 'Liberal Arts: The Elderhostel Plan for Survival', *Educational Gerontology*, vol. 2, no. 1 (1977), pp. 87-93.

34. Ivan F. Nye and Felix M. Berardo, *The Family: Its Structure and Interaction* (Mcmillan Co., New York, 1973).

35. 'Foster Grandparents Mark Ten Years as Champions for Children', unsigned, *Interaction*, vol. 4, no. 1 (1975), pp. 6 and 11.

36. Robert M. Grey and Josephine M. Kasteler, 'An Evaluation of the Effectiveness of a Foster Grandparent Project', *Sociology and Social Research*, vol. 54 (1970), pp. 181-9.

37. Vera Osidacz and Peggy Tanzer, 'Senior Volunteers in the School System', unpublished Master's Research Report, McGill University, School of Social Work, Montreal, 1977.

38. Raymond H. Speulda, *Gerontological Research Instructional Program, Final Report* (Office of Education (DHEW), Washington, D.C., 1973).

39. Lotte Marcus, 'Learning and Teaching between Old and Young', unpublished report, McGill University, School of Social Work, Montreal, 1976.

40. Margaret Mead, *Culture and Commitment: A Study of the Generation Gap* (Natural History Press/Doubleday and Company, Garden City, N.Y., 1970).

41. *Annual Report of New York City Community College,* Division of Continuing Education and Extension Services, New York, 1975-6.

42. Lowell Eklund, 'Aging and the Field of Education', in M.W. Riley *et al.* (eds.), *Aging and Society* (Russell Sage Foundation, New York, 1969), vol. II, p. 338.

43. Canadian Executive Service Overseas, Canada, December, 1976.

44. Yung-Huo Liu, 'Old People in New China', *Perspectives on Aging*, May/June 1974.

45. Marie Jahoda, *Current Concepts of Positive Mental Health* (Basic Books, New York, 1958).

46. Robert N. Butler, 'Successful Aging', *Mental Health*, vol. 58, no. 3 (1974), pp. 7-12.

47. Birren and Sloane, *Manpower and Training Needs*, p. 30.

48. Edward T. Hall, *The Silent Language* (Fawcett Publications Inc., Greenwich, Conn., 1964).

49. Sebastian DeGrazia, *Of Time, Work and Leisure* (The Twentieth Century Fund, New York, 1962).

50. Wilbert E. Moore, *Man, Time and Society* (John Wiley and Sons, Inc., New York, 1963).

51. David G. Gil, 'Social Policy and the Right to Work', *Social Thought*, vol. 3, no. 1 (1977), pp. 47-65.

52. H.L. Wilensky and C.N. Lebeau, *Industrial Society and Social Welfare* (Russell Sage Foundation, New York, 1958).

53. Margaret Clark and Barbara G. Anderson, *Culture and Aging* (Charles C. Thomas, Springfield, Illinois, 1967).

54.   E.F. Schumacher, *Small is Beautiful* (Sphere Books, Ltd, London, 1975).
55.   J.E. Birren and V.J. Renner, *A Brief History of Mental Health and Aging* (National Institute of Mental Health, Washington, D.C., in press, 1977).
56.   Robert N. Butler and Myrna I. Lewis, *Aging and Mental Health* (the C.V. Mosby Company, Saint Louis, 1973), p. 148.
57.   Barbara G. Myerhoff and Virginia Tufte, 'Life History as Integration', *The Gerontologist,* vol. 15, no. 6 (1975), pp. 541-3.
58.   Robert N. Butler, *Why Survive? Being Old in America* (Harper and Row, New York, 1973).
59.   Meyer Friedman and R.H. Rosenman, 'Type A Behavior Pattern: Its Association with Coronary Heart Disease', *Annals of Clinical Research,* vol. 3 (1971), pp. 300-12.
60.   Susan Carson, 'Sabbatical Time and the Leaving is Easy', *Montreal Star,* 29 January 1977.
61.   Carl Gersuny and William R. Rosengren, *The Service Society* (Schenkman Publishing Co., Cambridge, Mass., 1973).

Select Bibliography

Lorraine Altmann and Peter W. Oppenheimer, 'Education and the Older Adult' (unpublished paper delivered at the annual meeting of the American Gerontological Society, Louisville, Ky., 1975)

Philip Ash, 'Pre-Retirement Counselling', *The Gerontologist,* vol. 6, no. 2 (1966), pp. 97-9, 127-8

Daniel J. Baum, *The Final Plateau* (Burns and MacEachern Ltd., Toronto, 1974)

Walter M. Beattie, 'Gerontological Curricula: Multidisciplinary Frameworks, Interdisciplinary Structures and Disciplinary Depth', *The Gerontologist,* vol. 14, no. 6 (1974), pp. 545-9

J.E. Birren and B.R. Sloane, *Manpower and Training Needs in Mental Health and Illness* (Ethel Percy Andrus Gerontology Center, Los Angeles, 1977)

J.E. Birren and D.S. Woodruff, 'Academic and Professional Training in the Psychology of Aging' in C. Eisdorfer and M.P. Lawton (eds.), *The Psychology of Adult Development and Aging* (American Psychological Association, Washington, D.C., 1973)

Richard Blake, 'Counselling in Gerontology', *Personnel and Guidance Journal,* vol. 53, no. 10 (1975), pp. 733-7.

Christopher R. Bolton, 'Humanistic Instructional Strategies and Retirement Education Programming', *The Geronotologist,* vol. 16, no. 6 (1976), pp. 550-55

Robert N. Butler, 'Successful Aging', *Mental Health,* vol. 58, no. 3 (1974), pp. 7-12.

Robert N. Butler, *Why Survive? Being Old in America* (Harper and Row, New York, 1975)

Robert N. Butler and Myrna I. Lewis, *Aging and Mental Health* (The C.V. Mosby Company, Saint Louis, 1973)

Susan Carson, 'Sabbatical Time and the Leaving is Easy', *Montreal Star,* 29 January 1977

Margaret Clark and Barbara G. Anderson, *Culture and Aging* (Charles C. Thomas Springfield, Illinois, 1976)

W. Cohen, 'Report on the Demand for Personnel and Training in the Field of Aging', *Congressional Record,* vol. 65, no. 4 (1969), pp. 4465-8

Sebastian De Grazia, *Of Time, Work and Leisure* (The Twentieth Century Fund,

New York, 1962)

I.F. Ehrlich and P.D. Ehrlich, 'Higher Education and Gerontology', *Educational Gerontology*, vol. 1, no. 3 (1976), pp. 251-60

Lowell Eklund, 'Aging and the Field of Education' in M.W. Riley *et al.* (eds.) *Aging and Society* (Russell Sage Foundation, New York, 1969), vol. 2, pp. 324-51

Environics Research Group, *State of the Art: Research on the Elderly, 1964–1972* (Central Mortgage and Housing Corporation, Ottawa, 1972)

Paulo Freire, 'Cultural Action and Conscientization', *Harvard Educational Review*, vol. 15, no. 2 (1970), pp. 452-77

Carl Gersuny and William R. Rosengren, *The Service Society* (Schenkman Publishing Company, Cambridge, Mass., 1973)

David G. Gil, 'Social Policy and the Right to Work', *Social Thought*, vol. 3, no. 1 (1977), pp. 47-65

Robert M. Grey and Josephine M. Kasteler, 'An Evaluation of the Effectiveness of a Foster Grandparent Project', *Sociology and Social Research*, vol. 54 (1970), pp. 181-9

Louis Harris and Associates, *Myth and Reality of Aging in America* (National Council on the Aging, Washington, D.C., 1975)

Ivan Illich, 'Alternatives in Education' (Lecture delivered at the Ontario Institute for Studies in Education, Toronto, 1970)

L.H. Jarvik and D. Cohen, 'A Biobehavioural Approach to Intellectual Changes with Aging' in C. Eisdorfer and M.P. Lawton (eds.), *The Psychology of Adult Development and Aging* (American Psychological Association, Washington D.C., 1973), pp. 223-4

Jordan I. Kosberg, 'A Social Problem Approach to Gerontology in Social Work Education', *Social Work*, vol. 12, no. 1 (1976), pp. 78-87

Jacques Lebel and Maureen Lebel, 'A Continuing Education Program: A Case Study in Potential Relationships Between an Institution of Higher Education and an Elderly Community' (unpublished paper presented at the annual meeting of the American Gerontological Society, Houston, Texas, October, 1971)

John Lowe, *The Education of Adults: A World Perspective* (The Unesco Press, Paris and Oise, Toronto, 1975)

Lotte Marcus, 'Learning and Teaching Between Old and Young' (unpublished report, McGill University, School of Social Work, Montreal, 1976)

Margaret Mead, *Culture and Commitment: A Study of the Generation Gap* (Natural History Press/Doubleday and Company, Garden City, New York, 1970 1970)

Wilbert E. Moore, *Man, Time and Society* (John Wiley and Sons, Inc., New York, 1963)

Barbara G. Myerhoff and Virgina Tufte, 'Life History as Integration', *The Gerontologist*, vol. 15, no. 6 (1975), 541-3

Ivan F. Nye and Felix M. Berardo, *The Family: Its Structure and Interaction* (Macmillan Company, New York, 1973)

John Ohlinger and Colleen McCarthy, *Lifelong Learning or Lifelong Schooling?* (Syracuse University and ERIC Clearinghouse on Adult Education, Syracuse, 1971)

Vera Osidacz and Peggy Tanzer, 'Senior Volunteers in the School System' (unpublished Master's Research Report, McGill University, School of Social Work, Montreal, 1977)

Robert Peck, 'Psychological Development in the Second Half of Life' in J.E. Anderson (ed.), *Psychological Aspects of Aging* (American Psychological Association, Washington, D.C., 1956), pp. 42-53

David A. Peterson, 'Life-Span Education and Gerontology', *The Gerontologist*, vol. 15, no. 5, Part I (1975), pp. 436-41

Allen Pincus, 'Toward a Developmental View of Aging For Social Work', *Social Work*, vol. 12, no. 3 (1967), pp. 33-41

Carl R. Rogers, *Freedom to Learn* (Charles E. Merrill Publishing Company, Columbus, Ohio, 1969)

E.F. Schumacher, *Small is Beautiful* (Sphere Books, Ltd, London, 1975).

Gordon F. Streib and Clement J. Schneider, *Retirement in American Society* (Cornell University Press, Ithaca, N.Y., 1971)

D.M. Tibari and V.L. Boyack. 'The Effects of Pre-Retirement Education: An Evaluation' (paper presented at the Annual Meeting of the American Gerontological Society, New York, October, 1976)

Sheldon S. Tobin, 'The Educator as Advocate: The Gerontologist in an Academic Setting', *Journal of Education for Social Work*, vol. 9, no. 2 (1973), pp. 94-8

Pierre Vellas, 'L'Université du Troisième Age de Toulouse', *Annales de l'Université des Sciences Sociales de Toulouse*, vol. 22, no. 1 et 2 (1974), pp. 322-72

Ruth B. Weg, 'Concepts in Education and Training for Gerontology: New Career Patterns', *The Gerontologist*, vol. 13, no. 4 (1973), pp. 449-52

H.L. Wilensky and C.N. Lebeau, *Industrial Society and Social Welfare* (Russell Sage Foundation, New York, 1958)

5 AGEING AND HEALTH

John Brocklehurst

Health really means wholeness, or in more modern usage, fitness. It is a
positive concept meaning more than simply the absence of disease.
It is not just a normally functioning collection of cells, tissues and
organs and a clear rational mind, although it embraces all of these.
It involves also a personal congruity with the social environment.
These simple statements immediately lead to questions which indicate
that the matter is not nearly so simple as they would suggest. For
instance, is health then not possible in an unsatisfactory social
environment, as in many inner-city areas in our present industrial
society, where there is vandalism, fear, isolation? Is health possible
in an inimical political environment, as for instance for Jews in
Nazi Germany? And perhaps more pertinently for our present purposes,
is health possible within a body which is affected by the changes of
age?

Health is a relative quality. If it were not so, the only healthy
people might be those athletes who are fortunate to be living in a
benign society. Health is possible in a body which has been bereft of
one of its limbs, and indeed the restoration of health may involve
the surgical excision of certain organs. It may be assumed then that
health and old age are not mutually exclusive and this is a most
important lesson that has to be learned. To many, both old and
young, there is little expectation of health in old age and ageing and
disease are too easily confused with each other.

Health and Ageing

Ageing is a universal phenomenon and this is the principal characteristic which distinguishes it from disease. Individuals age at different
rates, so that chronological and biological ageing are certainly not
synchronous. However, the effects of ageing on body cells and tissues
will be apparent in everybody, provided they live long enough. Ageing
therefore has the quality of universality and it is this which
distinguishes it from disease. It has a number of other qualities which
it shares with disease; for instance, it is intrinsic, and its effects are
cumulative.

149

There are two major groups of theories about ageing. On the one hand that it is programmed and on the other that it is due to the accumulation of random errors. The former theories suggest that just as other stages in life are programmed; for instance, intra-uterine development, the growth of the body during its first twenty years of life, the reproductive period and the menopause, and as each marks a switching off of the preceding stage, so life itself is switched off by some mechanism residing in the genetic endowment of the organism, once the full life span has been achieved. The 'accumulation of random error' theories, on the other hand, are more akin to the processes of wear and tear. Interest has centred on the replication of DNA and the chance of random errors occurring in the template, messenger RNA, which will then affect the metabolism of the cell, and so gradually impair the competence of the organ and ultimately of the organism. There can be no doubt that errors of this type occur with ageing and it is very likely that ageing in fact is a multi-factorial process involving both groups of theories. The subject is reviewed by Davis and Schofield.[1]

The effects of ageing are apparent in all parts of the body. In the musculo-skeletal system for instance there is a diminution in bone density which may predispose to some compression of the vertebrae. There is a loss of water from the intervertebral discs so that they too become compressed, and so there is a gradual loss of height as a result of these two changes. At maturity, height and span are virtually the same (measuring span from fingertip to fingertip between the two outstretched arms). Loss of height in old age can be readily determined by noting the difference between it and span since span changes hardly at all with ageing. Muscle is a more specialised tissue, and muscle cells do not reproduce themselves. Age changes therefore produce a gradual diminution in the total number of muscle cells, although this may be compensated for by increasing the power and size of those that remain, with exercise. Both the grip and the lean body mass diminish with ageing and there is some increase in fat.

Skin

The skin becomes thinner and more transparent, and since the small blood vessels are less well supported they are more easily ruptured by relatively minor trauma, causing senile purpura.

Central Nervous System

The cells of the central nervous system or neurones are another group

of 'once and for all' cells which do not reproduce themselves. The
function of these cells is gradually impaired with ageing and there may
be a considerable diminution in their number. The effect of this is
perhaps most obvious in memory and particularly in committing new
matter to memory. This is one of the reasons why the older person
tends to dwell in the past. However, these changes also affect many
fundamental body processes; for instance the maintenance of the
upright posture is a highly complex feat developed late in the evolutionary scale. The upright human body has a high centre of gravity and
the area of its base is relatively small. If the centre of gravity is not
maintained over the base the person will fall: the upright posture
is maintained by the contraction of opposing muscles keeping the
joints extended. There is a constant tendency for balance to be lost
and this is immediately appreciated subconsciously through a
sensory mechanism built in to the skin, muscles, joints and bone
itself. As soon as the centre of gravity begins to move, this is
sensed and corrected by the action of opposing muscles. Posture is
thus maintained against a background of sway. This sway is very
apparent in the young child learning to stand, but it also increases
in old age because of a slowing of nerve conduction, and other
aspects of neuronal function (Sheldon).[2] For this reason the old
person has more difficulty maintaining the upright posture, is more
easily deflected and has greater difficulty in saving herself if she
begins to fall.

Other important regulatory functions through the central nervous
system are impaired with ageing, such as the maintenance of body
temperature, the maintenance of blood pressure on changes of
posture (see p. 160) and the excellence of control of the urinary
bladder (see p. 160).

Special Senses

While the organs of seeing and hearing are an extension of the
central nervous system, they are affected by age changes both
peripherally (for instance in the lens of the eye and the organ of Corti
in the ear), as well as centrally. These lead to the well known
phenomena of presbyopia (or long sight) and presbyacusis (high tone
deafness with normal loudness perception, difficulty in sound
localisation and sometimes tinnitus). The sensations of taste and
smell may also be somewhat blunted.

Cardio-Respiratory System

The cells of the myocardium and conducting tissues of the heart are affected by age change as well as by disease. Changes in the connective tissues of the chest wall together with some diminution in the area of the pulmonary alveoli lead to a gradual diminution of cardio-respiratory function. Exercise tolerance is slightly diminished, although in the practised or trained individual considerable accomplishments in exercise are still possible. In this system as in all body systems, the functional effect of ageing is much more apparent when the system is stressed than when it is at rest. This applies for instance to the excretory power of the kidney, to the ability of the body to deal with a high load of sugar taken into it and in many other ways.

Endocrine Glands

It is the endocrine system which shares with the central nervous system the whole regulation of body function and here again the changes are most apparent when the system is stressed. Another factor which may have some effect is the demand which is made upon the endocrine glands. The thyroid gland, for instance, maintains metabolism but the metabolism that is required depends, among other things, on the activity of the body. If the overall level of activity gradually diminishes in old age, then the demands made on the thyroid gland also decrease. The same applies to the pituitary and adrenal glands. These organs appear able to respond to stress normally, but their overall level of function in old age is diminished because of diminished demands made upon them.

The sex hormones show their decline in females at the time of the menopause and oestrogen, for instance, shows very much less decline after the age of sixty than between forty and sixty. The male sex hormone, on the other hand, (testosterone) shows a gradual diminution from the time of maturity onward.

These few examples indicate the basic and universal changes of ageing. Some of their effects on health will be apparent. The overall effect is an increasing frailty within the body, and a slowing of its functions, but none of these changes is in any way disastrous and indeed none is likely to be more than slightly inconvenient in its effects. Health may still be maintained against a background of these age changes.

The Effect of Chronic Disease

One of the things which distinguishes medicine in old age from medicine in younger people is the effect of accumulated multiple pathology. Many disease processes are slow in their onset but once they have occurred they can never be eliminated. Some, of course, are susceptible to surgical removal (if sufficiently localised), but many are generalised in their distribution and lead to a gradual loss of competence in body function. Perhaps the two areas where this is most apparent in Western society are in the blood vessels and in the joints.

Atherosclerosis

Atherosclerosis is a pathological process which produces varying degrees of change in the inner lining of arteries, consisting basically of the accumulation of fatty substances. This is associated also with changes in the middle muscular layers. The deposition of fat is accompanied by varying degrees of fibrous tissue and indeed of calcification. Atherosclerosis may be secondary to other diseases such as diabetes mellitus and hypertension, but in the majority of cases it develops independently. It is one of the conditions in which there is some difficulty in being sure that it is not an ageing change since it is almost universal among the elderly. However, it occurs also in occasional cases in very early life. Its prevalence has a geographical variation but basically this consists of it being a rarer condition in those parts of the world where life expectancy is short and commoner where it is long. Atherosclerosis appears to have environmental rather than ethnic associations, since it develops to a much greater extent among North American negroes, for instance, than among South African Bantu; these differences suggest a relationship with diet and cultural conventions. There is considerable support for a relationship between a diet high in saturated fats which is characteristic of the more opulent society and atherosclerosis. There is also some evidence for an association between high sugar intake and also the smoking of cigarettes and atherosclerosis. These three factors are all inter-related and the exact importance of any one of them is still uncertain.

The effect of atherosclerosis is to produce plaques within blood vessels. These diminish the calibre of the blood vessels and also serve as foreign bodies on which blood clots (thromboses) may form. Together these impair the circulation of blood to various parts of the body. If a blood clot forms it may completely obstruct the blood supply or a small part of it may break off to form an embolus which is swept forward in the blood until it comes to a branch of a blood vessel of smaller diameter than itself, which it will then obstruct. Thus the effect of atherosclerosis is ischaemia (loss of blood supply) which may be either acute or chronic. The effect of chronic ischaemia will depend on how widespread are the arteries involved and how effective is a collateral circulation. It is almost certain that some of the changes which may be attributed to ageing may just as well be due to ischaemia. For instance the effects within the central nervous system involving temperature regulation, maintenance of posture, bladder control and so on will be impaired by loss of function in the nerve cells (neurones) which could equally well be due to age changes or to impairment of blood supply. Indeed, these effects are likely to be additive and this is the particular importance of atherosclerosis as a chronic pathology in old age.

The acute complications of thrombi or emboli will produce sudden and evident loss of health. For instance a thrombus in the artery supplying the heart (coronary artery) will cause death of part of the heart muscle (myocardial infarction) with a serious and possibly fatal effect. Similarly, a thrombosis in the artery to the leg (femoral artery) with complete loss of blood supply to the foot, will be followed by gangrene of the foot. Thrombosis in an artery to the brain (cerebral thrombosis) may produce a stroke. Because atheroma is common these acute illnesses are also common in old age. Recovery is possible from many of them but recovery will never be followed by complete cure. It will generally be partial inasmuch as the loss of some degree of body function will remain; thus the person with a healed myocardial infarct may still have some degree of angina of effort or weakening of the wall of the heart, imparing his exercise tolerance; and a person with a recovered stroke may still have some speech disorder or weakness or paralysis which makes a resumption of his previous normal activities impossible. In old age, therefore, there is likely to be an accumulation of both the chronic and the acute effects of atherosclerosis and these may form a background to other disease changes.

The Joints

While most joint diseases occur in old age (as at other ages) and many of them, for instance rheumatoid arthritis, may have their onset in the seventh and eighth decade, the pathology which is most common in ageing joints is osteoarthrosis, a degenerative condition sometimes thought of as a 'wear and tear' phenomenon. Some degree of osteo-arthrosis has been found in 80 per cent to 90 per cent of people in Great Britain in the fifth and sixth decades of life and the condition

increases not only in extent but also in severity with advancing age.
Much of it is secondary to the stresses imposed on the large weight-
bearing joints by a lifetime of movement and is particularly likely in
individuals who are obese, whose occupation imposes special strains
on their joints (e.g. dockers, dancers, footballers and miners), or in
those who have had some acute episode of disease involving a joint in
the past. It is osteoarthrosis of the large joints which is particularly
disabling and contributes to disability in old age. Changes in the
spine (osteophytosis) are associated with disc degeneration (p. 160).
and while often included under the broad title of osteoarthrosis, are of
a different nature. Nevertheless, osteophytosis also may add something
to the background of disability and particularly where the
pressure from an osteophyte or bony spur impinges on a nerve root and
causes pain. Osteoarthrosis is a painful disease; its effects are not
catastrophic, but it is an important cause of disability and being so
common may again be one of a multiple group of causes of disability.

In both atherosclerosis and osteoarthrosis there is some
possibility of surgical intervention and replacement of the affected
joint or segment of artery, if a single area of this type can be defined
as being particularly hazardous.

Another related cause of disability lies in foot disorders,
particularly deformities, corns and callosities. These are much less
serious than either of the preceding pathologies but can cause
discomfort and sometimes total immobility. Again they may be one
among a multi-factorial spectrum of disability.

The sense organs, particularly the eyes, are vulnerable to a number
of age-associated pathologies. The commonest type of cataract is that
which comes on late in life. Atheroma leading to retinal ischaemia
may have an effect on this organ also and glaucoma is another
important age-associated disease of the eye. All of these are chronic
and therefore cumulative, although in the case of cataracts and to a
lesser extent glaucoma, surgical treatment is possible.

Dementia

Among the most important of all associated pathologies in old age is
that of senile dementia (see chapter 7). Fortunately, this condition
is not widespread as atheroma or osteoarthrosis but its course is
generally more rapid and disastrous, and for this reason it is a chronic
disease of the greatest significance in contributing to disability in
old age.

These are examples of the major chronic pathological processes which accumulate as age advances, but almost every bodily function may be affected to some degree. The survey carried out by Williamson and his colleagues in Edinburgh in 1964[3] demonstrated the extent to which disease was present in the normal elderly population of that city. They found disease of the respiratory system in 27 per cent, of the gastro-intestinal system in 20 per cent, of the urinary tract in 20 per cent, of the cardiovascular system in 19 per cent, of the central nervous system in 9 per cent, depression in 10 per cent and anaemia in 8 per cent, of a total population of people aged sixty-five and over.

Longevity and Health

Longevity might be thought of as the ultimate criterion of health, and there is no doubt that the familiar graphs which may be drawn for many body disorders showing a functional or structural decline through the sixth and seventh decades, often show this decline to be arrested and sometimes reversed during the eighth and ninth decades. This is not because people's bodily functions improve after the age of eighty but because the majority of these studies are cross-sectional rather than longitudinal, and are thus comparing different people of different ages with each other. Those who have survived to eighty and ninety have been called the biologically élite, or 'gerontocrats', and they exemplify the possibilities of health in old age. Indeed, Bromley[4] has suggested that the old saying, healthy, wealthy and wise is not entirely inapplicable among those who survive to a great age.

A study of those parts of the world where survival to 100 to 130 or 140 years is reputedly not uncommon, might therefore be expected to demonstrate the most healthy individuals of all. However, Davies' study *(Centenarians of the Andes[5]*) shows the interesting situation that very old men in Vilcabamba in Ecuador, while maintaining a remarkable exercise tolerance and cardiorespiratory function, have for instance, lost most of their teeth within the first half of their first century, and infectious and parasitic illnesses are common.

The Social Correlates of Health in Old Age

Deprivation and isolation are antagonistic to health at any age, and if these have more importance in old age it is because they are more common. Old people live in the oldest dwellings in the oldest part of cities; they are often less able to obtain repairs and indeed their old houses may be much more difficult to repair. They have less money and because of their diminished mobility they may be less able to make their own purchases at shops and thus have less stimulation to obtain a varied diet and perhaps the kind of household goods which are in common use with younger people. They expect to have a lower standard of life and they may be less sensitive to various types of deprivation.

For these reasons, for instance, large numbers of old people in Great Britain spend the winter in houses with temperatures which are well below those which are acceptable to younger people. This is partly because the property may be in bad repair, windows don't close properly, there are draughts under the doors and there is no modern form of heat insulation; partly because their heating appliances are more likely to be old and inefficient and they are fearful of spending an excessive part of their small pension on fuel; and partly because they are less sensitive to cold and therefore less aware of the need to heat the environment. However, the combination of a consistently cold environment and a body thermo-regulatory system which is functionally impaired means that the elderly are particularly vulnerable to the effects of cold, and the condition of accidental hypothermia is increasingly recognised as a cause of morbidity and mortality among old people in the winter time. The elimination of accidental hypothermia in an industrial country which suffers cold winters is a mammoth task. The universal provision of modern housing units with built-in heating systems where the cost of fuel is contained within the rent would be the ideal way of achieving this. Otherwise a great deal of make-do-and-mend is necessary, including the use of volunteers to assist in insulating old houses; the old person having a single bed-sittting room throughout the winter; and an effective form of heating being provided.

Isolation may prejudice good health in a number of ways — perhaps most obviously through depression and sub-nutrition. However, too hasty conclusions must not be drawn about these phenomena. There is little evidence of malnutrition among old people in Great Britain, and surveys such as those of Stanton and Exton-Smith[6] and the Department of Health Nutritional Survey[7] indicate an overall adequacy of nutrition. Stanton and Exton-Smith showed that dietary intake does not diminish with advancing age in those who are healthy and that a diminished intake is more likely to be a by-product of disability than its cause. However, this means that the small proportion of the population who truly are malnourished is likely to

be those who are disabled, housebound and isolated. For this group
the provision of 'Meals on Wheels' at least four times a week is
essential if nutrition is to be provided mainly from this source.
The aspects of diet which are most vulnerable are Vitamins C and D
and there is some justification for providing supplements of these to
isolated elderly people.

Again, depression may result from isolation but equally isolation
may be a result of depression. Loneliness and being alone are not the
same, nor are loneliness and depression. Depression may have many
causes including bereavement. The provision of voluntary visitors or
the ability to attend a club or day centre may be one factor which will
contribute towards improvement of depression. Fundamentally,
however, much depression is an endogenous disease which does not
have its roots in the social environment.

One of the truisms of medicine in old age is that social and
medical factors commonly both contribute to producing ultimate
breakdown. There are probably far fewer pure social problems in
the elderly than in younger people. The collapse of social competence
is generally associated with some element of ill health. This is
particularly the case among those elderly people whose breakdown
suggests the need for their removal to an institution. Both doctors
and social workers must therefore be very certain that all medical
and social factors have been discovered and dealt with as far as
possible before irrevocable breakdown requiring long-term
institutional care is accepted as necessary.

An old woman may be precariously supported living on her own
in the community. Housebound and perhaps barely able to move
from one room to another, she nevertheless maintains her social
competence in an independent dwelling with considerable support
from social services. Thus all her meals may be brought in to her,
she may depend on the Home Help Service for all the domestic work
and on the District Nurse for bathing. Even so, she retains her
independence until some medical disorder comes along which, in a
younger woman living in a family may only require a week in bed,
but in the case of this old lady is the ultimate factor causing breakdown
and her admission to hospital. The problem is thus both social and
medical. The danger in this situation is that, once in an institution,
even though the precipitating medical problem may be adequately
cured, the resumption of her limited independence may be completely
jeopardised because in the eyes of relatives, neighbours or
professional workers, a point has been reached from which it would

seem logical not to retreat and long-term institutional care is accepted by all concerned – perhaps most reluctantly by the old lady herself.

Or the combination of social and medical factors may be the other way round. A seventy-five-year-old woman may have been disabled by rheumatoid arthritis for many years, but able to retain her social competence because her husband is at hand to help her, in and out of bed, on and off the commode, with dressing and perhaps even with feeding. Her social competence, however, is dependent on his health. Should he become ill or die then there may be no alternative to admission to long-term hospital care for his widow, even though her own state of health has shown no change at that time.

Total Health in Old Age

These multivariate factors contributing to total health in the elderly may now be brought together and it will appear that health is a very different matter in the old from the young and very much more susceptible to breakdown. Illness in old age is often a combination of three things. First, the effects of ageing in diminishing or impairing a level of function but of itself not disabling. Second, a cumulative multiple pathology which may increase the background of disability but still permit independence. Third, social equilibrium maintained only with a good deal of help and dependency on another person. The final factor precipitating breakdown may then be an acute episode of illness, such as pneumonia, heart failure, a small stroke or a fractured bone which produces a disability and social incompetence as far as independent living goes. These four strands are closely bound together and this is the reason why health and disease in old age are the concern not of the physician alone, but may well involve social worker, family, priest and volunteer on the one hand and therapists and medical ancillaries on the other.

The Presentation of Illness in Old Age

Another difference between illness in old people and that in those who are younger is the altered presentation of illness in many old people. The most common presenting symptoms of illness in old age are mental confusion, incontinence, falls and immobility – presenting symptoms which are uncommon in younger people. These symptoms depend on the combination of factors already discussed above. Thus old people tend to fall because their postural mechanism is already impaired due to ageing, together in some cases with joint disease and disease of the central nervous system. They tend to become incontinent because of impairment of bladder function with old age; mental confusion is easily precipitated because of impaired cognitive intellectual function due to ageing and atheromatous changes – and immobility is an ever present danger because of age changes in muscles and joints together with arthrosis and other problems. In each of these cases, these age changes are the background, perhaps best called the predisposing factors. The actual incontinence, mental confusion, fall or immobility is precipitated by some additional – often acute – episode of disease. In younger people, these additional diseases may present in quite a different manner because the young do not have the underlying incompetence in these various systems. Therefore in the differential diagnosis of these presenting symptoms the following conditions must all be taken into account.

Falling

Predisposing factors: impairment of postural reflex and increase in sway; instability of the hip and knee joints and impaired vision; environmental factors such as badly lit stairs, dangerous mats and carpets. Precipitating factors: drop of blood pressure on changing from the horizontal to the vertical position. This is the consequence of the gravitational pull on the blood which brings it down towards the lower part of the body and diminishes the blood supply to the brain (causing postural hypertension). In the younger person this does not happen because of immediate corrective reflexes through the central nervous system, increasing the tone in the arteries of the lower part of the body and increasing the output of the heart. In old age this correcting system is defective. Another precipitating cause is a drop attack, i.e. the sudden occlusion of the vertebral arteries as they pass in the neck towards the brain. Because of their situation within the vertebrae themselves these arteries are particularly vulnerable to kinking in old people who have age changes in the vertebrae and intervertebral discs, causing a shortening of the spine. Drop attacks are precipitated in such elderly people by sudden movements of the neck. Another cause of falling is the Stokes-Adams attack – a sudden brief cessation of the heart's contraction – which occurs with increasing frequency in the elderly. Occasionally epilepsy begins in old age, often as the result of cerebrovascular disease, and falls due to this cause must be clearly distinguished from other causes since they are treatable with appropriate medication.

Incontinence

Predisposing factors: the uninhibited neurogenic bladder due to impairment of frontal cortical neurones of the brain; difficulty of access to lavatory or commode. Precipitating factors: becoming bedfast or admission to hospital and dependence on nurses; acute urinary infection, atrophic (senile) vaginitis, faecal impaction, prostatic hypertrophy, bladder neck incompetence.

Mental Confusion

Predisposing factors: impaired cerebral perfusion due to ischaemia and age change of the cortical neurones; sensory deprivation (deafness and blindness); subclinical dementia and depression. Precipitating factors: acute oxygen deprivation, toxaemia, the noxious effect of drugs and infection; environmental change; cerebral infarction and progressive organic disease.

Immobility

Predisposing factors: age change in muscle and postural reflex activity; osteoarthrosis. Precipitating factors: becoming bedfast as a result of a short illness which, in a younger person, would be followed by rapid resumption of ambulation; increasing pain; taking to bed because of social factors such as cold, loneliness, etc.

Important Aspects of the Management of Illness in Old Age

It is of the greatest importance to appreciate that the medical management of illness in the elderly (and particularly in those problems listed above) requires just as careful and detailed an examination as illness in people who are younger. Mental confusion and incontinence in particular are often accepted (sometimes even by doctors) as age-associated conditions for which there is no treatment. The contrary is the case. Both of these presenting symptoms present a host of treatable illnesses. Careful diagnosis is the first step, therefore, in their management.

Of course senile dementia is an important cause of mental confusion in old people and at the present time it is untreatable as far as specific therapy is concerned. However a great deal of help can be given to relatives to manage the confused and agitated old person in the home or else in a residential home by the skilful use of drugs, occupational therapy and social assistance. Similarly some cases of incontinence prove intractable to treatment. In these cases the informed physician will be able to assist with appropriate pads (a few of which are very good although many are almost useless), appliances and catheters. Again the use of catheters and appliances demands well instructed nurses for their successful management.

The Maintenance of Health and the Prevention of Illness

The maintenance of health and prevention of illness are not quite the same thing, if the definition of health discussed in the introduction is accepted. Thus the maintenance of health requires a wholeness of body, mind and environment and includes such important factors as good housing and recreation, social contacts, a degree of life satisfaction, as well as environmental hygiene, clean water, adequate food and fuel. The prevention of illness may be more specific involving for instance innoculation against influenza, smallpox and the other various infectious diseases. In addition to prevention there is associated the early ascertainment of developing disease by screening methods such as mass miniature radiography, cervical cytology and others. Thirdly, and equally importantly in old age, is the ascertainment of unreported illness.

Health Education

Health education in relation to ageing may properly be thought to begin with preparation for retirement. Retirement is a time of great change and for many men an event involving deprivation (consisting of diminished income, diminished purpose, diminished social contact and dominished status). The health educationalist and the geriatrician should therefore both have a role in preparation for retirement courses. Perhaps not the least important of the geriatrician's roles is being available for an hour or two on the course to answer questions and to discuss those misconceptions in relation to health which are still extremely common among much of the population. Most people in our society have no opportunity at any time in their lives to have a general discussion on matters of health with a doctor. Their contacts with the medical profession are likely to have been a series of consultations in relation to individual and quite specific matters of disease and with no opportunity to dispel other fears and phobias. The health educationalist would stress the importance of a safe environment, adequately lit and heated; a nutritious diet and exercise; as well as the development of some exciting creative or leisure activity which will impart purpose to life after retirement.

Health education in the old as well as in the young will seek to affect attitudes in relation to major health problems of today; for instance, cigarette smoking, obesity, accidents in the home and on the roads.

The Ascertainment of Unreported Illness

There is one aspect of the maintenance of health which is almost unique to the elderly and that is the question of the ascertainment of unreported illness. The question hardly arises in younger members of society, particularly when there is no financial barrier to the use of health services, because there are few young people who will not summon medical assistance when they are aware of something going wrong with their bodies or minds. If they do not, then their relatives are likely to encourage them or to do it for them. In old age, however, several factors mitigate against the self-reporting of illness. Perhaps the most obvious of these is the attributing of symptoms to age and not to disease.

The earlier discussion has already indicated that most disability in the elderly is multi-factorial and that while ageing brings some functional impairment, it is disease which causes breakdown. Old people will put up with their pain, incontinence, falling, depression and a host of other symptoms because they have such a low expectancy of health.

Other factors are important as well. It may be very difficult for an old woman living alone with few contacts and no telephone to make an appointment to see her doctor. She may have false ideas that he is 'too busy'. Or, lacking transport, the effort involved to present herself at the doctor's surgery may be more than she can face. These facts would suggest therefore that much illness in old people is likely to be unreported and several surveys have confirmed that this is the case. The best known of these is that of Williamson[8] and his colleagues. They selected a representative sample of the aged population in Edinburgh from the age-sex registers of a number of general practices. They then examined the old people in the sample, both medically and psychiatrically, in considerable detail and identified the extent of morbidity and disability among them. They then went back to the general practitioners' records and held discussions with the general practitioners themselves, to discover how much of the illness they had discovered was known to the general practitioner and how much was unreported.

Their findings showed two very interesting trends. Within the major systems there was a very high prevalence of disease, as has already been recounted (see p. 156). However, on average, 60 per cent of this disease within the cardio-respiratory, gastrointestinal, central nervous and other systems was known to the general practitioner. He would have been involved in its investigation, or else its symptomatic treatment. Another group of disabilities however, of a rather different nature, were those of impaired vision and hearing, foot troubles, urinary tract abnormalities, anaemia, depression, dementia and diabetes. Again a high prevalence was found (varying from 43 per cent with foot troubles to 4 per cent with diabetes) and in the case of these disorders, from 60 to 80 per cent was unknown to the general practitioner because unreported.

Perhaps the most important point to be made about these two different groups of disorders is that in the first, where much was already known, it might well be argued that a good deal of that which is not known is not remediable. In addition, in order to identify these major system disorders a full and detailed medical examination would be required and economic implications might well rule this out. On the other hand, in the second series of disorders which were mostly not known to the general practitioner, one characteristic is that they are to a large extent remediable and a second that they are of such a nature as to be discoverable on a much more limited examination, not necessarily carried out by a physician.

These findings suggested a form of a programme for the ascertainment of unreported illness in the elderly. This is now gradually being adopted in various parts of the country. The main responsibility for this work should fall to the health visitor. The role of the health visitor lies in health education and prevention and so this is an entirely appropriate task for her to undertake. Further, health visitors are increasingly being deployed through general practices and it is on the basis of the general practice that programmes for the ascertainment of unreported illness should be mounted. If the health visitor will obtain the age-sex register of the practice (from the local Family Practitioner Committee), she may then select all those in the practice over the age of seventy, and if she will arrange to call on each of these elderly people over a period of time, then it is likely that she could visit every person aged seventy and over in an average general practice (270 people out of an average practice list of 3,000), in two years, by devoting one afternoon a week to this work. On this basis she could visit three patients in the afternoon and she would be in a position not only to discover the social problems and their symptoms but to test their vision and hearing, examine their feet and teeth, assess their mental state and obtain samples of blood and urine. By this means alone most of the significantly remediable unreported illness in the old would be discovered and action taken on it through the general practitioner.

While this would seem to be the most economic method of the ascertainment of unreported illness, several different approaches have been considered in recent years. One important aspect, if the approach is to be more limited, is to try and bring into the net those who are particularly at risk and this should certainly include old people who are on the brink of institutionalisation. If admission to an old persons' home is being sought, then medical examination is essential (although at present not mandatory).

The Practice of Medicine Among the Elderly

A specialist system of geriatric medicine has evolved in Great Britain from the time of the inception of the National Health Service and within a quarter of a century there had developed a comprehensive geriatric service covering the whole country. This is probably twenty-five years in advance of any other geriatric service in the world, although in most countries a number of individual clinicians have trained themselves as geriatricians; most commonly these have been physicians on the staff of a special hospital for old people. At the time of writing the specialty of geriatric medicine is recognised in Great Britain, Eire, Denmark and Sweden (where it is called long-term care). It is also recognised as a specialty within the European Economic Community. In most of the rest of the world, however, it still does not have official recognition, although the situation in many countries (e.g. Canada, Australia, Holland and France) is moving swiftly towards a general availability of specialist geriatric care. The subject is reviewed in the book, *Geriatric Care in Advanced Societies*.[9] However, even in Great Britain, the geriatric service cares for only a minority of the elderly people in hospital. They are also treated by internists, psychiatrists, surgeons and their primary care is provided by general practitioners. The fact that old people make the most significant demands on the services in general practice is acknowledged by the National Health Service which pays an additional fee for every person aged sixty-five and over on the general practitioner's list. This fee is paid for the provision of normal medical services and at the present time general practitioners are not paid for any system of prevention, health education or ascertainment of unreported illness among their patients.

In Great Britain the system of primary medical care is undergoing a gradual evolution from the single-handed general practitioner working from his own house, to a group of general practitioners working together from a health centre. The health centre concept is encouraged and indeed financed by local authorities. It provides a centre not only for the general practitioners' consultation and treatment rooms, but usually a room for health education and possibly additional services, including chiropody and dentistry. The health centre is also the focus for the attachment of the health visitor and very often the community nurse. It is thus a natural and well-adapted focus for a comprehensive system of primary care. However, from the point of view of the aged, it may be a mixed blessing because of difficulties of access and non-availability of transport, together with a diminishing frequency of home visits by general practitioners, and an increasing use of an appointments system. The problem may also arise in relation to the prescription of medication within the National Health Service. Those in receipt of the retirement pension can obtain their drugs, their spectacles and dentures without payment of the additional fee which is required of the rest of the population. The drug prescription, however, usually has to be made up in an independent pharmacy and in rural and more scattered areas the number of these is diminishing.

The Geriatric Service

The geriatric service is hospital-based and organised by one or more consultant geriatricians. It is an area or district service and the only route for referral to the geriatric service is through the general practitioner. Old people may be referred to the geriatric out-patient clinic or a home consultation may be requested, or if they are an emergency, then direct admission is usually possible. The geriatrician runs a co-ordinated service which is usually based on the system of progressive patient care. All patients requiring admission come in the first place to the acute geriatric wards, usually situated in a district general hospital. Here are full facilities for X-ray and laboratory examination. The patient's clinical and social problems are analysed and treatment initiated. The average length of stay in the acute geriatric ward is two to three weeks and many patients go directly back to their own homes or to an old persons' home from here. If their problems and disability are more complex, then they may move to the geriatric rehabilitation ward for a period of more intensive physical rehabilitation and preparation for social resettlement which may involve changes to their home or may involve their moving elsewhere for continuing care in the community. The average length of stay in the rehabilitation ward is two to three months and again from here most patients go home or to an old persons' home. Some however remain so disabled physically or mentally or both, and their social circumstances are such that they have no one who can provide the care they need in the community, that they must remain in hospital as long-term care patients. At this point they are usually transferred to special long-term care wards. It is the objective of the long-term care ward to provide a homely and non-hospital atmosphere, which will allow a rich life with as much independence as possible, with opportunities for recreation and for privacy; for companionship and security within the hospital. Unfortunately, only too many long-stay wards are still far from this ideal. This is in part because they have not been designed for this purpose and in part because of nursing shortages which up to the present time have made it difficult to be selective in recruiting to long-term care nurses who have a particular vocation for this unique and important field of nursing. The average length of stay in geriatric long-term stay wards is two to three years.

Long-term (or continuing) care is a very special aspect of geriatric care. One of the great shortcomings at the present time is the near impossibility of achieving privacy. In future, long-term care patients should all have single rooms in which to sleep (or at the very most there should be three to a room). Relatives and visitors should be encouraged at any time. An activities organiser should provide a daily programme in which patients should be encouraged (but not coerced) to participate. For this purpose an art studio and a recreation room are essential. Access to a garden is also important.

Volunteers can help in many ways and the arrangement of holidays for long-term hospital patients is now quite possible and most desirable.

The consultant geriatrician is the person in overall charge of the patients in all these types of ward, and the responsibility rests with him to see that care and treatment are adequate and to initiate and develop new plans. In all of this, however, he is the leader of a team and all other individual members of the team have their own unique responsibilities. In each of the wards the ward sister is the key person responsible for the provision and quality of nursing, of the organisation of the patients' day, of the clothing and the serving of food. The attitude and personality of the ward sister is probably the most important fact in the happiness of the old people within the geriatric wards.

The role of the therapists is apparent at each stage of geriatric care but is most prominent in relation to rehabilitation. The physiotherapist maintains a full range of movement in the patient's limbs and teaches him to stand and walk, or else to use a wheelchair; to get up from the ground, to climb stairs and to develop as full a range of movement of all limbs as is possible. The occupational therapist makes a preliminary assessment of the patient's disability to determine whether special clothing or equipment is going to be needed and then teaches the patient to develop the normal activities of daily living — use of the lavatory and bath, cooking, dressing and taking part in recreation. The occupational therapist may well visit the patient's home, with or without the patient, in order to assess such adaptations as may be needed and the feasibility of the old person's return to the home. The speech therapist is concerned with elderly patients with strokes, both in the direct treatment of their disordered speech and also in assisting the relatives and other members of the staff to understand the patient's speech disabilities and what their approach should be.

The social worker is also likely to be involved with patients at all stages of geriatric care, but particularly those in the acute and rehabilitation wards. It is she who will discuss with patient and family their future plans and liaise with the social services department in the provision of special accommodation and equipment. At the present time, social workers in hospital are specialist rather than generic, but they are part of the local authority's social services department. This change since the reorganisation of the social services should make it possible for the social worker to be a much more effective link betwen hospital and community. For instance, she should be able to determine the suitability of patients for admission to old people's homes and it is hard to see that there should ever be a need for a second social worker to monitor her decisions. She should naturally have direct access to all other social services, although at the present time she will probably hand over the care of patients, once they leave hospital, to her colleagues in the district. Geriatric medicine is probably the field of hospital medicine where close relationships and team work between doctors, nurses, therapists and social workers is best developed and where each is aware of the importance of his own particular contribution. Within the field of long-term care other personnel are also prominently involved, the most important of these perhaps being the activities organiser. This person is responsible for what patients do throughout the week and ultimately the richness of their lives depends on her. Such an appointment is still uncommon in Great Britain, although it is well developed in many geriatric hospitals in the United States of America. The activities organiser will deploy volunteers and in addition to arranging a general programme of events for the ward as a whole, she will encourage individual arrangements for all patients who may wish to take advantage of the facilities.

The hospital chaplain also has a key role, particularly in relation to long-stay patients, although in many hospitals this is still a minimal part of his work. The conflicting demands on the time of the average hospital chaplain are such that he is unable to devote nearly as much of his work to geriatric long-stay patients as he almost certainly wishes to. The availability of a Chapel to such patients and the chaplain's relationship to their own former parish priest or minister are just two of the many aspects of pastoral care within a geriatric hospital which could well receive more recognition and discussion with other members of the staff. It is probably unusual for the chaplain to attend the case conferences at which all the other members of the therapeutic team meet to consider their work in relation to individual patients and this would seem to be a loss.

The Day Hospital

The geriatric service, in addition to its in-patient component, also involves a day hospital and here again the work is multi-disciplinary. The prime purpose of the day hospital is physical rehabilitation and the maintenance of such degree of independence as has been reached. It also provides some relief for relatives from the continuous demands which are inevitable when a disabled elderly person is being cared for at home. Medical and nursing procedures may be carried out here. The day hospital provides the therapeutic investigative aspects of geriatric care without the hotel service. Patients go home at night and at the weekend. It allows earlier discharge from hospital — and often prevents the need for hospital admission altogether.[10] It is also particularly supportive during the first few weeks immediately following discharge when the elderly patient is often most vulnerable.[11,12]

The day hospital must not be confused with the social day centre which, while providing social amenity, a midday meal and transport, is not part of the hospital service and does not involve doctors, nurses or therapists on its staff. The day hospital and day centre however should work closely together so that when the patients are

ready for discharge from the day hospital it is possible for them, if
they so wish, to continue to have the social advantages of day care by
being transferred to a social day centre.

The Training of Health Care Personnel

Geriatric medicine is now a well-established discipline in Great Britain
and nine University Chairs have so far been created in this field. These
form the basis within one third of the country's medical schools for the
instruction of undergraduate medical students in the particular
problems in the care of the elderly outlined in this chapter. It may
therefore be anticipated that, in future, general practitioners will be
better able to manage the problems of illness in old age and in the
long run the geriatric service also should benefit by improved recruit-
ment of doctors to it. As far as nursing is concerned, there is still
a considerable group of nurses who obtain the SRN without any
practical experience of geriatric departments. This deficiency may be
overcome by the special courses organised by the Joint Board of
Clinical Nursing Studies which are both a short course of fifteen days
and a long course of six months, available to enrolled and registered
nurses, both from hospital practice and from the community. The
intention of these courses is to help nurses to think critically and
constructively about the work they are doing in relation to old people
and again, in the long run, this cannot but have a beneficial effect.

A theme of this book is that while the interdependence and
working together of all those involved in health care for the elderly
is obvious and accepted, their training programmes are entirely separate
and disparate and that this apparent contradiction requires examination to see whether any advantage would be gained by bringing together, at some stage in their training, these various professionals. It is
possible to pick out from the brief review given in this chapter areas
which should be of common interest and concern to workers involved
in many ways in the promotion and maintenance of health. For
instance the effect of the environment is important and requires that
those who design and administer housing and transport should have a
familiarity with the physical and mental attributes of ageing and the
effects of illness on old people. Those who work with old people are
all too often aware of the deficiencies in the buildings and the
transport that are available and yet even after twenty-five years of
the National Health Service, there seems to be little communication
between these two very different groups of workers.

The interdependence of social and medical problems has also been emphasised and this would suggest a similar need for the knowledge of ageing and some of the effects of illness in old age on the part of social workers and hospital chaplains. There is an obvious common core of knowledge on anatomy, physiology, pathology and gerontology which should be available to all those whose work is clinical rather than social or pastoral (that is doctors, nurses, dentists, therapists and chiropodists), although in each case the emphasis and depth of know-ledge required is likely to be different. To what extent could two or more of these groups profitably join together in their training at this stage? Two things may make this more difficult — first, the numbers that are involved and, second, the fact that each of these different workers has a different perspective and their abilities in relation to different aspects of their training may vary considerably. Nevertheless, it is obviously desirable that they should understand each other and this is most likely to be achieved at an early stage in their career, if they meet together to discuss some of the elements which are common to their future work.

Notes

1. I. Davies and J.D. Schofield, 'Theories of Aging' in J.C. Brocklehurst (ed.), *Textbook of Geriatric Medicine and Gerontology* (Churchill Livingstone, Edinburgh, 2nd edition awaiting publication).
2. J.H. Sheldon, 'The Effect of Age in the Control of Sway', *Gerontologia Clinica*, vol. 5 (1963), pp. 129-38.
3. J. Williamson, I.H. Stokoe, S. Gray, M. Fisher, A. Smith, A. McGhee, E. Stephenson, 'Old People at Home — Their Unpublished Needs', *The Lancet*, vol. i (1964), pp. 1117-20.
4. D.B. Bromley, *The Psychology of Human Ageing* (Harmondsworth, Penguin Books, 1966, reprinted 1969).
5. D. Davies, *The Centenarians of the Andes* (Barry and Jackson, London, 1975).
6. B.R. Stanton and A.N. Exton Smith, *A Longitudinal Study of the Dietary Needs of Elderly Women* (King Edward's Hospital Fund, 1970).
7. Department of Health and Social Security, *First Report by the Panel on Nutrition of the Elderly*, Rep. Pub. Hlth. med. Sub. no. 123 (London, HMSO, 1972).
8. J. Williamson *et al.*, 'Old People at Home', *The Lancet*, vol. i (1964), pp. 1117-20.
9. J.C. Brocklehurst (ed.), *Geriatric Care in Advanced Societies* (MTP, Lancaster, 1975).
10. J.C. Brocklehurst, 'Role of Day Hospital Care' in *Medicine in Old Age* (British Medical Association, London, 1974).
11. Age Concern Liverpool, *Care is Rare* (Liverpool, Age Concern, 1976).
12. M. Skeet, *Home from Hospital* (London, Dan Mason Nursing Research Committee, 1971).

6 AGEING AND SOCIAL WORK

Paul Brearley

In recent years the development of social gerontology as a discipline
has been rapid and there has also been a great deal of change within
social work thinking and in the presentation of social care in Britain
over the same period. Attempts to link these two fields of thinking
have been disappointingly few and this perhaps reflects the status of
social work with elderly people. A number of studies have clearly
shown the unwillingness of many professional workers to become
involved with the old.

One such study was conducted by the Research Unit of the
National Institute for Social Work Training in a local authority
Social Services Department.[1] Sixty-nine area-based social workers
took part in the study and the researchers found that all except a
few workers were still carrying specialised case-loads, consisting
either of elderly and physically disabled clients, or of child care
cases, even though fieldworkers from the various specialisms had
been integrated into area teams. The highest proportion of the
department's clientele (62 per cent) consisted of physically disabled
and elderly and these were the client groups for whom the least
preference was expressed by social workers. Child care cases of all
kinds constituted 27 per cent of the department's clientele – and
these were the cases for which workers expressed most enthusiasm.

Work with the elderly appeared, from this study, to be
perceived in a stereotyped way by the young, qualified workers who
saw the tasks involved as requiring only practical services and
surveillance. In a study[2] of consumer reactions to social services the
same research group found that old people said they mainly
received practical services (and they were also the group who appeared
to be most satisfied with the services they received, particularly those
over seventy-five), while younger clients described receiving what
might be termed case-work.

Studies in the USA have reflected similarly negative mental
pictures of the aged among professional social work students and
medical students:[3] older people are characterised as disagreeable,
inactive, economically burdensome and dull. As has been discussed

172

earlier in this book stereotypes of old age are common. During 1974-5, for example, Age Concern England succeeded in encouraging the formation of around 800 local groups discussing various topics relating to older people with a view to creating a manifesto for the elderly. Just over eighty of these groups discussed the emotional needs of the elderly and, although the underlying assumption seemed to be that people are people whatever their age, all these groups tended to project the stereotyped ideas. The groups felt that the younger generation could learn 'courage, wisdom, loyalty, hard work, restraint and the importance of friendships and family life'.[4] The negative stereotypes are equally easy to identify: older people are irritable and self-centred; older people are self-assertive and dominating; older people tend to return to the past and refuse to try new things. The danger is that the elderly person may have no other yardstick by which to measure his behaviour and, in accepting the stereotyped behaviour pattern, fall into a habitual form of life which is less satisfying for him than would otherwise be possible.

It is not perhaps surprising that those professional groups which are concerned with providing care for older people should tend to focus on the problems experienced by old people. Recent work[5] has, however, shown the invalidity of describing 'the old' as often ill, alienated or deprived. Old people are usually fairly well integrated into their local communities by the services they provide for others and that they receive in exchange. In general terms some elements seem apparent. Stereotypes of old age are common but research has confirmed that the majority of older people are closely involved with others in their social environment. Many older people are, however, demonstrably less involved than they were when they were younger and for a fairly substantial minority this creates problems. The assumption that the industrial society has no real structural place for the old is not upheld but nevertheless considerable difficulties exist for the individual in making an adjustment to the pressures of society.

This paper will be concerned with the nature, problems and potentialities of social work with ageing people, in the light of the available information. An underlying assumption will be examined: that in providing a caring service for elderly people social, emotional, biological and medical factors are interdependent. Not only are they interdependent but they are inextricably linked and unilateral action to help an elderly person has only limited chance of success. Only with a multi-disciplinary approach can the elderly person who is experiencing difficulties be helped to lead a happy and healthy life.

The Social Work Content

During the last decade or more there has been a tendency to question
the applicability to casework, as it was practised and developed in the
previous twenty or thirty years, to the wide range of situations with
which social workers become involved. Confusion and disillusionment
with the appropriateness has been closely linked to the growth of the
demand for a range of social action that will take account of factors in
the wider environmental spectrum which prevents individuals achieving
satisfactory integration. The development of social services in Britain
in the 1970s has been based principally on a concept of genericism,
which refers to operating with a locality-based and family-centred
approach.

The sensitive development, use and perception of a relationship
that will help the whole individual towards autonomy in integrating
his own inner needs with his external situation is one approach of the
social worker. It is an approach that has been under critical review
and reappraisal. In addition to the skills of the case-worker social work
has seen an increasing interest in the techniques of using group
situations and group processes to help the individual and his family.
Beyond this social workers are active in much wider community contexts involving stimulating and guiding community groups to improve
their own material environment.

This does, of course, present social work in a rather flat unreal
perspective. In the real-life social service situation demand from the
consumer is for a range of resources in varied social situations. The
social worker's intervention may take many forms, from the provision of home helps or residential care to the development of an
individual supportive relationship, or to the stimulation of radical
social action. The social work task, therefore, is hard to identify but
there does seem to be a number of actions which are common to all
social work situations.

The basic situation presented to the social worker represents a
need about which a decision on involvement has to be made. The
decision-making process is set in motion by a stimulus which may
be a deliberate request, demand or a requirement or a more
accidental occurrence: this stimulus may be regarded as any person
or situation that has built up sufficient impetus to draw in a social
worker. In deciding what action to take the worker functions
within a range of influences including his own personal value system,

the theoretical knowledge available to him, the professional ethics involved, the helping techniques, the formal tasks of the agency he works for, and the information systems to which he has access. All of these influences operate within a wider framework of cultural and political expectations which operate to guide and direct the available options.

Within the process of deciding on, and carrying out action there are a number of sub-component parts: the collection and processing of information; the formulation of the problem; and evaluation of resources and deciding on achievable goals. The decision is then a result of identifying what is known, what is relevant, what is to be changed, what are the available forms of action, and finally of choosing a course of action (or non-action).

Clearly this mode of decision-making is not peculiar to the social work task and the importance of being purposeful in approach is ground that is common to all the helping professions. Within social work there has been considerable debate about the tendency to define action in terms of methods rather than purpose. There is no doubt that the pressured and often overworked social worker has little time to spare to consider purposes in detail but from every standpoint it is worth considering new and alternative approaches to social work with the elderly. Social work practice with this group of people has been very much concerned with the alleviation of problem states, often to the exclusion of the enrichment of the life-situation of older people and of the prevention of problems.[6]

The importance of clarity of objectives in the creation of change in the life of an older person cannot be too strongly emphasised. It is essential to be aware of the fact that perceptions of the extent and nature of the changes that can take place will be very different. In some senses to attempt to bring about change in the life of an old person is a daunting and depressing prospect, particularly in the light of the frequent lack of material resources. On the other hand change, from the viewpoint of the old person, can be very significant. Admission to hospital is an everyday experience for the doctor, nurse or social worker: for the elderly patient it is an often frightening, and always important life change. What seems to be an ideal solution to the doctor and social worker, or to the worried relative, may be totally unacceptable to the old person himself.

It should be remembered that bringing about social change is not necessarily a desirable objective but it is usually an inevitable result of intervention by members of the caring professions. It is important also to look carefully at who is bringing about the change, why it is being brought about, and in which area of the client's social functioning the change is taking place.

The usual task of the social worker has been seen as bringing about change in the elderly client's material situation and helping him to make attitudinal adjustments to his changed physical and environmental circumstances. This concept of the social worker must be carefully considered in relation to the overall functioning of a geriatric team. In addition to his own personal and professional attitudes each member of the team brings to the change situation a range of helping techniques which will be operated within the limits of the explicit and implicit tasks of the agency for which he works. It is plain that members of the geriatric team hold some skills, techniques, knowledge and objectives in common and it is equally clear that it will often be the doctor, nurse or health visitor who will bring about personal or social change.

The social worker cannot hold a monopoly as the agent of social change. An elderly person can be seen as functioning within a number of social systems. The introduction of a new person into any of these social systems inevitably leads to adjustments in the pattern of life. Each member of the geriatric team presents new facets to the life of the elderly individual and I shall suggest that part of the social worker's role is the interpretation of the patient's social functioning to the rest of the team and the organisation and direction of their individual interventions towards agreed social objectives.

It is important to reach an assessment of social data and to establish a set of objectives for personal and social development for the elderly person. A medical approach to a problem will have as its final objective the restoration of an optimum level of functioning. The solutions to social problems have very often failed to take account of the continuing needs of the older person. To put an old lady into an old peoples' home may meet her immediate need for physical care but without additional provisions for emotional support, continuing family contacts and regular reviews of her needs it will not be a solution. Ageing is of course a process, or rather a collection of processes; social interventions must take account of this and must aim to give on-going care that will provide for the developing needs of each ageing individual. The social work contribution to the team understanding of this developing need will be an interpretation of the client's, or patient's, previous social and emotional development (how he has become the kind of person he is),

of the way he sees his present situation, and of the way his attitude
to his illness, his family, the ageing process, etc., will influence his
future functioning in society.

The Social Worker and the Team

It is worth considering some of the situations in which the social
worker is likely to function as a member of a team in his work with
the elderly client. He is a member of his own professional team in
which he will be able to seek help and support and will also have the
opportunity to offer education to his colleagues in the sense of
demonstrating the value and possibilities of work with the elderly.
Related to this is his position as a member of the agency team, which
is likely to include administrators, support workers (home helps and
other domiciliary aides), residential workers, as well as other social
workers. In this team setting the social worker is concerned with
co-ordination and clarification of objectives: with ensuring that all
the team members are operating towards the same ends.

The team context which perhaps needs most thought and
development in relation to the role of social workers is the health care
team. This is particularly so of the community-based primary health
care team. The role of the hospital social worker has been relatively
clearly established — although the transfer of administrative responsibility for social work services in hospitals to the local authorities from
the National Health Service has created some ambiguities. In Britain
the general medical practitioner has traditionally been the significant
provider of primary health care, although some community-based
personal health services have been provided outside general practice.
Ninety-eight per cent of the population are registered with a general
practitioner, whilst 90 per cent of all illness is dealt with by general
practitioners without requiring specialist hospital services.[7] Hospital
and primary health care are closely interdependent in many respects:
expensive, technologically specialised hospital facilities can only be
economically deployed if the primary health services are able to refer
appropriately and to follow up hospital treatment after discharge.
In 1963 a working party[8] suggested that

> the general practitioner's field of work has no formal limit . . .
> The other health and welfare services depend on him for their
> effectiveness and he is in a position to influence their development
> by his identification and interpretation of the patient's needs.
> Above all, he has unique opportunities to husband the health of

his flock, to detect incipient disorder at the earliest point and to give advice that can reduce the risk of its occurring, postpone its onset, or lessen its 'impact'.

The opportunities and problems offered by the multi-disciplinary approach to community health care have been examined by several writers.[9] Some of the problems can be identified: social workers and general practitioners, for instance, seem to have limited understanding of each other's roles. This division is in some danger, in Britain, of being exaggerated by recent organisational changes in the National Health Service, and in the social services. Social work training has placed only limited emphasis on biological and medical information and medical training has placed correspondingly little emphasis on social and psychological instruction. Individuals often present psycho-social problems to their doctors disguised as physical illness, and also frequently present overt social problems with no medical content to general practitioners.[10] Similarly many problems presented to social workers – especially problems involving the elderly – have a significant medical component. Co-operation between professional groups is therefore essential if a full understanding of situations is to be reached.

Associated with the basic differences in training are differences in approach and method. The doctor is used to making quick and decisive diagnoses, while the social worker is more likely to work in conditions of uncertain causation and consequently less specific objectives: the speed of work is different. There are also real differences in authority and accountability in the ways in which the services are organised, and there are also issues involving relative status and remuneration. In spite of these potential conflict areas the benefits of co-operation are obvious and it is important that there should be a degree of role flexibility. At times a particular team member may be the most appropriate to deal with a problem because of an existing relationship with the client or patient rather than because of the professional relationship. For such flexibility to be possible there must be a degree of personal compatibility and trust between team members. As Dubos[11] has suggested: whatever the complaints of the patient and the signs or symptoms he manifests, whatever the medical problems of the community, diseases cannot be understood or success-fully controlled, without considering man in his total environment. Such a concept of interaction between health and the social context in which it occurs leads inevitably to the need for a team approach by the caring professions.

A final point of central importance to the concept of team care for the old person concerns where in the team the old person himself fits: how far is he enabled to take part in what is being done to and for him, and how far can he be enabled to take part? This will be considered in more detail later.

Knowledge for Social Work

Before he can begin to help older people the social worker must have a knowledge of behaviour in social situations. This knowledge will come primarily from the social and behavioural sciences but since, as is frequently argued, the problems of older people are almost invariably multi-symptomatic a familiarity with a range of knowledge about ageing is valuable.

Much of this knowledge is embodied in the present book: three particular factors seem important.[12]

1. As has already been discussed the formal actions taken by society tend to confirm the retired status of the elderly. In this group can be included the fixed retirement age, the awarding of a retirement pension, special concessions for pensioners, etc.
2. On an informal level social relationships are an essential element in the integration of older people. If supportive relationships are available to the older person he is more likely to make a successful adjustment to life changes. This has obvious implications for social work intervention.
3. A further vital factor which is significant for the position of older people as a group is the kind of material provision that is made for them. Many studies have highlighted the problems experienced by older people, often as a result of what has been called[13] the cluster of circumstances. Many demands converging within a relatively short space of time as an accumulation of relatively minor difficulties, at a time when resistance to stress is reduced leads to a need for outside help.

The picture suggested is that for most people ageing is experienced as a reasonably satisfying time. Only for a minority – although an uncomfortably large minority – is old age a time of problems. Nevertheless it should be recognised that there is a difference between ageing – as a process involving everyone – and the individual experience of ageing as a time when a number of characteristic problems occur. It is those people who are compulsorily, or involuntarily disengaged, those who are unable to achieve the level of activity they want and need who are likely to present problems to caring services and whom the social worker will be concerned with helping.

A discussion of the needs of the elderly for social work inevitably rests on a socio-cultural framework: needs are relative to circumstances and are, of course, shaped by social forces. Needs vary from one society to another; from age group to age group and from individual to individual. A concept of need implies some norm of satisfaction — a goal to be reached, but the same needs can be met in many different ways. I should like to suggest not necessarily that some attitudes and values are morally better than others but that certain conditions are necessary if older people are to live their lives with opportunities for personal happiness or satisfaction.[14]

The needs of older people can be looked at in at least two ways. First, some needs are related to the fact that they are growing older; for example children growing up, retirement, etc. These might be regarded as non-problematic needs. Second, other needs are not necessarily related directly to the ageing process but are related to the fact that older people are less well provided for and are less well able to deal with certain losses — in some situations this becomes problematic need.

A reduction in the range of choice is commonly a result of living longer: men, for instance, lose occupational roles, and women are more likely to be widowed. Lost roles vary in significance from major roles involved in work and marriage to lesser roles. Along with the loss of roles and their attendant relationships goes the loss of many material opportunities — loss of income, decrease in mobility, etc. — and each loss has a consequent loss of choice. Older people have the same need to be different as do younger people: they need to have room to choose the kind of people they wish to be. If choice is to be a realistic prospect then there must be a sufficiently effective information input: older people must know what is available to them.

Closely linked to the need of older people for choice in daily living is the need for them to retain independence and individuality. To be able to retain true independence they must be able to maintain an adequate income and a level of physical health and mobility. To remain healthy and mobile requires the meeting of many subsidiary needs — adequate services to compensate for loss of hearing and of sight, a proper nutritional standard (also implying adequate dental care), the maintenance of personal and household standards of cleanliness, care of the feet and a good, accessible health service. It is often suggested that old people treasure their independence and that every effort should be made to help them remain in their own homes. It certainly seems right that old people should have the opportunity to be in the right kind of accommodation but this does not necessarily imply an over-rigid insistence on remaining in the same house as they have lived in for many years. This kind of expectation has led to some old people living a lonely, unhappy existence in sub-standard accommodation when a move to newer housing might have meant a little more short-term effort for the social worker but much more long-term satisfaction for the old person.

Linked to this need for flexibility of approach to the concept of independence — which is so much more than a purely physical ideal — is the need for self-respect, dignity and privacy. Treating old people with respect involves looking behind the stereotype to the whole needs of the individual.

These fundamental needs for choice, respect, dignity, independence, individuality and privacy are only relevant in so far as they provide for satisfaction in old age. Satisfaction, in the sense of a subjective feeling of well-being, depends both on external, material factors, as well as the internal dispositions of the ageing person. This concept of satisfaction is closely related to the idea of adaptation to ageing. Adjustment is a very individual concept: in general terms there seems to be a spiral of sensory deprivation during the ageing process, which results from relative environmental deprivation and which leads to a characteristic under-performance in many older people. In consequence the role performance of these people includes an element of habitual under-performance: there is a reserve capacity which might be stimulated by a variety of approaches.

One view of adjustment to being old[15] proposes that the process of growing from childhood through adolescence and adulthood to old age requires the successful negotiation of a series of identity crises leading to a final stage of ego integrity. This achievement of ego integrity involves an acceptance of the past life — of all that has gone before — as unchangeable and inevitable; secondly, it involves a recognition that the present is real and meaningful in the light of what has happened in that past life; and finally it involves a realisation that death is an unavoidable appropriate conclusion.

In this sense satisfaction in old age is dependent on being able to see a total pattern in life — which will not always be easy in the light of the past and present deprivations that many old people experience. It is therefore not enough to see the achievement of inner satisfaction

as solely a matter for the internal adjustment of the individual.
Satisfaction and happiness are dependent on the congruence of
inner mental state with external circumstances. A helping strategy
that aims vaguely at achieving adjustment to old age has little
hope of success since few people have a clear concept of old age
per se. A strategy for helping should rather be aimed at overcoming
specific problems which are preventing the old person's life from
proceeding in the direction he wants it to go: a focused and
specific involvement is the most useful. Elsewhere I have suggested
that social workers should not be concerned with a static view of
problems in the here and now but with restoring a normal, on-going
process of ageing with the satisfactions that will imply.[16]

Social Work with the Elderly

It was earlier proposed that social work might be concerned with
issues of alleviation, prevention and enrichment. In order to achieve
these goals the selection of targets for intervention will depend on
what changes are possible: success in social work with the elderly
rests in a very practical sense on setting achievable goals. The
selection of targets will depend also on the nature of the agency
employing the social worker — its objectives and limits — and also on
the resources available.

I propose to examine a number of propositions in order to
elaborate on some of the courses of action which are open to the
social worker.[17]

*Proposition 1: A case-work approach to older people is at least a
possibility. This will involve a degree of psychological holding of the
ageing person but more especially an enabling role of clarifying
alternatives and supporting the development and relocation of
adaptive mechanisms*[18]

Whether he is deciding on an appropriate case-work treatment plan
or evaluating the strength of a tenants' action group the social
worker must begin by collecting information, which will be valuable
in so far as it is relevant to the recognition of the basic problem and to
the solution of the problem. The social worker will select information
that will enable him to decide whether the problem that is presented
is the problem that needs solving. 'Ms A. is just old', said the general
practitioner, 'she'll have to go to an Old People's Home.' Subsequent
investigations revealed that she had nursed a bedfast husband for three
years and immediately after his death she had become incontinent,

unable to walk and was hallucinating!

Having identified the cause of the social disturbance the next task is to identify the available resources. There has been a lack of research and evaluation of the effectiveness of techniques of intervention. Some recent studies[19] have pointed to the possible value of short-term focused involvement with individuals. In spite of this lack of evidence of success in social work it is important to be aware of the appropriateness of applying scarce resources to gain the optimum results. Assessment on the one hand is reaching a decision about the nature of the problem and the form of intervention: because of the changing nature of human situations this assessment must be fluid and open to readjustment. In his role as member of the health care team the social worker contributes to the team assessment of the patient's needs. It is with regard to the nature of the information that he will contribute that some confusion has arisen. There is some information about family background, home circumstances and social interaction which is obvious and is readily available to anyone. There is little skill in gathering, for example, information about the type of housing an elderly patient has, or about his income, number of children, etc. Perhaps it would be simplest to say that what the social worker contributes to the team assessment is not so much social information (although this is a part of the task) but an understanding of what that social information means to the individual person: the interpretation of information in terms of the individual's social functioning.

An adequate assessment of individual need can only be made if effective communication is established, and this can often be a problem in work with the elderly — although no more so for the social worker than for other professional workers. Good communication is an important part of the process of gathering information and attaching meanings to it and, beyond that, a part of building up relationships and providing practical help. In structuring an interview the first objective is to create an environment in which the client can feel free to express himself. It must also be an environment in which the worker can receive the message appropriately. Communication may be verbal or non-verbal, it may be through words or tone of voice, or through facial expression, or body movement. To recognise the meaning of the message may take time and patience and this is particularly true in the case of the elderly client. Chronic brain failure, for instance, will lead to confusion and forgetfulness: it is hard to establish a continuing thread of communication from one interview to the next when the client forgets after a few minutes.

It is similarly difficult to encourage confidences when the client is blind or deaf, or both: so much of the expression of caring and concern rests on non-verbal action. Speech loss presents similar difficulties in the one-to-one situation and reliance in social work with the elderly often has to be much more on non-verbal methods of communication. The use of touch and of silence takes on greater importance, as does demonstrating concern through simply spending time with the client, although this must be carefully controlled to avoid frustration.

The social worker seeks to relate to the whole individual and needs to look for a variety of ways of reaching out to him. Becoming aware of communication patterns between individuals within group situations is equally important, as is an understanding of intergroup interaction. In the geriatric setting, as in any agency setting, it is important for the social worker to recognise the ways in which patterns of organisational interaction (especially within the long-stay institution) impinge on the client. Labels attach themselves and even ostensibly 'good' labels ('sweet old thing', 'nice old boy') can be expressions of partialisation: of seeing the individual as a flat, cardboard figure. Only through good communication with colleagues and clients can the social worker amass sufficient information to create a rounded, fuller picture of the whole person.

Following directly from assessment and the fostering of communication is the use of relationships in social work. It is perhaps the controlled use of relationships which is at the heart of all social work and it is this that distinguishes the professional social worker from the sympathetic voluntary worker, or friendly neighbour.

In developing a relationship with the old person some problems can be identified. One difficulty may arise from the age difference itself. In one respect this will have consequences for communication: the life experiences, expectations and even use of language vary from one generation to the next. It may have consequences also for the kind of relationship that can be built up: a newly qualified social worker may have difficulty establishing trust in his competence, knowledge or skill in the mind of an eighty-five year old grandmother. Beyond this the dependence which a frail, old person may need to have accepted and to work through may not be possible in a relationship with a wide age gap. In fact this rarely seems to be a major problem and age or sex play only a limited part in the kind of helping relationship developed.

Another complication in working with older people stems from the limited time available. Often social workers become involved at a time of crisis and although at such times the potential for helpful change is great the vulnerability of this client group means that death is an important pressure on action. In addition to the objective limitation on time available to work with the older person which death imposes there are subjective limitations. The idea of personal death is one that many younger people do not consider in anything other than a remote way. To accept that one will inevitably die is an uncomfortable and unwelcome thought and for most people it is an idea that tends not to take on a personal reality, except perhaps at times of bereavement and in later middle age. If the young social worker is to help an elderly person to consider death realistically he must be able to face the inevitability of his own death.

In understanding his own and his client's needs in a situation of social disturbance the worker is able to direct and understand his use of the relationship. The worker will accept his client for his value as an individual while not necessarily approving of his behaviour in any particular situation. He will care about his client because he values the individual and in times of stress will try to understand how he feels without becoming caught up in the client's own distress or panic.

In being continuously aware of his relationships with clients individually or in groups the worker can help create an environment in which they can accept practical help, as well as allowing them to express strong feelings and discuss the situation realistically. It is this latter point which seems to be most frequently of value to the elderly client. As has already been suggested most elderly people who come to the notice of social workers do so at a time of crisis. This may be a crisis in the true sense of emergency as, for example, when a daughter who has been caring for an elderly mother is suddenly taken ill. Alternatively it may be the result of an accumulation of minor difficulties that together lead inevitably to a need for help, as, for example, when an elderly widow fails to feed herself properly following the death of her husband and because she fails to feed herself is unable to look after herself, creating a downward spiral of depression and debility. Sometimes problems presented as 'crisis' are made up not of the perceptions of the elderly client but of the perceptions of relatives, neighbours or friends. The so called crisis gathers momentum as daughter talks to neighbour who talks to the

doctor, etc. The final problem – definition, may bear little relation
to the reality of the situation.

Whatever the cause of the crisis, it is inevitable that the elderly
person at the centre of it is experiencing considerable stress. The
social worker's first task is therefore to relieve that stress so that
the client has sufficient breathing space to look more clearly at what
is really happening. At this stage the assessment should become a
joint experience. In discussion with the social worker the client can
be helped to consider the events that have led to the present
difficulties and then to examine the options that are open to him.
It is obviously vital that this discussion includes the opportunity to
consider the needs of all who are likely to be concerned: the
family, the neighbours, the doctors, etc. There are few situations in
which the needs and wishes of the old person can be reviewed in
isolation from those of the people who provide support for him. There
are, of course, occasions when the mental impairment of the old
person is such as to prevent rational discussion – but this cannot be
assumed until an effort has been made.

Most people have friends and relatives to provide them with this
service. Sometimes family problems have become so entrenched that
outside help is needed to find a solution. Some old people have
outlived their contemporaries and have few or no friends, or are
single, or widowed and childless. If this is the case an important
social work task is the provision for basic needs for caring concern
and support: tender loving care. Caring for the elderly client is
inextricably linked with the process of finding out about him: he will
only be able to feel valued if he believes that he has been understood.

In a broad sense the case-work relationship can be directed towards
helping the older person develop a feeling of life-satisfaction: to
help him adjust. Adjustment to ageing and to old age is very
difficult to measure: it seems to be entirely an individual matter.
Studies of attitudes after retirement have tended to confirm that
appropriate adjustment to retirement involves individual as well as
wider social attitudes and values. A study by Age Concern England[20]
of 2,700 people of pensionable age living in private households was
concerned with the attitudes of the elderly to the situation in
which they found themselves. Almost two thirds felt they did
help other people in some way and a majority felt that someone
relied on them in some way, but 8 per cent of the sample were
unable to think of anything that they 'look forward to nowadays'.
It may be that a majority make a good and satisfying adjustment to

retirement but up to seven in ten find the post-retirement period unsatisfying. The important factors in satisfaction or adjustment seem to be income levels and health standards and to a lesser extent social class and occupational variables.

In helping the older person towards a greater degree of satisfaction or to better adjustment the social worker can take a number of approaches. The importance of caring concern and clarification have been discussed and it has earlier been suggested that the achievement of ego-integrity involves being able to see a pattern in past, present and future. The function of reminiscence as a helping approach in this connection has been discussed by several writers.[21] Other writers[22] have discussed the implications for case-work of the concept of ageing as a developmental stage, the goal of the final stage of life being to find an inner meaning and integration in the pattern of life. Similarly others[23] have considered the importance of adaptive mechanisms in the ageing personality.

If the past and present can be seen as unified and logical then the prospect of the future (and death) can be viewed with acceptance rather than with resignation or fear. Contentment in old age seems to lie in the opportunity to live a slower life, concerned with relying on others but also with giving from a lifetime of experience. This adjustment will only be possible if emotional and physical supports are available. Case-work with the individual old person is therefore concerned with identifying possibilities, with the client, within a supportive and trusting relationship. For a few clients it may also be concerned with personal growth and adaptation through a reflective approach to insight – giving. However the view of adjustment presented so far rests on an assumption of the value of the withdrawal to what are essentially narcissistic, inner satisfactions. Whilst this is undoubtedly right for some clients, especially at a time of stress and personal vulnerability it does seem at least as important to consider social work techniques that help the old person within his family and encourage continued integration – if this seems appropriate after a full assessment.[24]

Proposition 2: If the importance of social integration of the elderly is recognised then it must also be accepted that a vital part of social work with older people will be concerned with family attitudes and interactions and the retention of a family role for the old person

In terms of physical activity the behaviour of older people reflects a degree of chronic adaptation: there is a reserve capacity. Older people

are expected to do less and so they become habitually less involved
in social interaction. If appropriate stimulation is available then it is
possible for old people to improve their level of performance. This can
be done both by calling on existing, under-used abilities, but also by
developing new abilities through the relocation of energies.
Recent evidence[25] shows a relationship between happiness and
social activity among the elderly. If the right kind of environment
and stimulus is available then increased activity and consequent
happiness will be a possibility for those who choose to become
involved.

The concept of interdependence relates closely to this: the most
vulnerable old people are those who are relatively inactive and who
are unsupported by significant others. It is important then to
recognise that the balance between interdependence (the need for
involvement with others) and independence can be very delicate.
Strong norms of independency are frequently expressed in families and
particularly within the middle-class conjugal group.[26] On the other
hand there is evidence that these same groups often receive considerable help and support from their extended family network. Families
usually do wish to provide support for their elderly parents or
grandparents, and in most cases are able to do so. It is precisely
because of this fact that many families do not ask for help until they
have reached their limits and are consequently in urgent need of help.
This is not to suggest that families and their elderly members are
usually on very good terms. In one study,[27] although a quarter of the
children reported cordial if not warm relationships with no serious
rifts or family alignment, three quarters of the children reported a
variety of family problems resulting from parental ageing.

As children grow up and parents age a number of changes are
inevitable. In most families these changes take place slowly and
gradually and adjustment within the family group is made over a
period of time. In some cases changes take place suddenly and
unexpectedly, as for instance, when the father is made redundant
or retires earlier than expected, or when a crisis illness occurs. In
these cases adjustment may be more difficult and rigid patterns
of response may develop which will eventually lead to family
divisions. The social worker may be called on to help either at the
beginning of the crisis, in which case he can help by giving support,
or after a period when attitudes have reached an entrenched position.
In extreme cases there may be no solution other than the removal of
the old person to a place of sanctuary: if this is inevitable the

objective should be to help all involved and to avoid leaving feelings
of guilt as far as possible. Ideally the social work approach should
be aimed at helping the older person to remain within his family
support network if at all possible. In order to do this similar
techniques of support, concern and clarification will be necessary but
of particular importance will be using practical resources to
reduce the pressures on everyone involved: for example, using a
home help to give the daughter a rest, arranging day care, etc. This use
of practical help will certainly imply an element of emotional support
and clarification: there is no point supplying meals on wheels to
someone who refuses to eat them because she has not faced her
inability to cook for herself any longer.

It should be remembered that this approach which emphasises
integration to the family may also have a segregating effect on the
family itself. The concept of integration should be viewed at many
levels: integration and independence are not desirable objectives if they
place an unbearable burden on a daughter. It may well be that most
elderly people and their families are prepared to accept a loss of
freedom and other forms of integration in order to provide for the
family integration of the old person. If this leads to integrated old
people but segregated families then we should not pretend that full
integration is a reality. There is no doubt that the full integration of
old people and their families into community life would require a
level of practical provision that would be very expensive: it would
certainly not be a cheap alternative to residential provision.

The social worker can make a contribution to both individual and
family integration by the flexible use of resources. If those practical
supports that are available can be used imaginatively they can be
directed towards the objective of maxmimum integration. It is a simple
and cheap enough matter, for instance, to provide care for an old
lady whilst her daughter takes a week's holiday, yet this may prevent
a breakdown of the whole family. This leads to a further proposition.

*Proposition 3: Work with both the older client and his family may
involve giving help with emotional adjustment but it is most likely
to be concerned with material support*

The flexible approach to using resources that has been proposed
inevitably implies a concept of team care. The administrative divisions
within the health and social services in Britain have created a number
of organisational problems for service to the elderly. It is therefore
vitally important that each member of the geriatric team is made aware

and remains aware of the impact of his own interventions on the patient's social functioning.

It should not be assumed that integration into the family and community is the best answer in all cases. A rigid insistence on this approach can lead to a small group of isolated and needy old people being compelled to live a lonely and unhappy life. For some people a change of accommodation will be a realistic answer to their problems. This may take a number of forms from self-contained housing in the community perhaps with a warden, as case-worker in occasional attendance, to full residential accommodation with meals provided, etc. The social worker will be involved in ensuring that the transitional stage from one life situation to the next is accomplished with the minimum of disruption. Studies have referred to various effects of admission to different forms of care and the nature of the adjustment that is made by the old person depends on several factors. The element of 'felt rejection' is one of the most basic influences: an elderly person is more likely to settle in a new environment if he feels he has freely made the choice to move.[28] There is a difference between freely making the choice to move and being able to accept the inevitability of change and this is the best that some old people can hope for. Admission to care occurs at a time of stress and vulnerability and exposes the older person to physical and psychological risk. The emotional responses to stress are aggravated by increased risk of infection and, for instance, hospital-related illness. Difficulties may be lessened if good substitute relationships are available within the communal group. Workers in the geriatric team of the hospital, the residential home and the community can reduce the stress by working together to prepare the client or patient emotionally and practically. It is particularly important that the institution is properly prepared to receive the old person and above all that support is provided at the time of admission.[29]

Even the best residential home is likely to rank as second best in the mind of someone who is admitted to it. Each individual brings with him his own needs to influence and affect other members of the communal group: to preserve a sense of personal identity and of 'self'. He will experience a conflict between the need to feel secure and wanted and the need to remain an independent being, and the problems that occur within the institutional group are likely to be accentuated by the closed nature of group living: this leads to ritualisation, standardisation and other institutionalising effects.

The residential workers' tasks will be concerned with three main areas of helping in his contact with the elderly resident. At the time of admission he will help with integration into the group and the repair of damage done before and perhaps during admission. After the initial need for rebuilding of strength has been met the resident will need a period of holding and maintenance before looking towards the next possibility of growth and development. Within these general needs the residential worker will be concerned at first with helping the resident deal with the new situation. This will involve helping him to deal with problems of relating to the group through the exploration of new roles and achieving socialisation into group norms and expectations. It will also involve the provision of an environment in which personal integrity and independence can be maintained by giving opportunities for self-direction through decision-making and exploration.

Linked to this is the worker's role in providing a warm, caring and controlling background. This implies physical care, controlled authority and help within the group in terms of opportunities for reflection and self-expression, help towards understanding the current situation, etc. No less important than all these is the importance of maintaining and fostering community links. It is therefore essential that field and residential workers should work closely together to build up a complete picture of the elderly person to facilitate admission and, hopefully, discharge; to facilitate a continuing relationship between field-worker and client and enable the client to retain a range of roles in the community; and to enable the development of mutual support between workers. There are real differences in the contexts in which these workers operate and in their relative status, but for the sake of both the client and the workers co-operation is essential. Similarly the social worker and the hospital team need to build up close relationships for the same purposes.

Residential care is one part of a whole range of services. Although there are many alternatives to residential care that can be provided in the community, residential or hospital care may be the best answer for some people – if only for a short period. In using institutional resources to the best advantage it is important to be aware of the way the internal social system of the institution can operate to build up routines and make its own demands on those who have to live within it.

*Proposition 4: Under-performance of the elderly person may result
from an under-use of capacities or from an inappropriate allocation
of abilities. The social worker can be concerned with both the
stimulation of and provision of materials for the under-used capacities*

In establishing a student social work placement in a small long-stay
geriatric hospital it has been possible to work with some of these
approaches.[30] From the patients' point of view there seemed to be two
primary needs: that they should be able to feel a part of what is
being done to and for them, and that they should have a degree of
choice. The way of achieving this latter objective in the particular
hospital has been to experiment with a range of alternative role
experiences which are available to patients. Discussion groups, activity
groups and opportunities to participate in staff administrative groups
have been offered to extend the social opportunities and involvement
of patients. It has been very apparent that the non-directive approach
taken towards the groups presented initial threats and anxieties. This
seems partly related to the fact that there had been a complete turn-
about in hospital practice and confusion resulted. This was not only
so for patients but also for members of staff and it has taken
considerable time for staff to learn how to enable patients to
participate and become involved just as it has taken patients a long
time to accept that they are able to act for themselves again. It seems
essential in a situation where it has been generally accepted that
elderly patients will function at a very inactive level to provide an
initial stimulus — and experience suggests this will generate some
initial hostility and confusion. It is perhaps also important to be
aware of the thin dividing line between providing stimulus and being
directive. Support and control may merge and a balance should be
sought between the two.

A strategy for institutional intervention must focus not just on
those people within the institution but also on the outside world
and the encouragement of integrative approaches. Support for
patients' relatives and the use of family members within the hospital
or residential home should be considered. Community participation
may also be extended from the usual organised voluntary
contribution: contacts at all levels of the community are important.

In order to achieve a programme of stimulation and self-help activity
there is a need for the setting of agreeable, achievable goals; for a
degree of choice of activities; and for the cues to come from the
consumers, the old people themselves, who must be allowed to work
at their own pace. There should also be a supply of people and

materials in the environment with whom older people can interact or engage: sensory impairment among the elderly means that stimulation has to be larger and louder than life to have an impact.

Proposition 5: Older people have a need for and a right to choice of alternative life-styles: they should be able to choose the kind of people they wish to be. One social work task is the opening up of new alternatives in many different contexts recognising that the withdrawn old person will need to be supported, encouraged and re-educated in the use of alternatives

The concept of self-help and participation is equally relevant to the community setting. A recent action research study in the London Borough of Merton was intended to test some of the possibilities.[31] The original concept was an open and flexible one, being to some extent dependent on the kind of person appointed to develop the study. In its original description the steering group suggested that

> the proposal differs in essence from existing employment and sheltered workshops run by voluntary agencies for the retired or disabled in the sense that its members would be totally responsible for the administration of the services which they would offer externally to the public (and internally among themselves) by involving men and women with as wide a range of professional, clerical, domestic, and trade skills as possible.

The outline of the scheme that evolved is very simple: any retired person who wants a job done phones in their request to the headquarters where it is recorded on a machine which is on operation twenty-four hours a day. At the same time they state what work and services they can offer and give their name and address. The staff at headquarters then try to match the various demands and offers. Payment for work is not made in money, but in stamp tokens at the rate of one stamp for each hour worked: the person who has done the work can then spend the stamps by getting another member to do some job for them.

That some people have seen the scheme in terms of voluntary work is suggested by the greater numbers of people offering rather than requesting help. However the scheme has differed from the usual community organisation or development approach in that a basic administrative system has been created, followed by a series of information-disseminating approaches to the community. The

retired residents in the community have therefore been entirely free to
decide for themselves whether to take up the opportunity offered. The
response has been relatively small but enthusiastic and although there
are problems of balancing supply and demand several other
communities are establishing similar link schemes.

A consideration of activity and the elderly in the community
cannot ignore the important role played by the volunteer in Britain.
A recent study[32] has shown that volunteers prove capable of coping
with crises and the demands of a caring situation and proposes that
some volunteers at least could be seen as offering a genuine alternative
to the professional social worker in a situation of scarce resources.
The volunteer organisation is also in a position to stimulate and
encourage community activity both to involve the elderly and to
provide for the elderly. Many voluntary organisations depend on the
services of older people although there does seem to be a connection
between income levels and the wish of retired people to be involved
in some form of voluntary work. Those with a better education and
a higher income tend to do voluntary work for charities and
organisations, while those in lower income groups tend to do their
voluntary work in the form of helping each other out.[33]

To advocate an increase in community activity for the elderly is
not to suggest that all old people should be involved in such activities.
It is important, however, for options to be opened up for older people
in order that they can feel and be a part of their locality and
community in the ways that they choose. Self-help has a preventive
component in the sense that those older people who are enabled
to remain actively involved with others are likely to improve their
performance — although the evidence for this is still sparse and rather
speculative. It also has relevance for the enrichment and improvement
of life: an active engaged old person may not be fitter or richer but
he may be happier. It seems likely that as time goes on a better
educated group of older people will move into retirement with
greater awareness of their consumer rights and a less passive view of
themselves. This will no doubt have an effect on perception of the
place of old people within the local, national and international
community.

Summary: The Social Worker and the Team

Social work is rapidly developing and it needs much clarification and
clarity. It does seem that the central objective is the alleviation of
stress in social situations through a flexible use of personal and

community resources. There will also be a need to consider the prevention of stress and the provision of enriched and improved life chances for older people. The social worker will be involved in direct and indirect intervention with the elderly individual, his family, the social systems within which he lives, the wide formal and informal organisation of the community, as well as the internal organisation of hospitals and residential homes.

In so far as they provide new and different relationships for the old person all the members of the geriatric team contribute to changing his life. In so far, also, as they live and work within the same community they play an important role in the ways in which the various social systems interact. It is vitally important that each member of the geriatric team is made aware, and remains aware of the impact of his own interaction on the elderly client's or patient's social functioning.

Notes

1. J.E. Neill, D.J. Fruin, E.M. Goldberg and R.W. Warburton, 'Reactions to Integration', *Social Work Today*, vol. 4, no. 15, 1 November 1973.
2. A. McKay, E.M. Goldberg and D.J. Fruin, 'Consumers and a Social Services Department', *Social Work Today*, vol. 4, no. 16, 15 November 1973.
3. M.L. Blank, 'Recent Research Findings on Practice with the Aging', *Social Casework*, vol. 52, no. 6 (1971), pp. 382-9.
4. K. Gilhome, 'Emotional Needs' in *The Place of the Retired and the Elderly in Modern Society* (Age Concern England, 1975).
5. See, for example, E. Shanas *et al., Old People in Three Industrial Societies* (Routledge and Kegan Paul, 1968).
6. P.B. Baltes, 'Strategies for Psychological Intervention in Old Age: A Symposium', *The Gerontologist*, vol. 13, no. 1 (1973), pp. 4-6.
7. *Gillie Report: The Fieldwork of the Family Doctor* (HMSO, 1963).
8. Ibid.
9. See, for example, L. Ratoff, A. Rose and C.R. Smith, 'Social Workers and GPs', *Social Work Today*, vol. 5, no. 16, 14 November 1974.
10. M. Jeffreys, *An Anatomy of Social Welfare Services* (Michael Joseph, 1965); B.G. Harwin, B. Cooper, M.R. Eastwood and D.P. Goldberg, 'Prospects for Social Work in General Practice', *Lancet*, no. 2 (1970).
11. R. Dubos, *Man Medicine and Environment* (Pall Mall Press, 1968).
12. For further discussion see C.P. Brearley, 'Social Gerontology and Social Work', *Brit. J. Social Work*, Winter, 1976.
13. S. Saul, *Aging: An Album of People Growing Old* (John Wiley and Sons, Inc., 1974).
14. For further discussion see C.P. Brearley, *Residential Work with the Elderly* (Routledge and Kegan Paul, 1977).
15. E.H. Erikson, *Childhood and Society* (Norton and Co. Inc., rev. ed., 1964).
16. C.P. Brearley, *Social Work, Ageing and Society* (Routledge and Kegan

Paul, 1975).

17. For further discussion see C.P. Brearley (1976), op. cit.

18. For detailed discussion of the ideas in this section see C.P. Brearley (1975), op. cit.

19. See, for example, W.J. Reid and L. Epstein, *Task-Centered Casework* (Columbia University Press, 1972).

20. *The Attitudes of the Retired and the Elderly* (Age Concern England, 1975).

21. See, for example, J. Liton and S.C. Olstein, 'Therapeutic Aspects of Reminiscence', *Social Casework*, May 1969; A. Pincus, 'Reminiscence in Aging and Its Implications for Social Work Practice', *Social Work*, vol. 15, no. 3 (1970), pp. 47-53.

22. M. Milloy, 'Casework with the Older Person and His Family', *Social Casework*, October 1964.

23. C.S. Ford, 'Ego-adaptive Mechanisms of Older Persons', *Social Casework*, January 1965.

24. A.O. Freed, 'The Family Agency and the Kinship System of the Elderly', *Social Casework*, vol. 56, no. 10 (1975), p. 579.

25. M.J. Graney, 'Happiness and Social Participation in Aging', *J. of Geront.*, vol. 30, no. 6 (1975), pp. 701-6.

26. C. Bell, 'Occupational Career, Family Cycle and Extended Family Relations', *Human Relations*, vol. 24, no. 6 (1971), pp. 463-75.

27. B.G. Simos, 'Adult Children and their Aging Parents', *Social Work*, vol. 18, no. 3 (May 1973), pp. 78-85.

28. S.R. Sherman, 'Patterns of Contacts for Residents of Age-Segregated and Age-Integrated Housing', *J. of Geront.*, vol. 30, no. 1 (1975), pp. 103-7.

29. For full discussion of the points in this section see C.P. Brearley (1977), op. cit.

30. C.P. Brearley (ed.), *Self-Help, Participation and the Elderly* (Conference Report, University of Southampton); C.P. Brearley and J. Richardson, 'Social Work in a Geriatric Hospital', *Social Work Today*, vol. 6, no. 8 (1975).

31. The Link Opportunity Study was established by a steering group comprising representatives of Age Concern England, the Parkhill Trust, the Employment Fellowship, the Pre-Retirement Association and the British United Provident Association. For discussion see: E. Walton, 'Information handling among the retired' in *Old Age – Today and Tomorrow* (British Association, 1976); C.P. Brearley, *Merton Link Opportunity Study: Report*, May 1976.

32. R. Hadley, A. Webb and C. Farrell, *Across the Generations* (Allen and Unwin, 1975).

33. *Age Concern on Accommodation* (Age Concern England, 1975).

7 AGEING AND THE MIND

Tony Whitehead

Old people are people. This statement of the obvious is only made because too frequently old people are not treated as people, and this is particularly so if they behave abnormally, or show other evidence that there may be something amiss with their mind. If an elderly person becomes agitated, miserable, expresses odd ideas, becomes a little forgetful, or in a multitude of ways appears to deviate from what some consider normal, it is likely that he or she will be considered 'senile'. The word senile carries an unpleasant and even censorious effect. 'You are going senile' and 'senile old fool' are expressions of abuse, and even when the word is used in a kindly context, such as 'You should make allowances, she is senile' or 'The poor old thing is going senile', the inference is still one that suggests that the old person is ceasing to be a person.

Ageing does not inevitably produce mental decay. The majority of old people with symptoms of mental disorder are suffering from the types of mental illness that afflict younger people and are not slipping into senility. Even when there is definite evidence of brain damage, presumably produced by ageing, the sufferer is still a person and can in fact be helped to function at some level, even if this is not as high as it had been in the past. Whatever happens to the mental functioning and behaviour of a person, it never changes that person into anything less than a person.

Having said this it would still be foolish to deny that age does affect the mind. As we become older, our thinking becomes mroe rigid and fixed, and it is progressively more difficult to absorb new ideas and new ways of looking at problems. This is of course an overall statement. Each individual is unique and there is a phenomenal variation, with some eighty-year-olds retaining a flexibility of thought rarely found in forty-year-olds. Intellectual deterioration is also considered a sequelae of ageing. In fact our intellectual abilities tend to decline from about sixteen or seventeen onwards, though of course this is compensated for by increased knowledge and experience. In the same way as mental rigidity varies, so of course does intellect, with some forty-year-olds giving up thinking, while some eighty-year-olds have intellectual abilities greater than most of us.

To complete the sad side of ageing, as far as the brain is concerned, there may be deterioration in memory, loss of control of emotions, and severe deterioration in the ability to reason. These things happen, but only to a small minority, and the fact that they happen does not prove that they are the direct result of ageing in these individuals. Many factors, known and unknown, may play their part. There is a belief that a lot of the mental deterioration that afflicts old people is not simply the result of physical changes in the brain, but more one of 'disuse atrophy'. If a muscle is not used it wastes, and some believe that the same sort of thing happens to the brain. Certainly if someone either young, middle aged or old is forced into a situation in which they are not allowed to think for themselves, they are liable in time to present a picture to the observer that would suggest that they were 'senile'. The inmates of backward mental hospitals, who have become victims of 'institutional neurosis',[1] show much in their behaviour and conversation that would lead you to believe that they were demented old people, except that very many of them are not old. If these same individuals are exposed to an enlightened regime, in which they are not only treated as people, but allowed to make choices and do things for themselves, they improve and start behaving like the people they used to be.

It has been said that man is a problem-solving animal and without facility to have problems to solve, goes into a decline. Our society encourages and forces the elderly into becoming non-problem-solving beings. Compulsory retirement and the general attitude of society towards the old both conspire to produce this result. On the one hand old people are neglected, while on the other attention is paid to them that is almost as equally destructive as neglect. Their views are ignored, decisions are made for them and they are given few chances for maintaining their dignity and feelings of usefulness. This does not mean that they should be treated as superior citizens, since such an approach would be equally damaging. All they are entitled to is being treated as equals with the rest of us. Because of society's attitudes, and their own defensive reactions, many old people do appear to expect special treatment, particularly from children and young adults. This reaction naturally generates a reaction on the part of the child or adult, which is one of either annoyance or anger, so society's attitude towards the elderly is reinforced, as is the old person's attitude to society.

A number of other things happen to people as they grow older.

We tend not to improve with age and there is considerable truth in the statement that 'If you want to be a charming old lady, you have to start off as a charming young lady'. The same statement of course applies to men. Thus personality traits, both acceptable and unacceptable, do not disappear or change with ageing, but simply intensify. The kind young man becomes the very kind old man, while the suspicious, bad-tempered youth becomes the paranoid, irritable old man.

Man is subject to emotional conflicts, inhibitions and other emotional maladjustments. Sometimes emotional problems occur in young people, which produce unresolved conflicts, but as the individual becomes involved with the problems of daily living, these problems are pushed into the background and cease to have a significant effect upon his behaviour. However, with retirement and old age the problems come back again, now often intensified. In the same way an individual may have difficulty in his inter-personal relationships, which are partially disguised by his working life-style. For example, a man may marry and never adequately relate to his wife. If he becomes very much involved in his job and his wife in hers, this problem of inter-personal relationships is never worked through, until suddenly retirement forces them together. Now the problem is dramatically resurrected, with all kinds of emotional repercussions. This has sometimes been referred to as the 'sailor home from the seas' phenomenon.

None of the things mentioned occur in isolation, since they are part of an interwoven complex of emotion, bodily functioning or malfunctioning and interactions with other people and society, both parochial and general. It is quite futile to try to help those that are in difficulties without realising all this and acting upon it. One useful way of guarding against trying to offer help in isolation is not to be isolated as a helper. Clearly most old people who have difficulties are helped by their friends and neighbours, who are much less likely to take a narrow view of the problem than professionals. When, however, professional help is necessary it is important that this help be provided by a group of professionals, who are members of different disciplines. This is described in modern jargon as a multi-disciplinary team and the usefulness and effectiveness of the team approach will be considered later in the chapter. For the present it should be emphasised that most old people do not have all these unpleasant things happen to them, but for those that do there are solutions, which at least improve the quality of the individual's life and at best produce a cure, which means that the symptoms are removed, the conflict resolved, or a good inter-personal relationship established or re-established.

It has been said that there are serious disadvantages in considering one facet of an individual in isolation. However, for descriptive reasons, it is necessary to describe the types of mental illness that can and do afflict old people, so that they can be recognised and then placed in the context of the whole individual and his life situation. With this in mind some of the common psychiatric disorders will be considered and then methods of help that encompass the total life situations will be described and discussed.

Psychiatric Disorders in Old Age

Some of the common emotional problems of the elderly have already been considered. It is often forgotten that the elderly have sexual problems, which are both emotional and physical. Old age should not take away sex life, and impotence and frigidity, when they occur, are more likely to be due to social and emotional reasons than any ageing process. The ageing man may become impotent because he has never come to terms with sex and had always viewed it as something rather unclean. The ageing woman is liable to be affected in the same way. Sometimes physical disorders play a minor role. For example, impotence may occur following prostatectomy. This should only be a temporary phenomenon, but if other factors are in operation it may become permanent. In the same way hysterectomy may leave the woman with some degree of frigidity, which again should go away, but if for example she has always viewed sex as something unclean, it is likely that frigidity will continue. It is important that old people are helped with their sexual problems and difficulties, since they are as liable to respond to help and treatment as younger people, and if they do respond an important and joyful dimension of life is restored to them, or perhaps given to them for the first time.

Specific Disorders

The problems of defining normality and abnormality are real and their discussion would require a large text book. Remembering this and the variety of abnormal behaviour that is possible, it can be seen that any attempt to systematise mental illness is both hard and hazardous. This explains why some psychiatrists are loth to apply diagnostic labels to patients, preferring to consider each individual as unique, with problems and difficulties that are equally unique. Such an approach is certainly seductive, yet there are advantages to attaching labels to patients provided the uniqueness of the individual is also remembered and continually considered when trying to provide them with the help and support they may need. There are many theories about the causation of different types of mental illness. There are also a small number of facts, some of which support the idea of defining certain specific mental illnesses. In our present state of limited knowledge, with our small number of therapeutic tools, it would appear that defining specific illnesses makes treatment a little more effective and perhaps slightly more rational. Here the generally accepted psychiatric disease entities will be considered and their specific and not so specific treatments considered. Consideration of these specific treatments should not detract from the need not only to treat the individual as an individual, but also to make every effort to provide the unique help he or she may require.

For example, an elderly lady may suffer from a classical attack of psychotic (endogenous) depression, the specific treatment for which may be electro-convulsive therapy, antidepressants, or a combination of both. The same old lady may have led a lonely, isolated, purposeless life for some years prior to developing this severe depressive illness. Some psychiatrists may consider that the illness was the direct product of this type of life, while others of a more organic and genetic persuasion would say that the illness was due to biochemical changes, with the environment and life-style contributing little, if anything, to its aetiology. Whichever attitude is taken, most of us would use the specific treatments mentioned, because an attack of severe endogenous depression requires urgent treatment or the patient may die from malnutrition, dehydration, intercurrent infection or suicide. Attempts to correct the defects in the environment and life-style, together with intensive psycho-therapy, if this was available and practicable, would be unlikely to produce a rapid improvement, even if it did so in the long term. On the other hand, simply giving the specific treatment and ignoring all the other problems would only partially help the patient and, if the cause of the depression did include psychological and social factors, a recurrence of the illness is almost inevitable. The sensible approach would be to deal with the immediate illness, using the specifics mentioned, and follow this up by attempts to combat loneliness, restore purpose and provide an opportunity for the patient to discuss her problems in a psychotherapeutic situation.

Old people suffer from most of the psychiatric illnesses that affect the young and middle aged, the only difference being one of incidence.

Neurotic Reactions

It is conventional to divide psychiatric illness into various main groups, including the neuroses, the psychoses, personality disorders, organic brain diseases and mental handicap. At one time it was taught that the difference between neuroses and psychoses was that in the case of neuroses the patient had a mental illness and realised he was ill, while the victim of psychoses was ill but did not recognise this to be the case. Such differentiation is quite meaningless, since some sufferers from neurotic reactions have little realisation that their illness is of psychological origin while many, if not all, victims of psychoses at least have some appreciation that things are amiss. Effective definitions are difficult to come by, and it is perhaps best to describe what is meant by the various disease groups and leave it at that.

Neurotic reactions can be considered under a number of headings, though this does not mean that an individual patient may not suffer from more than one of these varieties.

Anxiety

Everyone experiences anxiety, but when the term is used in psychiatry, it means something slightly different from what is experienced, say, before a difficult interview, an examination or a potentially embarrassing speech. Anxiety as an illness or a symptom of an illness is much more intense than the normal anxiety that we all feel, and occurs for no apparent reason. The sufferer feels anxious and tense, and may even feel that he is going to die. Associated with these subjective feelings, a variety of somatic phenomena may occur. These include an increase in pulse and respiratory rate, dryness of the mouth, sweating, particularly of the palms, a feeling of weakness, tremor, a tight feeling in the chest, a tight feeling around the head, a sinking sensation in the abdomen, a desire to micturate or defaecate, and a general feeling of unwellness. Everyone who suffers from anxiety does not necessarily get all these symptoms, and it is possible to get a number of combinations, often with subjective concern about one or two. Anxiety may occur in acute attacks or can be with the victim all the time, with perhaps occasional upsurgings of symptoms. It may be apparently unrelated to anything else, or may be associated with specific situations. In the latter case it will be described as phobic anxiety. Phobic anxiety is anxiety which is brought on by something definable. For example, some people may become extremely anxious when they are confined to a small, closed space (claustrophobia), while others become anxious if they are out in the open (agoraphobia). A large number of phobias have been named but the actual names are of no great significance provided that the immediate cause of the anxiety can be indentified.

Some consider that the free, non-phobic anxiety is always associated with depression as an illness or some other psychiatric disease entity. Others consider that anxiety can exist as an illness in its own right.

Anxiety in old people can often present as an organic illness, the patient believing that he has heart disease, abdominal problems, organic brain disease, etc. Often the patient is investigated for some organic disease and as a consequence becomes more anxious, the anxiety not being allayed when the doctor says nothing 'physical' can be found amiss.

The possibility of anxiety should always be considered when a patient complains of any of the symptoms of this disease. The presence of organic pathology, though warranting treatment, does nor necessarily exclude anxiety, which also requires treatment.

The treatment of anxiety consists in attempting to discover the cause, the treatment of any associated disease, be it organic or psychiatric, coupled with specific therapy for anxiety. The judicious use of tranquillisers, such as diazepam (Valium) or thioradazine (Melleril) can be quite effective provided a serious attempt is made to discover the cause of the anxiety. If the cause is a depressive illness, this requires treatment in its own right while, if the cause cannot be discovered, symptomatic treatment with a tranquilliser is both necessary to relieve stress and can be an effective cure, since it breaks the vicious cycle of anxiety provoking more anxiety, and so perpetuating itself even when the original cause, discovered or undiscovered, is no longer acting.

Phobic anxieties can be very effectively dealt with using the techniques of behaviour therapy. The techniques of this type of therapy cannot be described here, but they are based upon concepts of conditioning and de-conditioning discovered by Pavlov and elaborated on by Watson and Skinner. The interested reader can obtain information from a number of sources.[2]

Techniques of relaxation can be effective, while individual or group psychotherapy, if available, can be extremely useful.

Obsessional Compulsive States

The word obsession, like anxiety, has a special meaning in psychiatry. In ordinary usage, it means that as individual is abnormally pre-occupied with something. For example, someone may say that a friend has an obsession about his mother. When obsessional is used to describe a neurosis, it is possibly better to use the phrase 'obsessional compulsive' since this clarifies the situation a little. The sufferer from this condition either experiences a recurrent thought that is usually unpleasant, or must carry out a repetitive action or a complex ritual. Attempts to suppress the thought, or not carry out the repetitive action or ritual, results in the generation of considerable anxiety, and it is this anxiety that pushes the individual into the repetitive action. There are many possible recurrent thoughts, and even more repetitive acts or rituals. An example of the former would be the thought that the patient would kill someone, or himself, while repetitive actions can range from having repeatedly to wash his hands, to complex manoeuvres when entering a room, or dressing or undressing.

Obsessional symptoms are fairly common in the elderly, and may be associated with a depressive illness. Some old people have had the condition all their lives, while others develop it in later life.

People who suffer from obsessional compulsive states usually have a so-called obsessional character. This means that they have a tendency to be unusually neat and tidy in their behaviour, their thoughts and their morals. The unpleasant recurrent thoughts are usually completely foreign to their overt personality, and they never act them out. There is one important exception to this statement in the case of thoughts of suicide. Recurrent attacks of depression are common in this condition and in one of these the patient may attempt, and sometimes succeed, in taking his own life.

Treatment is often difficult since the patient tends to respond badly to psychotherapy and only gain a degree of relief from medication. Depression when it is present should obviously be treated, and its successful treatment often produces considerable relief of the obsessional symptoms, though they may still continue at a lower key. Leucotomy is sometimes recommended for this condition in younger patients, though many psychiatrists would object to the use of this mutilation. There are very few who would recommend it for the elderly.

Hysteria

In psychiatry and medicine hysteria describes a whole range of symptoms and signs that appear to suggest physical disease, but in fact have their origins in the psyche. Paralysis, with the loss of use of an arm or leg, loss of sensation in different parts of the body, loss of memory and odd uncontrolled spontaneous movements, are some examples of symptoms that may be of organic origin, but can equally be the product of hysteria. A very rare manifestation of hysteria is the Jekyll and Hyde phenomenon in which the patient has two or more very different patterns of behaviour, and switches between them without apparently having any conscious knowledge of what is happening. This great rarity is mentioned, not because of its importance, but because some people confuse this phenomenon with schizophrenia. Schizophrenia is not an illness in which there is a split personality but is an illness in which there is fragmentation of the personality.

It may be thought that what has been described could equally well be categorised as malingering. Some people malinger particularly if they are unwilling members of an armed service, prisoners or in other unsatisfactory situations. Malingering means that the person consciously and purposefully tries to mimic some illness to achieve some benefit for himself. Hysteria describes an unconscious mechanism with the patient completely unaware that the symptoms are being generated by his own psyche.

Very many psychiatrists are now doubtful of the existence of hysteria and it certainly can be a dangerous diagnosis to make. Present evidence suggests that hysteria is excessively rare as an illness in its own right, but hysterical symptoms may occur against a background of some other illness. For example, someone with a cerebral tumour may develop hysterical symptoms on top of the symptoms produced by the tumour itself. Psychiatric illnesses, such as depression and schizophrenia, may also generate hysterical symptoms. Elderly people are slightly more likely to develop hysterical symptoms than younger patients, but almost always there is an underlying pathology which can range from organic brain disease to severe depression. The presence of hysterical symptoms should always result in a very careful search being made for some other pathology. Such a search, properly carried out, usually reveals that there is in fact some other disease.

From what has been said it should be clear that the treatment of hysteria is often the treatment of the underlying condition.

However, hysterical symptoms *per se* can often be removed by hypnosis and provided the underlying cause is dealt with — be it another illness or some emotional conflict — the results can be most impressive.

Depression

A number of different types of depression are described by pscyhiatrists, and there is continuing debate as to their relationship to each other. It is usual to talk of four main varieties, which are:

1. Grief reactions.
2. Reactive depression.
3. Neurotic depression.
4. Psychotic or endogenous depression.

Grief reactions are normal phenomena and describe reaction of the individual to bereavement, loss or some other tragedy. This type of reaction is not pathological and should never be treated as such, though obviously help, support and comfort are necessary. Support and comfort are usually provided by relatives. If the victim is alone it may fall upon the shoulders of a social worker or doctor to provide this comfort. In the past, priests were the people to turn to, but now for many people with no interest or belief in religion, the social worker or doctor takes on the role of the priest.

Reactive depression describes the misery engendered by intolerable life situations. Sometimes grief protracted beyond its normal span may then take on the features of a reactive, neurotic or psychotic depression. Individuals vary considerably in their reaction to stress and disaster, some not becoming depressed until their life situation is truly intolerable, while others develop depressive reactions when things go a little amiss. The features of so-called reactive depression are very similar to those of neurotic depression, and some psychiatrists would not differentiate between the two. Those who do differentiate would expect the depressed person they label as suffering from neurotic depression to have a past history of neurotic adjustment, while the ones that they would describe as suffering from reactive depression would not have this past history of neurotic adjustment, but would have factors in their life situation which would be expected to produce misery in the exposed individual.

The symptoms of reactive and neurotic depression need to be compared with those of psychotic depression, though the latter condition will be described in the next section. A sufferer from neurotic or reactive depression will experience subjective feelings of misery, which vary from time to time and tend to be dependent upon circumstances. Endogenous depression produces variations in these subjective feelings of misery, but these variations appear to be more related to the time of day than circumstance. Typically, endogenous depression produces considerable misery first thing in the morning, with some alleviation as the day goes on. Neurotic and reactive depression tends to produce more misery towards the evening, or in special circumstances such as being alone in the house, and it is usually possible to cheer up the individual, be it only temporarily. Similar attempts to cheer up an individual with an endogenous depression are usually doomed from the beginning. Sleep disturbances occur in both types of depression, with a tendency to awake very early with endogenous depression, while there is difficulty in getting to sleep with the neurotic or reactive type. Anxiety is likely to be present in both types of depression, and both types can lead to suicide attempts. Loss of appetite is an important symptom of endogenous depression, but with neurotic or reactive depression the appetite may not be affected. A variety of organic symptoms can be produced by either type of depression, which are either the products of anxiety or depression itself. These will be considered in more detail under the heading of endogenous depression.

The treatment of reactive and neurotic depression must consist of a number of different approaches. Attempts may be made to improve the unsatisfactory life situation of the patient. Psychotherapy should also play a part, and physical and medical intervention should not be eschewed. The latter would consist of the careful use of an antidepressant drug, and many would consider that this should be a so-called monoamine otidase inhibitor. As distinct from other antidepressants described as tricyclics and quadricyclics, there is some evidence to suggest that these are the antidepressants of choice in the case of reactive and neurotic depression, but unfortunately use of these preparations carries certain dangers if the patient does not carefully follow a variety of prohibitions on certain foods and a number of other drugs. Because of this it is often not possible to treat old people with monoamine oxidase inhibitors, because they may ignore the prohibitions on certain foods and may have to take other drugs which are incompatible because of other illnesses, such as asthma or heart disease.

Psychotic Depression and Manic-Depressive Psychoses

Depression in its various forms is a very prevalent illness among the elderly, and some people would consider dividing it into different types is both unnecessary and misleading. There is evidence to suggest that different types of depression only describe differences in degree, but other evidence shows that the different types are in fact different disease entities. It is obvious that both these pieces of evidence cannot be true. Whichever is true does not distract from the apparent need for different therapeutic approaches for the different types.

Endogenous or psychotic depression describes a type of depression in which the subjective misery is severe, with loss of appetite, loss of weight, sleep disturbance manifest in early morning wakening, considerable slowing up of the individual's thoughts and actions, and a preponderance of morbid, unhappy thoughts which can develop into frank delusions. The patient may believe that he has committed some dreadful offence for which he will be punished, and should be punished. I once treated a patient who believed that she had contracted a virulent type of venereal disease which would spread to anyone who came near to her, and that already large numbers of people had fallen victim to her presence.

Coupled with these symptoms, there may be a whole variety of physical complaints and dysfunctions. Constipation is common, together with the various symptoms of anxiety already described. Some patients develop delusional beliefs about their bodies such as the conviction that their inside is putrifying and rotting away.

Attacks of psychotic depression may occur throughout the life of the individual, or he may only suffer one attack which may occur in youth, middle or old age. Sometimes attacks of depression alternate with attacks of elation, the latter being described as either mania or hypomania. Roughly, hypomania and mania are the opposite of depression, with subjective feelings of elation, over-activity, talkativeness and a general tendency to rush around trying to do a whole variety of things, including quite often spending phenomenal amounts of money, which the patient may or may not possess. Some individuals never develop attacks of depression, and only suffer from recurrent attacks of mania or hypomania. The term manic-depressive psychosis describes both depression of a psychotic variety in the absence of any attacks of mania, mania occurring on its own or, the least common, attacks of depression alternating with attacks of mania or some other variant, in which the patient experiences at one time depression, and at another time mania.

The elderly, though frequent victims of depression, rarely develop mania or hypomania, but sometimes suffer from a rather odd condition in which there is an intermingling of depressive and manic symptoms occurring almost at the same time. This illness presents, as can be imagined, a strange picture and may be mistaken for organic brain disease or schizophrenia. The patient may claim that he has achieved great things because of his prowess and, having said this, may weep because he believes that someone has deprived him of the rewards of his imagined achievement. There are thus symptoms of hypomania and depression with a paranoid flavour.

Depression is often missed in the elderly, either because a patient describes physical symptoms and plays down his emotional feelings, or because the doctor views any psychiatric illness in old people as a manifestation of senility and organic brain disease, so concerning himself more with where the patient can be placed for care than with the provision of effective treatment.

Psychotic depression and the rarer hypomania and mixed manic depressive state can all be effectively treated, regardless of the age of the patient. The specific treatment for psychotic depression is either an antidepressant, electro-convulsive therapy, or a combination of both. The treatment for mania and hypomania is either a tranquilliser, lithium carbonate or, with a rare intractable case, electro-convulsive therapy. The mixed manic depressive condition tends to respond best to electro-convulsive therapy. It has been emphasised before that the specific treatment is of little avail by itself, since there is likely to be a need for various types of social intervention and the provision of company and activity.

Paranoid Reactions

Old people often become suspicious. This suspiciousness is not infrequently a true appreciation of reality, but some people develop what appears to be a specific illness, where there is pathological suspiciousness. This condition has some of the features of paranoid schizophrenia, and there has been, and continues to be, debate over what category it should be placed in. Since we know little about the causation of schizophrenia, arguments as to whether this paranoid reaction occurring in the middle aged and elderly is, or is not, related to schizophrenia are rather academic. Without doubt a condition exists in which the individual comes to believe that strange things are being done by neighbours or other people and these activities are directed at the individual concerned. It is usual to describe the condition as paraphrenia.

The usual sufferer is a widow, widower, spinster or bachelor living alone, or occasionally the victim has a spouse or is living with relatives. A common story is that the patient over a period has come to believe that a neighbour, frequently of the opposite sex, is spying on her, either through holes in the walls or ceilings that no one else can see, or using some strange machine which makes visualisation through walls possible. One old lady described such a machine as a 'main brain'. As well as being spied upon she may believe that noxious substances are squirted or forced into her room. She may hear the neighbour or person involved saying unpleasant things about her, which may be comments on her morals or statements that they are going to come and kill her. There is often a strong sexual flavour to these delusional beliefs. Occasionally the beliefs are that neighbours are indulging in all sorts of immoral acts which in no way are directed at the patient but simply cause considerable annoyance.

Apart from these delusional beliefs, the patient is essentially normal, though may complain of mild depression engendered by the goings-on and sometimes has difficulty in sleeping, again because of what she imagines is happening in the house next door or across the road. Occasionally elderly people are seen who have more florid schizophrenic illnesses, with or without paranoid symptoms. These individuals have usually suffered from schizophrenia since they were young or middle aged, and have either previously received treatment, or for some reason have gone through most of their life without being caught in the psychiatric net.

Paraphrenia is an eminently treatable condition, and as with most mental illnesses in the elderly, can be successfully treated without the trauma of admission to hospital, provided adequate services are available. The specific treatment for the condition is the judicious and careful use of a major tranquilliser. One of the injectable long-acting tranquillisers can be very useful for this condition, provided it is used by an expert who develops a relationship with the patient that makes regular monthly injections an acceptable procedure. Coupled with any specific treatment there is the usual need to deal with the social, economic and psychological problems of the patient that may or may not be related to the specific illness.

Organic Brain Disease

For many doctors, including psychiatrists and geriatricians, the presence of any psychiatric illness in an old person suggests he has, or is developing, organic brain disease. This is of course untrue, since the old are as entitled as anyone else to develop neurotic and psychotic illnesses without having any organic brain disease. Because of this misconception, organic brain disease is diagnosed more frequently than it occurs. However, brain-damaging diseases do occur fairly frequently in elderly people. This does not mean that they are beyond help, yet many services for the elderly operate as if this was the case.

Organic brain disease means physical disturbances of the brain itself, as distinct from psychological disturbances of function. There are two main groups which can be further subdivided:

1. Acute toxic confusional states, or to use the fairly recently introduced American term, acute brain syndrome; and
2. Dementia, or the American equivalent, chronic brain syndrome.

Acute Brain Syndrome

When some people become physically ill, particularly with infections or diseases that may affect the cerebral circulation and the transport of oxygen to the brain, they develop a collection of psychiatric symptoms that make up the picture of acute brain syndrome, or acute confusional state. These symptoms include a clouding of consciousness, which may vary from time to time, disorientation, restlessness, anxiety, the misidentification of things and people and occasionally a liability to aggressive behaviour if they are badly handled.

This condition is fairly common in the elderly and can be produced by a whole range of organic pathologies, including chest infection, heart failure, cerebral thrombosis, haemorrhage or tumour, vitamin and other deficiencies and, perhaps most common of all, drug intoxication as the result of ill-advised prescribing.

The treatment of this condition is the treatment of the underlying disease. The psychiatric symptoms are almost always reversible and if the underlying disease is one that is either self-limiting or responds to treatment, there is no reason why the sufferer should not make a full recovery.

There are no permanent changes in the brain, but transient changes can be discovered at post-mortem if the patient dies. These changes involve swelling of the cerebral nerve cells.

Chronic Brain Syndrome

The term dementia, or chronic brain syndrome, should be confined to a description of illnesses that have produced irreversible and usually progressive physical brain damage. The overt manifestations of these conditions are disturbances of memory, reduced ability to reason, disorientation, and a tendency for the patient to over-react emotionally. In some types of dementia, particularly the so-called arteriosclerotic dementia, the patient may have difficulty in finding the right word to express anything he wishes to express, and in the extreme appears to talk rubbish.

There are two main types of dementia afflicting the elderly. These are the so-called senile dementia and arteriosclerotic dementia. Many patients with dementia have both types.

The basic differences between senile and arteriosclerotic dementia are that in senile dementia there is a generalised diminution in the number of brain cells spread reasonably evenly throughout the cortex, while in arteriosclerotic dementia areas of degeneration occur in relationship to disease and occlusion of arteries supplying these areas. In senile dementia it appears that something affects the brain cells directly, while in arteriosclerotic dementia disease of the arteries affects the brain cells.

The patient with senile dementia tends to have an overall and progressive deterioration in all cerebral function, while the course of arteriosclerotic dementia is a more fluctuating one with periods of acute disturbed mental function followed by some recovery and later by another acute attack. This varying picture is due both to changes in the blood supply to the brain and to obstruction of small arteries by degeneration of their walls.

It can be very dangerous to the patient to have the label of dementia attached to him, since it often means that he will then be looked upon as someone beyond help or hope, and the only concern will be in finding a place for him in some institution where he can be ignored and forgotten. The diagnosis of dementia can be very difficult, since an individual may have certain symptoms of dementia, or apparent symptoms of dementia, which are the product of other illnesses or maladjustments. If the true situation is ascertained, and the patient exposed to the correct treatment and helped with appropriate social and psychological intervention, the symptoms disappear, so giving the lie to the diagnosis of dementia. However, if these symptoms are taken as definite proof of dementia, a search for underlying illness, psychological problems, and social difficulties will not be undertaken. Nothing will be done about the symptoms, and the patient will be treated as if he was demented. If someone is treated as if he is demented and placed in some institution where everything is done for him and he is allowed no say in occupation or expression of individuality, it is likely that his behaviour will further deteriorate and become even more apparently demented. In every mental hospital in the country patients can be found who were once labelled demented yet following a programme of rehabilitation ceased to be demented, or having been labelled demented, still appear to be demented until someone decides it is worthwhile at least trying to help them. The existence of a definite dementing process still does not mean that nothing can be done to help the patient. Failing memory makes the individual even more dependent upon the familiar, so the first principle in providing help for patients with dementia is to try to maintain them in their own familiar environment for as long as possible, using what services may be available. Admitting a patient with dementia to hospital or other institution never does the patient any good and usually does considerable harm. Coupled with maintaining them in their own environment, every effort should be made to ensure that they are able to use their remaining abilities to the utmost.

This has been a brief outline of the types of psychiatric illness that may affect old people. Further information is outlined at the end of the chapter.[3]

When an elderly person suffers from one or other of the so-called disease entities mentioned, it must be remembered that he or she has developed this illness against the background of a long life and may have many other problems, emotional, social and physical. Because of this, provision of effective help may be rather complex and difficult. It also means that a variety of help and assistance may be necessary. There is a common belief among professional workers that no one but professional people help old people. In fact the vast majority of elderly people who have problems and needs receive what help they get from friends, relatives and the general public. Professional workers tend to get a rather distorted view of reality, since a disproportionate number of their clients are ones who for one reason or another have difficulties with relatives, friends and neighbours. Most families do help and support their elderly members, while most communities do the same. There really is little truth in the belief that children no longer care for their ageing parents. In this context it should also be remembered that the children of many elderly people are elderly themselves. It is not uncommon to find that a daughter who is trying to help to support her mother has similar emotional, physical and social problems to those of her mother.

When families are not helpful and supportive, it is not because the elderly are rejected by the young. Even a superficial look at these families will quickly demonstrate that there has always been conflict and tension within the family group. Such a superficial look can lead you to believe that the old person is really to blame because of her behaviour in the past and her continuing reaction to her family. However, playing the blame game is neither realistic nor helpful and it is equally mistaken to blame either the family or the elderly relative. They are all victims of a complex of emotion, inter-personal conflict and misunderstanding.

Providing Help

A large number of different services, both official and voluntary, provide varying types of help for old people. Some of this help is provided specifically for those with psychiatric problems, while other services help, or try to help, all old people regardless of any label that may be attached to them. Some services almost specifically exclude those who are considered to be mentally ill. Because a variety of agencies and services are involved in providing various types of help, overlap and conflict is not uncommon and a situation too frequently occurs in which two or more agencies provide conflicting help, or a number of workers become involved with one elderly person, not necessarily to the advantage of that individual. When it is remembered that there are considerable shortages of facilities, and more important, personnel, it seems unbelievable that these limited resources and too few people should be so badly organised that overlap, duplication and pointless conflict is still a commonplace phenomenon.

In the United Kingdom, some people believe that the reorganisation of social work on a generic basis, together with a rationalisation of both the National Health Service and local government services, would at least have solved this problem as far as the public sector services were concerned. This has not happened. The family doctor service still operates independently from the hospital service and it is still commonplace to find little, if any, liaison between the providers of health service help on one side and local authority social service department help on the other. This is bad enough, though at least understandable, but even with a local hospital service there may be conflict and overlap, with considerable misunderstanding and resulting distress to the elderly victim of the system. An old lady may have been successfully supported at home by a social service department social worker helped with the usual services such as a home help, meals on wheels and attendance at a local day centre. She then becomes physically ill and is admitted to a general hospital. Here she may have very good treatment for her illness, but this will be carried out without much regard for her as a person. Within the isolation of the hospital, it may then be decided that she will be unable to live alone again. Now to use the terrible jargon of the hospital service, she becomes a problem for disposal. It is likely that her physician will refer her to the department of geriatric medicine. If this department is hard-pressed because of shortage of personnel and accommodation, the old lady may be briefly seen and stuck on a waiting list for a long-stay bed. By now she is becoming rather distressed by her prolonged stay in hospital. It is very likely that she has a strong desire to return home, but realises that the hospital staff are against this, and are trying to 'put her away'. She becomes anxious, depressed and perhaps a little muddled. Because of the development of these symptoms she is likely to be referred to a psychiatrist. He may have no special interest in the elderly, not because he is a bad psychiatrist, but because of his involvement in running a general psychiatric service with all its complicated problems, involving younger people. He sees the old lady, perhaps prescribes a tranquilliser or antidepressant, and either recommends that she waits for a long-stay bed in the geriatric department, or perhaps offers to take her in to the local psychiatric hospital. As yet no one will have asked her what she wants to do, or made much enquiry about the possibilities of her support at home. If in fact this had been done, it is very possible that she could have returned home, with perhaps a little more support than she had been having before. If this is not done, she is likely to deteriorate further, and finally end up in a long-stay ward to end her life in misery. Ironically her belief that people are trying to 'put her away' can be used as evidence of mental deterioration and so ensure that she is 'put away'.

People working in well-organised and effective departments of geriatric medicine, or geriatric psychiatry, will say that such an account is out of time. This sort of thing used to happen in the past but never happens now. This is not true; it is still happening. It is not as common as it used to be and many parts of the country do have services that do interlink and are able to offer elderly people the kind of treatment, help and support that they want and require.

A Service for the Elderly Mentally Ill

There is now considerable evidence that old people with mental illness
are best helped and supported by a special psychiatric service developed
with their problems and needs in mind.[4] However, there are many
cogent arguments against developing special services for special age
groups and some would claim that specialisation, sub-specialisation and
super-specialisation are diseases of present day society, that should be
prevented and not encouraged. The development of special facilities for
the elderly is likely to isolate old people from the rest of society and
produce various types of geriatric ghettoes. However, it is possible to
develop special services that bring with them advantages and prevent
these kinds of ill effects. Such a service will now be described.

When considering mental illness in the elderly, it should be
remembered that over half the beds for the mentally ill in this
country are occupied by old people. They have either got into such
accommodation because they developed illnesses in their youth,
which have kept them in hospital ever since, or they have become
mentally ill in old age. Both of these groups are equally in need of all
the help, treatment and support that is possible. The fact that someone
was unfortunate enough to develop a mental illness when there was
little treatment available, must not exclude them from receiving all that
is now possible. To have spent forty or fifty years in a mental hospital
does not mean that they should be beyond the interest of society.

Because there are such large numbers of elderly people in mental
hospitals, it is clearly incumbent upon psychiatry to involve itself in
helping the elderly. There are some psychiatrists and psychiatric
nurses who believe that old people should not be their concern,
claiming that it is wrong for old people to be admitted to psychiatric
hospitals. This view seems to be based on a strange misconception of
what psychiatry should be about. There is an inference here that
psychiatric hospitals are bad places and that old people should not
be punished by being brought into them. This is a sad commentary
upon the professional's view of their own specialty.

Every psychiatric service should develop a special facility for the
elderly. Such a facility must encompass both the community and the
long-stay patients from the past.

The Community

The vast majority of elderly people in our society are helped, treated
and supported in the community by relatives, friends, neighbours,
voluntary organisations and the family doctor service. This is as it

should be and must continue. Improved education of doctors, social workers, nurses and other professionals involved, plus the proliferation of various types of voluntary activity, should mean that even greater numbers of old people will be helped and supported without the need of hospital care. The proliferation of various types of neighbourhood and community schemes for helping old people is a great encouragement of future hope.

The family doctor service is becoming much more effective, since the development of the primary health team concept. Now the family doctors do not work in isolation, but are becoming members of multi-disciplinary teams, including social workers, health visitors and home nurses. The team approach is slowly becoming a reality, with little place for individual professionals working in isolation. As far as the hospital service is concerned, a lot of lip service has been paid to the team approach, but it is still very much in its infancy, with many hospitals continuing to function along the lines of professional isolation.

A service for the elderly mentally ill must encompass everything from the street to the hospital. As far as the hospital facet of the service is concerned, this should also be primarily involved in the community, with the actual hospital facility on the periphery. The service itself requires psychiatrists, social workers, nurses, occupational therapists, physiotherapists, psychologists, chiropodists, etc., who are able to offer help, support and advice in the community. This help should be available to any old person in need and any worker, official or voluntary, who is involved in helping old people. The next service such a facility must provide is day hospital care. The majority of elderly people who require assessment, treatment, help and support for mental problems can receive all this in a day hospital. A day hospital should provide everything that a hospital provides, except for beds at night. The provision of help in a day hospital means that an old person can be treated and supported without the trauma of removal to hospital. It cannot be denied that the majority of old people are upset and sometimes permanently harmed by simply admitting them to hospital. Their fears of being put away are confirmed, the web of support in the community is broken, confusion is produced by the dramatic change of environment, and there is always the danger that new disease processes may be started.

The Day Hospital

Day care for the elderly is now well established and is provided in a great variety of ways. Day centres, which are usually run by either voluntary organisations or local authority social service departments, are not day hospitals. Day centres provide companionship, occupation, food, entertainment and comfort. Day hospitals should provide all this, plus treatment in the hospital sense of treatment. Because day hospitals must provide facilities for assessment, diagnosis and treatment, it is necessary that they are either part of a hospital, or very near to a hospital. Some day hospitals for the elderly mentally ill are in psychiatric hospitals, but on the whole this is not the best site for them. It is best that they be accommodated within the general hospital complex. In fact all hospital services for the elderly mentally ill should be provided within the general hospital complex. This will be discussed later. As far as hospital-based services are concerned, the day hospital should be the centre and headquarters of such a service. As well as providing day hospital care and treatment, it should also provide out-patient facilities. Most out-patient departments are rather dreary, noisy, troublesome places, which old people find disturbing. When out-patient facilities are part of a day hospital, most of these disadvantages are removed. The old person can wait in comfort, perhaps be involved in some of the activities of the day hospital, so that not only is the visit pleasant, but much more informative and useful as far as assessment is concerned. Within the day hospital milieu it is possible to obtain a multi-disciplinary approach, so that the out-patient visit becomes more meaningful and helpful.

It can be claimed that the similarities between day centres and day hospitals are such that it is difficult to draw the line between the two. This is certainly true, and because it is true, there are strong arguments in favour of providing the whole range of day care on one site. Thus there would be day centre facilities and day hospital facilities all within the same building. The day centre would be separate, but at the same time together with the day hospital. Part of the complex would provide the usual day centre services, while the other part would provide the day hospital services, with considerable interchange and communal usage. Not only should there be this close physical relationship between the day centre and the day hospital, but the day hospital itself should have two parts, one serving the problems of mental illness and the other the problems of physical illness. Again there would be separation, coupled with common usage.

In-Patient Facilities

In spite of an emphasis on helping and treating old people in the community, there is still a need for in-patient facilities. Some old people need to come to hospital for a period, while others require long-term care. As far as the first group is concerned it is important that an in-patient facility be provided adjacent to the day hospital. For those people who require prolonged care there are many possibilities. At the present time the majority are accommodated either in long-stay wards in general hospitals, or in similar wards in psychiatric hospitals. This is not the best answer and we should be making very different plans for the future. Small units scattered throughout the community served, and closely integrated with that community, are a much better solution, In fact the majority of local authorities' old peoples' homes now accommodate residents who are little, if any, different from the residents of long-stay wards for the elderly mentally ill. The only difference is that the homes for old people usually provide a much better and happier environment. This is not a plea for local authorities to take over the present responsibilities of the hospital service. It is a plea for the hospital service to develop similar facilities to those created by those forward-looking social service departments. There is a need for co-operation and co-ordination, so that both the hospital service and the local authority share their responsibilities in a more sensible and client-orientated manner. Everything possible must be done to eliminate for ever the long dreary wards filled with beds and people waiting apathetically for death.

Geriatric Psychiatry and Geriatric Medicine

Geriatric medicine is now a well-established part of the hospital service. Since there are obvious clear links between geriatric medicine and geriatric psychiatry, it is important that the hospital facilities for the elderly mentally ill be provided close to the department of geriatric medicine, and the two services be run closely together. Such services have been developed, and the result has been to everyone's advantage, not least the client. Experience has shown that in spite of all the present difficulties it is possible to remove the department of geriatric psychiatry from the mental hospital into the general hospital complex and develop a combined service with the department of geriatric medicine. Failure to do this will mean that mental hospitals will continue to be geriatric ghettoes, and that elderly people in the community who are unfortunate enough to develop mental illness will not receive the help, treatment and support that they must have.

Not only should there be this close liaison between geriatric psychiatry and geriatric medicine, but there is also a need for an equally close liaison between these two and the community, which of course includes social service departments and voluntary organisations. Real liaison, co-operation and co-ordination between the hospital service and the rest of the community is much easier when the hospital facility is within the general hospital complex.

Old people often find themselves in crisis situations. At the present time crisis often leads to admission to either hospital or old people's home. Sometimes such a move is the only answer, but too often this is not the case. Admission to hospital or old people's home occurs because there are no satisfactory crisis intervention provisions. This is particularly likely to be the case in the evenings, at night, or at weekends. It is incumbent upon any hospital service for the elderly mentally ill that it develops a crisis intervention service. The expertise of the staff of the service must be available to the community twenty-four hours a day, seven days a week. It is possible to develop crisis intervention services in co-operation with community services, provided the will exists to do so.

What About the Long-Stay Patient?

It has been said that there are large numbers of elderly people in psychiatric hospitals who have been there for a very long time. Many of those people could leave hospital and end their lives in a more normal and happier environment, provided accommodation could be found. It is of considerable importance that any service for the elderly mentally ill develops facilities for doing this. Many voluntary organisations are interested in providing hostels and group homes. It is also possible to find people who are happy and willing to take in an old person as either a paying guest, or actual member of the family. This is sometimes described as boarding-out, and boarding-out schemes should always be attempted. It is surprising how successful they can be if, as always, there is sufficient interest and enthusiasm among the staff trying to develop such a scheme.

Experience suggests that the view that someone who has been in a mental hospital for forty years cannot, and should not, be discharged, is totally incorrect. Some of the happiest people I have been fortunate enough to meet have been long-stay patients, who were successfully placed back in the community in either a group home, or under a boarding-out scheme.

Old people who have emotional problems or specific psychiatric disorders can be helped in a great variety of ways. Help can only be effective if it is provided by groups and not individuals. As far as the professional hospital side of help is concerned, it needs to be provided by a so-called multi-disciplinary team, which relates closely to the family doctor service and the appropriate voluntary and official agencies in the community. Perhaps most important of all, it should relate closely to the actual people in the community. When such a service is fully developed it is possible to help the majority of old people, without incarcerating them. Those that have to be accommodated within a sheltered environment can be pleasantly housed provided there is imagination about the type of accommodation and its location. A long-stay ward in a mental hospital can be turned into a home and there are no excuses for not so doing. When this happens it is still not the best place, and there must be forward plans for providing small units in the community. Failure to develop special services for the elderly mentally ill and make plans along the lines suggested could be catastrophic, with more and more old people ending their lives either unhelped or incarcerated.

Notes

1. Barton Russell, *Institutional Neurosis* (Bristol, Wright, 1966).
2. K.D. O'Leary and G.T. Wilson, *Behaviour Therapy*.
3. D.B. Bromley, *The Psychology of Ageing* (Penguin Books, 1966); Pitt, Brice, *Psycho-geriatrics* (Churchill, Livingstone, 1974); J.A. Whitehead, *Psychiatric Disorders in Old Age* (Harvey, Miller and Medcalfe, 1974); J. Pearce and E. Miller, *Clinical Aspects of Dementia* (Balliaire and Tindall, 1973).
4. J.A. Whitehead, *In the Service of Old Age* (Harvey, Miller and Medcalfe, 1977).

8 AGEING AND THE SPIRIT:

Paul Gaine

Lord, you have been
our refuge age after age . . .

Our days dwindle under your wrath,
Our lives are over in a breath
— our life lasts for seventy years,
eighty with good health.

. . . make our future as happy as our past was sad,
those years when you were punishing us.

(Psalm 90, *The Jerusalem Bible*)

A friend of mine used to say that the most pleasing thing about passing the age of forty was that one ceased to be a man of promise. My *Dictionary of Quotations* offers me many other pieces of folk wisdom about this particular age: that it is the time by which one should have acquired judgement; that all men over forty are scoundrels; that life begins at forty. The quotations are not merely recording the subjective experience, but also how it appears to others. Shakespeare in his second sonnet could warn his mistress of the approach of old age:

When forty winters shall besiege thy brow
And dig deep trenches in thy beauty's field,
Thy youth's proud livery, so gaz'd on now,
Will be a tatter'd weed of small worth held . . .

John O'Keefe (1747–1833), who has recently been rediscovered as 'England's Molière', could however write that 'Fat, fair, and forty were all the toasts of the young men'.

Ageing as a Mythology: The Ageing Process

This slight literary excursion is intended to suggest that age knows no

absolute, empirical criteria. One could make the same point in more
technical, social scientific terms. In a recent book, *Aging in American
Society*, the author, J.D. Manney, suggests that there is an 'American
view of aging' which falsely regards it as primarily a biological process.
He dismisses this as a myth, or a stereotype, which his book now
replaces with correct empirical data which concentrates on 'the social
situation of older people'. Jaber Gubrium reviewing the book in
Contemporary Sociology[1] suggests that a myth is not simply a mistake
which is to be remedied, but is rather one version of social reality.
The everyday lives of people are based upon innumerable practical
theories or accounts by which they give meaning to the various
incidents which they have to cope with. These myths constitute the
reality of everyday life: we all have our myths. Manney's positivist
account of ageing is only one myth among others, and is neither
more nor less correct than the others. A famous sociologist, W.I.
Thomas, put the matter succinctly: 'If people define a situation as
real it is real in its effects.'

Traditionally anthropologists have tried to explore how people
actively but tacitly make sense of each aspect of their lives. Recently
new schools of sociology have begun to concentrate their attention
on the processes whereby people negotiate the social reality of their
lives.

It has always been a function of religion to provide men with such
myths to give meaning to their lives, or to offer its comment on
other mythologies. One would perhaps expect religion to provide
mythologies for such an important aspect of life as the process of
ageing. However, despite passages in the Bible mentioning both
the sorrows and the potential of old age, books on pastoral theology
and pastoral counselling rarely discuss ageing explicitly, except
with reference to death and bereavement.[2] Similarly technical
treatises on ageing and the elderly usually make no mention of the
role of the churches or the part that the minister can play in helping
people to cope with the ageing process, or with the problems of old
age.[3] There have been several studies, largely American, of religious
practice and belief among older people,[4] and church programmes
of service.[5] Age Concern England published a booklet in 1968
reporting points raised by a working party convened to discuss the
role of the churches in the care of the elderly.[6] A Church of Scotland
minister, W.S. Reid, has recently completed a Ph.D. thesis on religious
attitudes of the elderly and the role of the church in their life.[7]

It is interesting to speculate on the comparative dearth of written material about the role which a minister of religion could play. In doing so I shall suggest that there are certain potential strengths available to the minister which could be consciously developed. To some extent my speculation will relate explicitly to my own specific experience as a Roman Catholic priest in an English diocese.

In a very practical handbook for health visitors and others concerned with the elderly, a consultant geriatrician, speaking of hospital care says:

> The next requirement is a properly constituted team of workers. Doctors, nurses, clergy, auxiliary workers of all kinds, voluntary workers, visiting hairdressers and domestic staff have their part to play and their attitude will add to or substract from, the success of the project. Some unobtrusive kind of educational policy is needed to ensure that the right attitudes are adopted by all who enter the [hospital] community in any capacity.[8]

It is a pity that he nowhere develops this throwaway mention of the clergy as part of the therapeutic community which he envisages an ideal hospital to be. It suggests that the clergy might have a role not only in dealing directly with the elderly, consoling and counselling them, but also in supporting other members of the team helping them to cope with the various tensions and problems associated with geriatric work.

I suspect that there is no literature developing this theme because, in these days of increasing specialisation, society has often lost confidence in the omnicompetent clergyman who can be called in to offer advice in any situation. I find this attitude clearly reflected in a United Nations report which, in commenting on organised social and health-related services for the elderly, wrote, 'Few members of the clergy are prepared or have sufficient knowledge of the aging processes, psychological, sociological and physiological, to adequately provide the required counselling.'[9] This is all the more surprising in that the report at this point is speaking explicitly of preparing elderly people for death, which is an area where one would have thought that most professionals would feel their own lack of relevant expertise, and where a minister should have much to offer in terms of a framework of belief which transcends this world and this life. I will return to this topic at greater length later in this chapter.

The loss of confidence on the part of society seems often to be reflected in a role crisis within the ranks of the clergy. To put it

simply, using the example of the Roman Catholic priesthood,
sacramental theology taught that Holy Orders did not merely confer
certain powers and duties on the individual, but that it altered his
nature fundamentally: he became a priest and would remain so for
ever, regardless of whether he exercised the functions of that office
or not. In a society which was interested in the question, 'What are
you?' it was completely satisfying to be able to reply, 'A priest.' In a
society which is more functionally orientated, and which asks rather
the question 'What do you do?' the priest is less satisfied that he can
give a fully satisfactory answer which accounts for the range of
his professional activities and sufficiently distinguishes him from
others in the caring services. Marc Oraison in an article summarises
one line of thinking when he writes that 'offering sacrifice,
preaching and leading in prayer are the only specifically sacerdotal
functions'.[10] He might well have added 'administering the
sacraments', but the point remains that this is a limited functional
area which occupies comparatively little of the priest's time.

Personally, I believe that a partial solution to this problem of
identity lies within the remarks I made earlier about the function of
religion as a myth maker, and the traditional approach of the
anthropologist in mapping these myths in the society he is studying.
If we take ageing in the broadest sense we can view society as a drama
in which ordinary people are 'making sense' of age and accounting
for and evaluating their own age-related activities and those of others.
Some of these are culturally predetermined and transmitted. (One
has only to think of the implications of phrases such as 'precocious',
'act your age', 'mutton dressed as lamb', or 'second childhood', or to
recall medieval theories of climacterics, to realise how intricately
woven is the social fabric of ageing.) At another level each
individual interprets and negotiates the meaning of age for
himself and others.

An important element of Christian evangelisation must surely take
place at this level of myth making: the myths must be identified and
examined in the light of the Bible and Christian tradition. Such a simple
sentence ignores the problems of a cross-cultural comparison of
values. It is certainly not intended to advocate that form of cultural
colonialism which so often occurred in the case of the foreign missions
of European and American Christian churches. Hopefully, Christianity
will be able to adopt and baptise many of the human values which it
identifies. In other cases it will be seeking to preach basic Christian
values, for example about the value of human life, to understand

them in the light of prevailing social and technical conditions, and to build them into people's *Weltanschauung*.

Such an abstruse description sounds too complicated to serve as an answer to the problem I have outlined. But in fact it is the description, rather than the role, which is complex. Many clergy have natural gifts of empathy which help them 'tune in' to the mentality and life-style of those to whom they minister. They also have some very clear advantages for such work compared with other professionals who may be caring for the same people. Often their contact with people is long term rather than being crisis-based, as it is for many social workers for example. Often the minister lives among his congregation. Where the congregation is in a working-class or a deprived area, he may well be the only professional person to live in that area. He may well be the only professional person who has time to talk to people about the routine events of their daily life and the personal interpretation which they put upon them. Often such a minister may realise intuitively that it can be his task to articulate the needs and aspirations of those in his flock who cannot easily express their own feelings.

This sounds closely akin to the situation so assiduously created by anthropologists in their field work. If only ministers could be persuaded that they have a professional skill as participant observers, which could make a genuine contribution to the work of any inter-professional team. This suggests that some of the simple techniques and concepts of anthropology and ethnography should be built into their training, if not as a separate subject discipline, at least as a dimension of pastoral training and the pastoral analysis of particular problems. They would then have a language in which they could explain their role more clearly and convincingly to other professionals with whom they were co-operating. They might also feel that, at least in part, it provided them with a more satisfying and more extensive answer to the question 'What do you do?', even as a part of their own self-image.

Current discussions of pastoral strategies in many Christian churches attach great importance to adult education in the broadest sense, sometimes called Christian formation. Often such education may simply take the form of involving people more practically in the work of the congregation, or consulting them more effectively as regards its pastoral needs. In other cases it consists of helping people to look at ordinary situations in their workaday lives and to judge them in the light of the Gospel. Obviously such a methodology could add an extra dimension to all these approaches.

Although ministers have great potential advantages in adopting such an approach, they may also be faced with their own specific difficulties. Thus, training in moral theology in the Roman Catholic tradition furnishes the priest with clear, logically co-ordinated sets of moral principles. It is based on an Aristotelian model of man as a rational animal who has to apply such principles to his situation in a real social and material world. Although the footnotes in the manuals qualified the abstract principles with such phrases as *humano modo* or 'in the common estimation of men', the training syllabus provided little help in giving substance to such phrases. The danger is that the priest in providing moral guidance may define the situation from outside using scholastic categories, rather than seeing it through the eyes of the individual whom he is counselling. Paradoxically, scholastic epistemology can give rise to a positivist view of the world as a given reality. Moral education becomes a more feasible project if one accepts that the actor lives in a world which he has socially created, and if one starts from his own interpretation of his behaviour.

In the context of this article the scholastic approach would encourage a priest to ignore the process of ageing as a category which is irrelevant to moral discussion. As a lifelong continuing process it is part of the common lot of mankind, rather than a special category for inclusion in moral converse. In such a view it is only when the process is subsumed under other categories, such as adult, or parent, that it becomes relevant to moral discourse. This is unfortunate because ageing is part of a continuous process of maturation as one learns to come to terms with increasing and then decreasing powers, both physical, mental, and spiritual, in a fluid formula from which the individual is continually trying to create a personal equilibrium. Here surely is an opportunity for Christian formation.

Otto Pollak, writing about the training of those in the helping professions, says that the essential problem is how to develop

> an ability to decrease the barrier of difference between physician and patient and social worker and client without making this decrease dependent upon belongingness to the same demographic category. One result of professional training must be to enable a younger person to empathize with an older person, a woman to help a male client, a male physician to help a woman patient . . . One problem of training is, therefore, to develop the

ability to gain out of one's own experiences an understanding of
somebody with another experience and to convey this understanding in such a way to the client or patient that he feels not
only understood but also respected in his difference.[11]

He outlines some of the problems which have to be overcome by a
professional helper dealing with older people.

The problem seems to lie primarily in the fact that young
people and probably people well into their middle years are under
the spell of the dramatic growth and maturation experienced
during their first twenty years of life. Although physical growth
comes to an end at roughtly that time, social development
seemingly continues the experience. Increasing professional
status, increasing income, the experience of marriage and
parenthood, the widening web of relationships and experiences
suggests a continuation of growth which conceals the fact that
physiological decline may well be on the way.

He suggests that professional careers cannot allow themselves the
luxury of such ignorance, but should consciously reflect on the
first signs of physical deterioration in themselves — the general loss
of tissue elasticity in a woman, the decline in the capacity to run in
a man. Such self-awareness can help the professional to appreciate
the impact on an older person's self-image of a deteriorating body.
    So too, in the approach I am recommending, the minister will
first have to become sensitive to his own experience of ageing, to
reflect upon its significance and his reaction to it: his declining
physical powers, and later his loss of mental agility. Does he face up
to these things as part of God's providential care for him, or does he
ignore them as a defence mechanism? How does he relate to other
ministers, and to lay people, who are younger, or older, or the same
age as himself? How does he speak to the very old or senile members
of his congregation, and what does this reveal about his practical
belief in individual autonomy, and the dignity of each individual
as a child of God? Such reflection and the learning which comes
from it will be a continuing process. It could be greatly facilitated and
enhanced by the practice of frequent meditation which is part of the
rule of life followed by many ministers of religion. Such hard-won
self-knowledge provides a good basis for empathising with the
experiences of others, and a source of insights which can be offered

to them in counselling situations.

Although ministers will have to deal with people of all ages in an ordinary congregation or parish, it can be argued that any clergyman who has to specialise in working with the elderly as chaplain or visitor will need special qualities of temperament and powers of empathy. The Age Concern Working Party wrote, 'Those selected should have a specific vocation for this aspect of parochial care; when chosen they should not be harassed by too heavy a burden of other parochial commitments, but should have time to listen, to counsel, and to bring comfort, reassurance, restoration and a degree of rehabilitation to those for whom they care.'[12]

The ideology of particular churches can predetermine the nature of the contacts which the minister will have with members of his flock. (The use of the possessive pronoun 'his' in this context, or the use of a word such as 'flock' can be indicators of taken-for-granted relationships which are rarely stated explicitly.) Thus the role-definition of a Catholic priest as minister of the Sacraments may well lead him to think of his parishioners in sacramental categories: adolescents due to be confirmed; young couples to be prepared for marriage; the old and infirm who are suitable candidates for Extreme Unction, now called the Sacrament of the Sick. This may account for some glaring gaps in the typical pastoral provision in a Roman Catholic parish; for instance, there is rarely strong supportive work with young families, although much evidence suggests how vulnerable contemporary marriage is in its early years.

A writer in the *American Sociological Review*[13] argues that Congregational ministers are less likely than Episcopalian ministers to have close friendships with parishioners. His point is that Episcopalian theology puts a strong emphasis on the priestly, sacramental duties of its ministers. Outside of the exercise of his sacramental ministry the Episcopalian clergyman is likely to make contact with his parishioners on a purely social basis. The Congregational clergyman, on the other hand, has no sacramental role, and is trained to regard *all* his contacts with his parishioners as purposeful, ministerial ones. His contacts will to that extent be formalised.

In another way, a sacramental theology can influence the relationship of the priest, particularly with the very old, since it provides him with a pretext (and often a duty) for visiting the very old and inform — to bring them Viaticum and to assess their condition so as to decide if and when they should receive the Sacrament of the Sick.

Ageing as a Social Problem: The Old and the Very Old

Recent sociological literature on social problems has turned its
attention away from the characteristics of the 'problem' situation or
the 'problem' individual, and has concentrated on the social processes
whereby this has been identified and labelled as a problem. This new
approach brings with it some undoubted benefits. It emphasises the
fact that the nature of a problem cannot be taken for granted:
different groups will see a problem in a different light according to
their position in the social structure and in the specific process. It
demonstrates how a society can create, or aggravate, or endorse the
very problems which it publicly deplores: every society gets the
problems which it deserves. One consequence of this has been to divert
the efforts of some committed professional careers away from
individual relief work towards more political action to alter the
structures of an unjust society.

Such a change of emphasis can be salutary because charitable relief
may be dangerous: it may blunt the demands of those who are
suffering, and it may serve to assuage the twinges of the social
consciences, to allow us to connive more easily with the manifest
inequalities of our society. In a much-quoted sentence in *The Sociological Imagination*[14] C. Wright Mills says that it is the task of a
committed sociology to turn private sorrows into public issues.

Traditionally, since Biblical times, the church has exercised two
duties with regard to those in need: the caring and the prophetic.
It has always sought to care for 'the halt, the lame, and the blind'
and for those who are 'weary and heavy laden'. It has also
challenged society to judge itself in the light of the Gospel, and to
find itself condemned for its blindness and hardness of heart. In
recent centuries the Christian churches have perhaps concentrated on
charitable relief work at the expense of their prophetic role. In the
West this role has to some extent been undermined by the rise of
statutory welfare programmes. While some are content to regard
the churches' charitable work as self-liquidating (the churches' task
is fulfilled once they have persuaded the state or other organisations
to take over the comforting role), others would argue that the
church must always be a visible witness to the charity of Christ. In the
Third World particularly, the churches inspired by a theology of
development and a theology of liberation, have begun to see their
role in that setting as being one of challenging the political structures
and ideologies.

In the light of these modern sociological insights, and the example

of the Third World, it seems important that the churches should review
critically their response to suffering and need. There will always be
cases of loneliness, bereavement or mental handicap for example,
where there will be need for individual caring. Even here the churches
should consider whether their traditional charitable works are not
too exclusively oriented towards relief when they could now properly
move into the field of social work.[15] There may be other times when
the churches should help those in need to articulate effectively their
demand for justice, and should help their members to assume their
practical and political responsibilities in this regard.

Currently the mass media in Western countries have identified old
age as a social problem, and have sensitised the public conscience to
its existence. However, because the media excel in concrete
description and pictorial representation there is the very real danger
that they may define the problem largely in terms that can readily
provide a picture, very often in terms of other social problems such as
poverty, homelessness, hypothermia, isolation or squalor. Such a
picture can easily ignore the psychological aspects of the problem,
old age as it is experienced by the elderly. Pollak comments on the fact
that the global phenomenon of fatigue as a concurrent aspect of ageing
seems to have escaped even the specialist writers in the field of
gerontology.[16] It certainly does not feature prominently in popular
descriptions of the problem of ageing. Nor does the possibility of
angry reactions to the feeling of relative weakness or the awareness of
sensory decline, to the experience of social devaluation, or the threat
of nothingness. To some extent this results from the fact that the
image is presented by an interviewer, a journalist or a research worker,
who has shaped his questions in the light of his own preconceptions
and categories. Very rarely are we presented with a description
expressed spontaneously by old people themselves. Indeed, age may be
only a very incidental part of an old person's self-image. As Marjorie
Fry wrote, 'To the administrator an individual may be just "that old
woman – I think her name is Jones", but to herself she is the Katie
Jones who won a prize for Scripture and had the smallest waist in the
class – with a thousand other distinctive features – who just happens
to be old.'[17]

As I have already suggested the empathetic minister has great
potential advantages at this level for he has probably known the old
person over a long period and is aware of his/her past history to which
age is peripheral. He has had the opportunity of listening to the old
person in a more leisurely context than members of other caring

professions who are so often summoned to a crisis situation precipitated by one of the concomitant social problems of old age. There is the danger in this latter situation that this presenting symptom may be allowed to become the defining characteristic of the old person.

For many purposes it seems important to clarify that old age presents two quite distinct sets of problems. The churches as organisations with strong roots in the community, and with con-siderable material resources at their disposal, may wish to make a pastoral contribution in each of these fields: the problems of the old and of the very old.

Old age is a relative concept which varies very much from one culture to another. In industrialised societies with statutory welfare provisions and a fixed age for retirement, the latter serves almost as a *rite de passage* defining a total change of role and status. Unfortunately, the role of 'old person' does not automatically contain any activities which would give purpose to the individual's day, nor is the status of the elderly high in a society which attaches so much importance to independence and maturity. In general, this change is more marked for a man than a woman, and consequently is often more traumatic. The man has often defined himself as bread-winner for the household, and in terms of his competence at his job. Overnight he can be robbed of this self-definition. Usually the change is less abrupt for a woman because she has tended to fulfil several roles as spouse, mother and housewife as well as in terms of any occupation which she may have had outside the home. She loses the former roles gradually over a period of time so that she does not lose her self-image as abruptly as if she had to retire from work.

Society at large is only now becoming aware of the demoralising effect that this process can have. As has been pointed out in other chapters in this book, various firms have introduced the idea of a 'staggered' or gradual retirement so that individuals can acclimatise themselves gradually both to the idea and the reality of retirement. There are an increasing number of pre-retirement courses designed to prepare people for the change and to encourage them to acquire a new range of interests and skills which will enable them to occupy their newly-acquired leisure in a useful and enjoyable manner. Counselling services, too, are taking more explicit account of the domestic tensions which can so easily be associated with retirement.

While the sympathetic minister may have a role to play as a general practitioner in counselling, it is perhaps at the level of an educational service that the church can best offer a pastoral response to this specific aspect of ageing. Many churches have halls or schools which could be made available at different times for educational programmes in the widest sense, which would both initiate people into their retirement, and provide them with a new social network. At a later stage in their retirement this could provide them with a programme of continuing activities, and even involve them actively in local community affairs. Some ministers, aware of the need, and conscious of the fact that their church buildings are used for prayer and liturgical services for only brief periods during the week, feel it proper to give them over to such social purposes at other times as a testimony of the Church's caring role. In other cases, because of dwindling congregations, ministers have divided their church buildings so that part of it is available all the time for social uses. The concept of the multi-purpose church building or the flexible parish unit presents architects with new challenges in terms of imaginative adaptation and design. Many of them are accepting this challenge with a real sense of social obligation.

Often advancing years are accompanied by physical disability. Whether or not churches and halls are being adapted for use specifically by the elderly it is important that access to these buildings should not present an obstacle which further cuts them off from the wider community. In September 1976 the National Conference of Priests (of England and Wales) passed a Resolution, 'That this Conference urges priests to pay more attention to facilities for the handicapped in and around churches, and, where necessary to improve these facilities.' Although the discussions on this proposition were wide-ranging and covered such matters as the provision of hearing-aid devices for sermons or in the confessional, obviously ease of access is of primary importance. The Central Council for the Disabled have a department concerned with 'Access for the Disabled' which has issued detailed guidelines on this matter. Help in planning architectural solutions to access problems will also be found in 'British Standard Code of Practice CP 96'.

Ministers are aware of various individuals in their congregation, or neighbourhood, who would be willing to contribute time and skills to providing such educational programmes. However, in this context especially, it is important that the minister should see himself not as an organiser, but as a catalyst and an enabler who makes the resources available so that old people can take an active part in defining their own needs and in making suitable provision for them.

To take over this role which many of the old are capable of fulfilling perfectly well, would only further entrench society's definition of age as helpless and useless. Nevertheless, it may require constant restraint and self-denial for a minister to adopt merely a supportive function when he takes a much more direct role in other aspects of the daily life of his parish or congregation, or when he sees that he could arrange a programme much more quickly, or feels that he could devise a 'better' programme. Such an attitude ignores the fact that the planning and arranging can be a part of the therapeutic exercise. It would also fall into the error of not letting the elderly speak for themselves.[18] It might well prove to be the case that many old people would enjoy and benefit from something much more leisurely than any organised programme — just the incentive to get out of the house, and the opportunity to meet other people socially.

Another useful function of the clergy in this field would be to ensure that there was good liaison with local authorities and old people's welfare committees so that the awareness of local needs can be extended and the danger of leaving gaps unfilled or of overlapping with other services be avoided.[19]

I said above that the social problem of ageing was at least two-fold. The situation of the very old often presents a whole complex of physical and material problems. Although these can be thought of as logically distinct, for practical purposes it can be useful to subsume them under the umbrella title of the problem of old age, provided always that one makes it clear that it is not the old people who are the problem, but rather the situation in which they find themselves. This situation is often to a large extent created by the attitudes and practices of our society.

The various problems associated with very old age (physical decline, loss of mental powers, frustrations, poverty, poor housing, isolation and loneliness) are dealt with in detail elsewhere in this volume. Here I should just like to emphasise that these problems cannot be dealt with in isolation by separate specialists both because they are mutually interconnected, often as reciprocal cause and effect, and also, equally importantly, because they intersect in an individual who needs to be known and treated as a person.

Once again the fact that the minister may well have known the old person over a long period suggests that there are several useful functions he can perform. These functions in their turn require that ideally he should be possessed of certain information and skills.

Because of his long-term, pre-crisis knowledge of the individual, he is likely to be the 'professional carer' who is first to notice the onset and accumulation of these problems. He may well be in a position to help the individual (and the family, if the old person is living at home) to consider the implications of these problems and possible solutions. To do this adequately he will need to be familiar with the structure of the social services, and with the resources available locally. Although it is desirable that his initial training should contain some basic information about the range of welfare provisions, and ideally should give him some direct experiences of working with the very old, this can only be a partial answer. Statutory provision changes rapidly; local resources and attitudes vary enormously from one area to another; many interest groups are making competing demands on initial training time; such knowledge is best grasped by practice in the field. For all these reasons I am inclined to put more emphasis on what the minister can learn once he is on the job — from the accumulated wisdom of other clergy and ministers in the area, from the existing societies in his parish or congregation, and from social workers themselves. In some cases, ministers have provided facilities for a weekly or monthly luncheon club for local social workers. This can provide a welcome opportunity not only for social workers and teachers to meet each other informally, but also for them to meet the local clergy. Social workers could help in this process of informal education of ministers by calling on them and introducing themselves, by informing clergy of cases where their ministrations would be welcome, or asking them for specific help for individuals. There are obstacles to such co-operation, but it is important that both sides should seek to create a partnership in which professional skills and potential are mutually respected, and professional confidences can be exchanged. Various experiments in inter-professional training offer some hope that bridges could be built during initial training.

Another strength which is available to the minister is that his approach has traditionally been family-centred. Although the tradition may vary from one denomination to another, and the link becomes more tenuous with increasing geographical mobility, the minister often has privileged access to the family. This may mean that he can support a family in the problems connected with caring for an aged parent or relative, advising them of community resources that are available. In families that have a strong church commitment he may be welcomed as an impartial but concerned arbiter between different branches of the family when it comes to allotting the burden of care; an acceptable ombudsman to adjudicate over the personal grievances created by tensions and conflicts arising in caring for the very old. It would be a pity of this enviable status betrayed the minister into making authoritarian decisions on behalf of the individuals concerned. The pastoral training of ministers should surely include an introduction to the values of social case-work and some of its skills. In situations where families have to decide whether an elderly relative will have to give up her independent accommodation, who will care for her or whether she should enter a residential home, one of the minister's main contributions may be to provide the basis on which decisions should be made. His long-term friendly knowledge of the family may give him intimate knowledge of the domestic situation and of the strains under which particular individuals find themselves.[20]

The frequent and regular house visiting which was a major element in the pastoral care of RC parishes[21] is on the decline for a variety of reasons (including patterns of TV viewing which can make evening visits unwelcome). For other denominations, too, the above description could appear excessively idealistic. At least it suggests the desirability of such frequent contact. If the busy minister cannot achieve it unaided it could be made one of the tasks of untrained auxiliaries (who might even be full-time members of group or team ministries such as are being introduced experimentally by some churches). It is unlikely that the minister or even his organised congregation is going to be able to meet all the demands of special categories of people. Since some form of selection of need, and concentration of effort is necessary, one could suggest that those ministers who keep a census of their congregation could at least arrange for a focused visit to every member as they reach the age of, say, seventy-five, and periodically thereafter. Some medical practices do this with profit.

Many churches attach great importance to family life. This can be a strength if it leads to a well-informed pastoral strategy of support for families at various stages of their existence. It can be dangerous if it leads to platitudinous exhortation, or to recommendations based upon a false picture. Thus it is easy for the preacher to suggest that children have a duty to care for their parents in their old age; that this was always done in the past; and that it is only the selfishness and materialism of the present generation which could allow old people to live isolated and lonely lives, or which could consign them to institutional care. There are, of course, problems; and children may neglect the duty of *pietas* towards their parents. But such a facile analysis would misrepresent the past. Peter

Townsend has argued that probably our picture of the frequency of
three-generation households in pre-industrial society is mistaken.
'There seems to be comparatively little evidence of a steady atrophy of
social relationships . . . In Britain [now] there are more bedfast aged
people at home than in all hospitals and institutions put together.'[22]
One can find plenty of contemporary evidence of neglect of parents
in nineteenth-century rural England.[23] Both the absolute numbers and
the proportion of very old people in the population of England
and Wales has increased throughout the century; many of the very old
are the spinsters and widows of the First World War; there are many
more four-generation families in our population than ever before.
One cannot fairly compare the situation or the obligations of families
then and now.

At the opposite extreme would be an uncritical acceptance of disengagement[24] theory as a basis for planning a pastoral programme for
the care of the elderly. In brief the theory states that growing old
involves a gradual and 'inevitable mutual withdrawal or disengagement
resulting in a decreased interaction between an aging person and others
in the social systems he belongs to'. It suggests that society and the
individual prepare in advance for the ultimate disengagement of death
by a mutually satisfying process of social disengagement prior to
death. It is almost portrayed as though both sides, society and the
individual, collaborate to lessen the ultimate shock and loss of death
by making it a gradual and voluntary process. The individual 'wants'
to disengage and does so by reducing the number of roles which he
plays, lessening the variety of roles and relationships and weakening
the intensity of those which survive. The remaining relationships are,
also, different in quality; they are more emotional and expressive
rather than active and achievement-oriented. On its side, society
offers the individual freedom from structural constraints and
'permission' to withdraw.

I regard this theory as dangerous, not merely because critics attack
it both on theoretical grounds and because of conflicting empirical
evidence,[25] but more so because it could give rise to a policy of
non-interventionism. The churches must surely speak out prophetically
here, and condemn a society which can allow so many material
problems to accumulate for the individual at this point of dependency. The churches must become sufficiently concerned to challenge
a world which views old age as repellent and dirty; which regards
it as a threat, and thinks of old people as better dead; which
sentimentalises old age while robbing it unnecessarily of dignity and

independence; and which despises it because it fails to recognise
the common humanity of all men. The current concern to facilitate
euthanasia although ostensibly a concern for individual dignity can
represent a too easy capitulation to such attitudes and values.

I have not devoted any space to institutional care, though
obviously specific sets of problems will cause an individual to enter
a residential home or geriatric hospital. It does not seem appropriate
to make detailed recommendations where local circumstances will
vary so much, although the local minister should feel a responsibility
to ensure that he and his congregation adopt some routine,
methodical procedures for visiting and supporting the aged in these
institutions. While demand is so much greater than supply and
statutory supervision is limited the conditions and ethos in some
residential homes leaves much to be desired.[26] Faced with such conditions a minister may at times feel that he should intervene to speak in
defence of the dignity of an old person. On the other hand he must
also realise how much stress is involved in the continuous nursing of the
very old and of chronic geriatric cases, particularly where facilities are
inadequate. In such circumstances his care for the aged may well
involve a supportive concern for other members of the caring team.

Under the pressure of such demands a minister and his congregation
must seek to establish priorities for action. W.S. Reid suggests certain
principles to guide this choice.[27]

> We may say broadly that the Christian Faith has a four-fold
> task in helping the elderly as they adjust to the situation
> presented in their latter years, namely:
>
> (1)   to help them face impending death and overcome anxieties
>   and fears,
> (2)   to give them a meaning and purpose for later life,
> (3)   to assist them to accept the inevitable losses of age, and also
> (4)   to help them in the discovery of compensatory values.
>
> In the light of this the Minister must have some principles of
> selectivity as well as priority for the direction of his pastoral
> work amongst the elderly. When he visits the elderly he arrives
> as a representative of the Christian congregation showing the
> concern of the fellowship for them, and in particular the lonely,
> the recently bereaved, and those recently discharged from
> hospital. He goes to them as one who is ready and willing to listen,

and if his listening is creative then it is likely to bring release for pent-up feelings and give the person a new perspective on the situations that trouble them.

. . . While it is true that all groups in the Church should be considered in the list of ministerial priorities, in the case of the elderly he will remember those at greatest risk as well as the call of special needs. We have already mentioned those living alone, recently bereaved and recently discharged from hospital. To this list it is possible to add those who have become disabled in a physical sense and those who have mental impairment, with also consideration for those showing a tendency to isolate themselves for some reason or other. But in the organisation of his pastoral visitation, he will probably be guided by the categories of crisis, continuous strain or routine calls. In this sense the list under crisis for the elderly must be enlarged to include not only illness and bereavement, but also retirement, moving to a new house and financial restrictions. Under continuous strain we could find chronic illness, housing difficulties or interpersonal tensions.

. . . if we seek to determine priorities then for the pastor it is essential that he spends his time not only upon those with the greatest need, but mainly upon those who have the capacity to respond to help. Other categories should still receive the patient, supportive help that comes from a truly 'caring' fellowship, and the opportunity may then emerge for successful counselling and help.

The Aged and Religion

There is a large amount of research data but it is difficult to interpret.[28] Often the concept of 'religiosity' is differently defined, and results are contradictory. The results of cross-sectional research which show an age gradient as regards ritual practice, personal devotion or belief, could reflect the results of the ageing process, but might equally reflect generational differences. Over the last two decades it seems to be generally true that the over-sixties go to church less as they get older. Information such as this is unlikely to win wide acclaim for the insights provided by research techniques. One would only compound the damage if one appealed to disengagement theory as an explanation of what can more easily be explained as a result of increasing physical disabilities. Much of the evidence suggests that religious practice does not voluntarily alter much in old age, but tends to reflect the habits of a lifetime. W.S. Reid in his Scottish Survey found that old people, previously regular church-goers, who were prevented by infirmity from attending church were very unhappy and stressed how much they missed seeing their friends at church. (This social factor in church attendance appears to be of considerable importance, and is an additional argument for congregational concern for and visits to those who can no longer attend a church.) A large number of elderly regularly follow religious broadcasting both on radio and television, but tend to regard it as a substitute for 'the real thing' — although a consoling substitute for those who were housebound.

This interpretation is supported by the fact that most studies have found a great increase in private prayer with age. In Reid's research many respondents explained their practice of prayer as arising from teaching or from the example they received in childhood. Some remembered the family prayers of their youth; others had a definite prayer outline to which they adhered strictly. This practice of prayer could provide a useful link between a minister and those who had lapsed from the more formal practices of their religion. It could provide a formal religious content for the minister's visit as opposed to making it a purely social friendly call. Interestingly, several studies have found that when asked what more their church could be doing for them, the majority of elderly respondents have put home visitation at the top of their list. Their expectations have been simplified, and their needs have become expressive rather than instrumental: they seek from the church a feeling of community, of interest and concern.

If the age differences revealed in these studies are part of a regularly recurring pattern the implication for pastoral policy is that the churches should make long-term provision for special care for roughly the same proportion of old people in the future. If later studies show that the present picture results from the disappearance of a generation of Christians with a strong religious commitment, the problem will rather be one of a declining clientele.

Ageing as a Preparation for Death

Perhaps surprisingly, some research shows that there are only slight differences between older and younger people as regards firmness of belief in God.[29] Belief in an after-life on the other hand shows a dramatic increase in the older age groups (although it is not clear whether this is due to ageing or simply reflects that the older

generation have had greater certainty about traditional beliefs
throughout their lives). In many denominations this is coupled with a
belief in an automatic heaven without any judgement. Argyle and
Beit-Hallahmi write,

> The heightened religion of age is very different from the
> heightened religion of adolescence. In adolescence there is a great
> intellectual perplexity and doubt coupled with emotional
> turmoil: young people suddenly change their whole orientation
> one way or the other. In old age when both intellect and emotions
> are dimmed, there is no worry about the niceties of theology, nor
> is there any emotional excitement about religious matters.[30]

Often this faith played an explicit part in the adjustment of the
elderly after personal crises such as bereavement (but sometimes
explicitly in the case of retirement also).[31] This supportive function
usually derived from a combination of a strong belief in God's
comforting and loving presence, and an active involvement in church
life. The latter was sometimes deliberately suggested by a minister.
It helped them to make a re-entry into social life (maybe after a period
of isolation caused by illness in the home) in a context where others
felt supportive. It helped them realise that others too had suffered
similar bereavements, and sometimes it led them to realise that they
could support others in their loss, or to cope with secret fears of
bereavement.

In other cases, people found their faith threatened by the
experience of bereavement. In Reid's sample elderly people at home
found it more easy to adjust than did those in institutions. He
suggests that the churches should give much greater priority to
counselling and care of the bereaved. Loretto Lynch in *The Experience
of Death*[32] outlines the spiritual and emotional needs of the bereaved
and some of the ways in which counselling and care for them is
organised by different associations.

The majority of respondents in these surveys had no fear of death.
In Reid's study this sense of acceptance was expressed in religious
terms like 'my appointed time', 'going to meet my Maker', or 'when
God calls me'. They did, however, express a real fear of the *process*
of dying, sometimes as a fear of a painful and protracted death,
often with reference to the experience of someone close to them.
At other times it was lest they become a burden on those who
cared for them. There was also the fear of losing their faculties and

becoming a helpless invalid. Clearly there are many different
emotions involved in this stage of a person's life: fear, refusal to accept
a situation; a sense of lost possibilities; grief at the gradual loss of
contemporaries as they die; sorrow at the prospect of leaving one's
friends behind, at never seeing children growing up or getting
married; frustration and anger at this loss — a sense of anger which
may be directed against God, or against those who are close to the old
person. It is important that the elderly should be helped to
express and work through these various emotions rather than have to
repress them lest they shock others. Obviously it is painful for anyone
to share such feelings with an old person, especially since there is
often little that one can do in practical terms. Not to do so,
however, would be to leave them alone with their anxiety.

Many psychoanalysts believe that everyone carries in their mind
a basic anxiety about death. This is not made any easier to deal with
by the fact that our society treats it as a taboo subject even now when
many other taboos have been exorcised. People are reluctant to talk
about death because it is a very emotional subject, and they
anxiously avoid mentioning those things they feel most emotional
about. Yet these are the very things they need to talk about if they are
to cope maturely with these anxieties, and to share with family and
friends this most important aspect of their lives. That is not to say
that one should ask people abruptly or bluntly whether they are
worried by the thought of death. They would very probably deny
their anxiety because they may not be explicitly conscious of it,
and once again we would be reduced to conniving at their defence
mechanisms of spurious gaiety or irrelevant conversation.

Rather than interrogate the old about their feelings we need
to listen attentively to what they are saying, interpreting silences
or sadness sensitively. Here a clergyman could be at an advantage
since he is concerned explicitly with the after-life. His presence
should provide a context in which the death taboo does not operate,
and in which the old person should not feel constrained to hide
his anxieties, nor fear to disturb his audience. It is sad that the
United Nations report quoted above finds clergymen unable or
unwilling to cope effectively with such a situation. Loretto Lynch
in *The Experience of Death*[33] suggests that recent changes with
regard to the Catholic sacrament of anointing, while salutary in
themselves, could become part of the general conspiracy of silence
about death. The new pastoral regulations about this sacrament state
that it may be administered to all who are seriously ill, not

exclusively to those sick who are in danger of death. By overstating this new emphasis the preacher, or the chaplain to the elderly, can confirm people in the view that the prospect of death is not to be discussed in personal terms.

Paul Tournier in *Learning to Grow Old* writes with great insight about the problems of facing up to death, and much of what follows is based on his ideas. When people look for 'the meaning of their lives', or of their old age, they are asking two questions. One is about the present significance of their actions, or their existence. The other is about their destination. Where is their life, their old age, leading them to? That is why, although they are theoretically distinct, the discussion of old age cannot be separated from a discussion of death. The meaning of life, of old age, in the second sense, is death. And as Tournier writes, the meaning of death is the religious question *par excellence*. Does there exist something other than the visible world in which we are enclosed from birth to death? 'My old age has meaning, I can live through it with my gaze still fixed before me, and not behind me, because I am on my way to a destination beyond death . . . we may say that acceptance of old age is the best preparation for death, but also, conversely, that the acceptance of death is the best preparation for old age.'

Inevitably this raises the question whether the acceptance of old age and death is easier for believers than for unbelievers. The answer to this cannot be an unqualified 'Yes'. In the first place, faith can mean different things ranging from an intellectual assent to a creed and gospel to a warm and trusting commitment to friendship with a loving God. Certainly the former type of faith, together with its associated pattern of 'correct' responses such as 'resignation to God's holy will', may simply serve as an extra defence mechanism. It may inhibit the believer from expressing or exploring his repressed anxieties, sorrows and resentment. At the opposite extreme I still remember vividly one of the first death-beds I attended as a young priest. It was an old man who was impatient to die so that he could the sooner meet in Heaven the God whom he had loved and served all his life. 'That we may be dissolved and be with Christ.'

Tournier believes that the cultural tradition and psychological determinism play a more important role than faith in the acceptance or non-acceptance of death. Thus American Christianity tends to be much less dogmatic than European Christianity, yet at least impressionistically one senses that Americans suffer much more from a complex about death. There is a growing literature which describes how the American funeral industry exploits this fear by marketing a facade behind which the harsh realities of death can remain discreetly hidden and unacknowledged.

Tournier suggests that the Christian churches have over the centuries exploited the fear which men feel when they are confronted by death. At its worst, their emphasis on the Four Last Things (death, judgement, heaven and hell) has been used by preachers as a system of rewards and punishment, as a form of conditioning moral and spiritual responses, long before Bentham or Watson. One can see how the tradition of preaching hell-fire sermons during missions, retreats or revivalist meetings, could be psychologically unwholesome. Fortunately most churches have improved in this respect, and nowadays one hears much more often sermons about God's mercy and forgiveness. Tournier discusses the case of one of his patients who was left permanently and neurotically obsessed with the idea of death as a result of the sterner form of religious upbringing. He had been unable to protect himself against anxiety by making the macabre jokes about death and hell which had served as defence for his more robust companions. His case had proved particularly intractable despite help from a succession of priests and psychiatrists, who all in turn abandoned the case. Interestingly Tournier writes: 'They have given up, whereas I persevered, perhaps because I find failure easier to bear.'

Faith, even when strongly internalised, does not exclude anxiety, despite its triumphant message of hope based on the Resurrection of Christ. On the other hand, however, one must not undervalue the support that faith can provide, especially for those who are temperamentally anxious people. One can think of the victories over anxiety achieved by the faith of men such as St Francis of Assisi, Pascal, Luther and Kierkegaard.

Christian faith invites people to a more realistic acceptance of death than do many other philosophies which are to some extent an attempt to eliminate anxiety. Christ, as our archetype underwent the anxious anticipation of death, leaving his life's work apparently uncompleted and insecure. In his distress in the garden of Gethsemane just before his arrest he sweated 'drops as it were of blood'. He had plenty of time in which to experience and suffer the agonies of his painful and lingering execution. In his suffering he called on God in the words of the Psalm which expresses both distress and the conviction of ultimate salvation and triumph: 'My God, my God, why have you deserted me?' (Matthew, 27, 46).

The fact that Christ shared our human condition to that extent should give the Christian courage to accept the prospect of approaching death with all its fears and sense of loss, of weakness and impotence. Death ultimately establishes the equality of all men in the eyes of God. It reminds us of our physical, animal nature: that we are not pure spirits despite all our high aspirations or elevated preaching. It is our physical weakness rather than our spiritual virtues which wins for us the compassion of God.

Georges Bernanos in his *Dialogue des Carmélites* describes the death of the strongly religious Sister Blanche. A young sister who had admired her qualities of strength and piety is overcome by amazement that she had found it so hard to die. As Tournier says 'Death is indeed the moment of truth which upsets all our vain categories. It is only our preconceived notions which are surprised by unexpected, but quite natural reactions.' He goes on to add 'what man needs most is not to be alone when he faces death, as if a human presence, even that of an unbeliever, were a pledge of the divine presence . . . The American doctor K.R. Eissler puts it admirably: . . . "What you can really do for a person who is dying, is to die with him".'

If the minister or clergyman wishes to perform that ultimate charity, there could be no better preparation for it than also to have 'grown old' with that person.

Notes

1. Volume 5, no. 5 (Sept. 1976), pp. 578-9. The book under review was: James D. Manney, Jr., *Aging in American Society: an Examination of Concepts and Issues* (Ann Arbor, Institute of Gerontology/University of Michigan, 1975).
2. Notable exceptions are Steers' *Caring for the Elderly*, and Tournier's *Learning to Grow Old*. The last decade has seen the rapid growth of a new literature on the pastoral care of the dying and the bereaved.
3. Exceptions to this statement are: Paul B. Maves, 'Aging, Religion, and the Church' in Clark Tibbitts (ed.), *Handbook of Social Gerontology* (University of Chicago Press, Chicago, 1960), pp. 714-20, and Philip Hammond 'Aging and the Ministry' in Riley, Riley and Johnson, *Aging and Society*, vol. 2, pp. 293-323, although both deal largely with church provision of services for the aged.
4. Some of this evidence is conveniently summarised in Michael Argyle and Benjamin Beit-Hallahmi, *The Social Psychology of Religion* (Routledge and Kegan Paul, London, 1975), pp. 68-70. See also D.L. Scudder (ed.), *Organized Religion and the Older Person* (University of Florida Press, Gainesville, Florida, 1958); R.M. Gray and D.O. Moberg, *The Church and the Older Person* (Eerdmans, Michigan, 1962); D.O. Moberg and M.J.

Taves, 'Church Participation and adjustment in old age' in A.M. Ross and W.A. Peterson (eds.), *Older People and their Social World* (F.A. Davis, Philadelphia, 1965).

5. See E.T. Culver, *New Church Programs with the Aging* (Association Press, New York, 1961); White House Conference on Aging, 1961, *Background Paper on Services of Religious Groups for the Aging* (Government Printing Office, Washington, D.C., 1960).

6. Age Concern, *The Role of the Churches in the Care of the Elderly* (Age Concern, Mitcham, Surrey, 1965).

7. See Select Bibliography. Much of his findings are summarised in an article 'Religious attitudes in later life', *Age Concern Today*, no. 17 (Spring 1976), pp. 29-30.

8. T.N. Rudd, *Human Relations in Old Age: A handbook for health visitors, social workers and others* (Faber and Faber, London, 1967), pp. 87-8.

9. Department of Economic and Social Affairs, *The Aging: Trends and Policies* (United Nations, New York, 1975 ST/ESA/22), p. 36.

10. It is significant that the article was entitled 'Un homme sans metier', *Christus* (October 1965), pp. 462-75. Marc Oraison's own biography is interesting in this respect. Born into a family that had lost several children by death he deliberately chose to become a surgeon like his father in order to combat death. As a surgeon he soon realised that while medicine can delay death it cannot solve its problems. He became a priest feeling that the problems of death called for spiritual answers. As a priest he became interested in the psychological dimensions of the problem, and subsequently trained as a psychoanalyst. However, few could be so versatile, and his example does not solve the more general problem of the priesthood. This problem is explored in more sociological terms in John D. Donovan, 'The Dilemma of the Christian Priesthood', *Actes de la IX Conference International Clergy in Church and Society* (CISR, Rome, 1967), pp. 115-26.

11. Otto Polak, *Human Behaviour and the Helping Professions* (Spectrum, N.Y., 1976), pp. 58-9.

12. Age Concern, *The Role of the Churches*, p. 8.

13. Luke M. Smith, 'The Clergy: Authority, Structure, Ideology, Migration' in *American Sociological Review*, vol. 18 (1953), pp. 242-8.

14. Oxford University Press, New York, 1959.

15. The practical implications of this distinction are developed in Una Cormack, *The Church and Social Work* (Liverpool Institute of Socio-Religious Studies, Liverpool, 1977).

16. Pollak, p. 60.

17. *Old Age in the Modern World* (Livingstone, Edinburgh and London, 1945).

18. See the emphasis put on independence, choice, self-realisation, and participation, as basic ingredients in any programme of care for the elderly: D. Hobman, *All Our Futures*, pp. 10-16; and by Age Concern England in its *Manifesto*.

19. Age Concern, *The Role of the Churches*, p. 9.

20. See T.N. Rudd, *Human Relations*, pp. 20-21, writing of the role of a health visitor: 'In listening it is essential that the worker should not attempt to form moral judgements or to allocate blame between the parties; to do so, is both unjustifiable and harmful to good social work. It is, furthermore, generally unwise even to attempt to formulate the situation in psychological terms. What we need to know is the extent to which the conduct complained of is "trying" or intolerable in itself and how much is caused by the interplay of clashing temperaments . . . Careful questioning of the individual and the household sometimes

illuminates the situation for the first time and enables firm action to be taken. Sometimes, however, the old person on whom the blame is placed does not appear on questioning to be so very abnormal. Further inquiry may then show that the person at fault is the apparently normal marriage partner or daughter who is herself a victim of a psychoneurotic anxiety state or of a compulsive obsessive neurosis. In such an instance it is the affected person who needs, treatment. Removal of the person originally blamed will not cure the real sufferer, although separation of the parties may be desirable at the onset.'

21.   Conor Ward in *Priest and People* (Liverpool University Press, Liverpool) gives a graphic account of how this system operated in one traditional Liverpool parish.

22.   P. Townsend, 'The Place of Older People in Different Societies', *Age with a Future* (Copenhagen, 1964), p. 36.

23.   The following quotation is sufficiently interesting to quote at length. The writer, W.H. Roberts, claims that the English agricultural labourers, unlike the Irish poor, had scarcely any regard for their parents, and goes on to say: 'Abundant evidence might be adduced . . . that . . . whatever their circumstances may be, the children of worn-out agricultural labourers will do nothing for them except on compulsion, having a fixed idea that that duty pertains solely to the parish. Repeated instances have come under the writer's own observation in which unmarried sons, earning good wages . . . have not only not contributed towards the support of their pauper parents, but have actually lived with them rent free, and filched from them all they could of the parish allowance. Not even the smallest offices of filial duty will they render without being paid. When, as frequently happens, an out-pensioner of the parish lives with a married son or daughter, if the poor old creature falls ill, an instant demand is made at the Board for an allowance for nursing. As a rule this demand is granted; but when exceptions occur, it is not an unheard-of thing for these unnatural children to send the aged sufferer at once to the work-house.' (*Fortnightly Review*, April 1875, vol. 17, pp. 519-20, quoted in C.S. Devas, *Studies of Family Life*, Burns and Oates, London, 1886, p. 251.)

24.   This typology of the ageing process derives originally from an article by Elaine Cumming, Lois Dean, Dean Newell and I. McCallfrey, 'Disengagement: a tentative theory of ageing', *Sociometry*, vol. 23 (1960), pp. 23-5. Elaine Cumming and William Henry elaborated the concept in *Growing Old* (Basic Books, New York, 1961). It has subsequently been expanded, and modified by these authors and later commentators.

25.   See George Maddox, 'Disengagement theory: a critical evaluation', *The Gerontologist*, vol. 4 (1969), pp. 80-83; and Arlie Russell Hochschild, 'Disengagement Theory: a critique and proposal', *American Sociological Review*, vol. 40 (October 1975), pp. 553-69. The latter author argues that Cumming's and Henry's theory as stated is logically unfalsifiable (because it provides itself with escape clauses); that it is unhelpful because its major variables are composed of too many independent sub-parts; and finally because it ignores the meanings which the actors attach to what they do.

26.   P. Townsend, *The Last Refuge*.

27.   Quoted by permission from W.S. Reid, thesis, pp. 106-10.

28.   The discussion which follows is based on Argyle and Beit-Hallahmi, *The Social Psychology of Religion*; Hammond, 'Aging and the Ministry'; and Reid, 'Religious attitudes in later life'.

29.   D.O. Moberg, 'Religiosity in old age', *Gerontologist*, 5 (1965), pp. 78-87.

30.   *The Social Psychology of Religion*, p. 70.
31.   The generalisations in this paragraph are based largely on the findings of
       W.S. Reid's survey of the elderly in Edinburgh.
32,   Loretto Lynch, *The Experience of Death: Care of the Dying and the
       Bereaved* (Liverpool Institute of Socio-Religious Studies, Liverpool, 1977),
       pp. 27-31.
33.   Ibid., p. 6.
34.   Paul Tournier, *Learning to Grow Old* (SCM, London, 1972), pp. 215-41.
35.   Georges Bernanos, *Dialogue des Carmélites* (Editions du Seuil, Paris,
       1949).
36.   Tournier, *Learning to Grow Old*, pp. 223 and 224.

Select Bibliography

Age Concern, *The Role of the Churches in the Care of the Elderly* (Age Concern,
    Mitcham, Surrey, 1965)
British Association of Social Workers, 'Social work with the elderly', *Social
    Work Today*, vol. 8, no. 27 (12 April 1977), pp. 7-15, and a separate leaflet
Norman Autton, *The Pastoral Care of the Dying* (SPCK, London, 1966)
Norman Autton, *The Pastoral Care of the Bereaved* (SPCK, London, 1967)
D. Bromley, *The Psychology of Human Ageing* (Pelican, Harmondsworth, 1966)
Department of Economic and Social Affairs, *Aging: Trends and Policies*
    (United Nations, New York, 1975)
Philip E. Hammond, 'Aging and the ministry' in Riley, Riley and Johnson, II,
    pp. 293-323
D. Hobman, *All Our Futures: The Care of the Elderly* (Liverpool Institute of
    Socio-Religious Studies, Liverpool, 1976)
Loretto Lynch, *The Experience of Death* (Liverpool Institute of Socio-
    Religious Studies, Liverpool, 1977)
Bernice L. Neugarten (ed.), *Middle Age and Aging: A Reader in Social
    Psychology* (University of Chicago Press, Chicago, 1968)
Otto Pollak, *Human Behaviour and the Helping Professions* (Spectrum, New
    York, 1976)
W. Scott Reid, 'The Role of the Church in the Life of the Elderly — studies of
    the attitudes of the elderly in Institutions and those domiciled privately',
    unpublished Ph.D. thesis, Faculty of Divinity (New College), Edinburgh
    University, 1974
W. Scott Reid, 'Religious attitudes in later life', *Age Concern Today*, no. 17
    (Spring 1976), pp. 29-30
Matilda White Riley, John W. Riley, Jr. and Marilyn E. Johnson (eds.), *Aging and
    Society, Volume one: An Inventory of Research Findings* (1969); *Volume
    two: Aging and the Professions* (1969); *Volume three: A Sociology of Age
    Stratification* (1972)
H.P. Steer, *Caring for the Elderly* (SPCK, London, 1966)
Paul Tournier, *Learning to Grow Old* (SCM, London, 1972)

9 AGEING AND THE ARCHITECT/ DESIGN FOR LIVING — A CASE STUDY

M. Jenks and R. Newman

> But, if we have learned anything from the failures of recent years, it is that architecture is equally a social art, whose successful practice is totally dependent on the active participation of non-architects, ranging from the architect's technical collaborators at one end, to his clients, the users of his buildings, and the general public at the other.[1]

The marked increase, in recent years, in the use of sociological and psychological knowledge and concepts in the field of architectural design has largely arisen from the recognition that a much more systematic and thorough enquiry into user needs is more necessary than has been thought important in earlier decades. The criticisms that have been made of modern architecture can be listed under many headings, but the primary complaint has centred largely around the unfeeling architectural insensitivity that has often failed to recognise the behavioural and social consequences of designs which have largely failed to meet the requirements of the people who will live and work in the buildings that emerge from these designs.

The reasons for this apparent reluctance by many architects to both recognise the importance of user needs and their reluctance, even today, to incorporate social and psychological research into their design are many and varied. Explanations that are put forward include an over-emphasis on aesthetics; the class and status separation of architects from many of their users; the architects' artistic self-image and an over-emphasis on an intuitive approach;[2] 'the design sub-culture ['s tendency] to design for itself without considering the values, images and ideals of other groups';[3] lack of research findings in a useable form and deficiencies in environmental design education;[4] and finally, the bureaucratic structure of the public authority which often interposes itself between the architect and the building users.[5]

Yet in all the discussion of the effects of insensitive design on users there is a curious paradox. On the one hand there are writers who argue that the effect of the built environment on human beings is extremely limited. The idea of architectural determinism, 'in which the physical environment is the independent variable and human behaviour the dependent variable',[6] a belief which often appears to underlie many architects' thinking has, in recent years, been so heavily criticised that, for the most part present-day architects have little hesitation in emphasising the extremely peripheral effects of the built environment on human behaviour. The most recent proponent of architectural determinism,[7] in the form of drawing a direct casual connection between the height of a building and the crime rate of its residents has now largely come round to a recognition of the influence of the social, economic and political variables that must inevitably affect and complicate the simple connection between these two factors.

The other side of the paradox is that given that the built environment has often only a peripheral effect on human behaviour, why is such great importance now being attached to user needs? The answer is, of course, that it is a matter of scale and detail. There can be little doubt that the design of a prison, for example, is intended to, and will indeed drastically, affect the human behaviour of its residents. Although the findings are still rather muddled and contradictory, there is some evidence that high-rise buildings affect some of their residents in a socially undesirable manner. But rather than just considering buildings, when one also considers the different characteristics of the users involved a completely different perspective emerges.

Whilst many design features and factors have little or no effect on the ordinary active person, clearly when one considers the design requirements of special groups such as the elderly and the handicapped a quite different design problem is involved. A badly designed series of steps, a heavy door, a poor spatial arrangement of rooms or an electric socket at floor level may well be, for the average person, faults which he or she may not even notice, yet these will represent for the elderly, handicapped, frail or mentally ill person sometimes insuperable obstacles. In other words: 'Environmental factors have a proportionately greater effect on behaviour as the respondent's state of competence decreases.'[8]

Thus in designing for special user groups, such as the elderly, special care must be taken to try to meet their needs in a sensitive way based on both a recognition and knowledge of the special requirements involved. At the same time, in both this country and overseas an increasing proportion of accommodation for the elderly is being provided by public authorities where, as has been mentioned earlier, the bureaucratic structure may so often represent a barrier between the architect and the building users. There have been many suggestions as to how these problems might be overcome and indeed a great deal of research is being done in this field[9] but one direct way would clearly be to try to overcome the gulf between user representatives, experts on the requirements of the elderly and architects and architectural students by bringing them all together in a multidisciplinary learning situation. The remainder of this chapter is a description of such a situation and an analysis of the lessons that may be learnt.

Educational Context

Architectural education in Britain is generally divided into three distinct stages that are characterised by the RIBA examinations Parts I, II and III before a student can finally qualify as a practising architect. In the Department of Architecture at Oxford the course is split into three years, academic training leading to a B.A. (Arch) degree with RIBA Part I exemption; this is followed by one year in practice and then the students return for a further two years graduate training to gain RIBA Part II exemption and a Diploma in Architecture. A final year of practical training is then required before the RIBA Professional Practice exam (Part III) can be taken, and it is on passing this exam that students become fully qualified architects. Training thus lasts a total of at least seven years.

The project that will be examined and analysed in this chapter was programmed for the first term of the undergraduate third-year students. For the first two years of their course the students were given a varied education, concentrating in the first year on a process of acclimatisation involving graphic communication, designs working directly with building materials (and sometimes even scrap) to produce operational prototypes (e.g. disaster shelters, children's play equipment, etc.) and introductory lectures from various specialists involved in the field of architecture — sociology, psychology and environmental engineering, for example. The second year was more concerned with projects emphasising the design of single buildings, with a concentration on designing for environmental factors such as heating, acoustics and lighting. These projects ran in parallel with courses of specialist lectures. The third year represented a widening of the criteria to be considered by the students in designing, and a synthesis of the many varied strands of learning gained from the previous two years of study. The first project of the third year is designed to give a wider context for students to work within, allowing them the opportunity to examine the needs of a particular group of disadvantaged people within society at large, and, theoretically at least, giving rise to the possibility of indicating solutions outside the narrow boundaries of purely architectural proposals. How was this opportunity grasped, and what influence did it have on the students' approach to designing for people with special needs?

The Objectives of the Project

The organisers of the project had a number of objectives in mind and these ranged from architectural and training purposes to a mixture of academic, educational and social aims.

Schools of Architecture, like most academic institutions can, unless great care is taken, become 'ivory towers' — cut off from the outside world. In a sense, such a process is inevitable, for if the student, during this first three years of his course is to be given adequate opportunities to receive and ingest the enormous amounts of the necessary data and instruction he or she must be introduced to, this information must be given in relatively small and ordered packages. In addition, as this process continues the students must also have opportunities to practise and organise their increasing abilities and skills in the form of design problems of slowly increasing complexity. Necessarily, therefore, the introduction of additional variables and data must take place at a controlled rate in these early years, and with the ever increasing areas of study that architectural students must today absorb, the inevitable consequence is that the realities and complexities of the real world and the associated multifarious factors that will affect design solutions, are left to the end of the course.

Naturally, many will argue about the rate and timing of the introduction of not only the external realities but even the internal academic subjects. Some will even argue that in some schools of architecture many aspects of the external realities, particularly social factors, are excluded almost totally by an over-emphasis on, for example, narrow design and aesthetic considerations.

This concern with the realities of the world outside the academic institution was very much in the forefront of the minds of the project organisers and such concern took a number of forms. First, the degree of over-simplification necessary in evolving design problems for students presents a difficult problem posed to test and stretch the student's mind, yet, at the same time, it must not be too complex for the stage of ability and training that the student has reached. One purpose, then, of the project was, under relatively carefully controlled conditions, to give the students a glimpse of the complex system of the departments of local and central government that would be involved in such a project in real life. In addition to these institutions of government, the students were required to take cognisance of a number of organisations and individuals, such as local social interest and pressure groups and interested persons, which would also be acting upon and affecting the situation. The student would thus, it was intended, be given a brief glimpse and experience of the numerous and often conflicting forces that would provide information and possibly influence the briefing and subsequently, the ultimate design process. Rather than the ordered, relatively narrow range of conflict that must necessarily exist in architectural academic design problems, the student was, so it was intended, to be given a partial introduction to the complex and often conflicting values, interests and opinions of the external world.

Moreover, unlike the relatively neat packaged site that is invariably the product of an architectural school design problem, the students were presented with a variety of sites which meant that they were encouraged to see design in a wider context. All too often designs proposed for one chosen site tend to end up as self-contained, monumental designs, isolated and unrelated to their surroundings, and hence divorced from the social and physical environment, which in the real world interacts with the design solution.

An associated purpose was intended to counteract any tendency that tends inevitably to arise in a school of architecture that a building is necessarily a solution (if not the best one) to a problem, social or otherwise. This objective was intermingled with giving the students an opportunity to explore and expand their often existing personal concern with social problems. Rather than representing the situation as it occurs to the practising architect, who, for example, is instructed to 'design an old people's home' the students were given an opportunity to consider and question whether a building represented the solution at all. For perhaps the only time in their lives, the students' minds were addressed to considering the total context of the social problems of, in this case, elderly people and to asking such questions as: 'Who are elderly people?' 'From what social and economic factors do their problems arise?' 'Can these problems be totally, or even partially met by a building?' In other words, the students had to consider the overall and total social and political framework and factors which affected their client groups and to try to gain at least a partial comprehension of the effects of the built environment. Within the context of the project, only a limited consideration could be given to this novel approach but possibly, it was thought, it might lead to a better understanding of the underlying problems; it might educate and inform their social concern for the client group and thus conceivably might lead to a clearer and more realistic assessment in their design considerations.

This over-emphasis on the often disproportionate role that buildings might play is a common feature of the thinking processes and values system of not only architectural students, but of many mature architects. It emerges, perhaps inevitably, from a lifelong interest in building design and form. This belief is implied in quite subtle ways, ranging at one extreme from the idea that if a community centre is visually attractive enough it will gather in all the people of the community and thereby solve the community's problems. At the other extreme, it takes the form of believing that if a building in a high street or main square has an exciting staircase, entrance or facade it will sweep people up into the building and thereby affect the success of the enterprises in the building, irrespective of the economic, commercial, social or political purposes the building is designed to serve — after all, it might be a police station!

The final and most important purpose or objective was to try to bring the students into contact with a potential client group — elderly people. This would be achieved in a number of ways, such as in vacation visits to different types of existing accommodation used by elderly people, by a symposium at which representatives of the various departments, groups and individuals concerned with the welfare of this client group would express their views, and finally by informal contacts during the project, and formal contacts at the end of it. The extent to which this objective was achieved — of gaining structured and useful information on the client groups, in the brief time available — was, as will be seen, the most debatable question which emerged from the whole project.

Description of Project

The project, entitled 'Provision for old people in Banbury' (a town a few miles from Oxford) was programmed to cover a period of eight weeks, with a pre-briefing period of one week and, in addition, some extra work was required from the students in the long summer vacation, prior to the commencement of the project. The project can conveniently be described in separate stages and these were broadly: (i) Pre-briefing, involving inputs of information from various multi-disciplinary sources, and some personal experience gained by students visiting and working with old people. (ii) Research and brief formulation — a stage where problems associated with old people were examined in general, and then in more specific terms related to the village of Grimsbury, a suburb of Banbury. Briefs were then prepared, based on this research and policy proposals formulated. (iii) Design — the implementation of policies proposed on specific sites in Grimsbury. (iv) Feedback — which was obtained, from an exhibition held in Grimsbury of the students' work, from the specialist advisers who were involved in the formal assessment of the student's final designs, and in a seminar held after the completion of the project.

Pre-Briefing

Personal Experience

The first, and perhaps rather overwhelming, contact the students had with the problems of frail and elderly people stemmed from a requirement that they spent a number of weeks of their vacation working in an old persons' residential home. There were two underlying purposes for this, the first was so that they would discover at first hand some idea of the everyday needs and problems of a group of disadvantaged people, the second was to observe the effects of the built environment and to discover from the points of view of the warden/matron, the residents and the local social services department, as well as from their personal point of view, what was thought of the building and what faults could be identified. Findings were included in a report written by individual students giving each a point of reference which could then be raised in discussion groups at the start of the term.

To add to these very personal experiences organised visits for all students were arranged to local buildings that catered for old people, namely two old peoples' homes and one sheltered or grouped housing for the elderly project. These visits were preceded by an introductory talk. The choice of buildings to visit was a conscious one to demonstrate a range of building provision and their associated problems.

The first old persons' home was a country mansion conversion, an example of the many conversions that took place in the early fifties after the 1948 National Assistance Act. This home was in its own grounds on the edge of a small village with a busy main road running through the village centre, largely separating the home from the village. The converted home was not only overcrowded, but had to operate within a basic physical envelope which was unsatisfactory for those elderly people who were not physically able and mentally alert. Bedrooms were shared between four to six residents, and lounges were segregated by sex and furnished with rows of chairs arranged around the edge of the rooms. In brief the building exhibited many of the classic features of an institution with highly dependent residents.

The second old persons' home was a purpose-built home from the middle 1960s and was situated within the boundaries of Banbury itself. The home was a typical example of a purpose built residential home with single bedrooms, a proportion of double bedrooms, shared bathrooms and WCs and separate large lounges and dining room.

The sheltered or grouped housing scheme with independent housing units and a warden, was a development of bungalows with a communal hall, and linked to the warden's house by an alarm system. This was situated within the centre of the chosen study area of Grimsbury in close proximity to shops and a church.

The visits thus gave the students a partial insight of two of the basic and often conflicting problems that occur when attempting to provide built solutions for the care of the elderly — the often debilitating effects of institutions (institutionalisation), and the alternative approach seen in the concept of independence embodied in the sheltered or grouped housing approach. Even with such a small and carefully selected (and arguably biased) sample of buildings, the extremes could be seen even at the superficial level of a short visit. These two general areas of concern were reinforced by the content of the talks by the specialist advisers, speakers at a symposium shortly afterwards, both of which provided essential multi-disciplinary information inputs to the students.

'Care of the Elderly'

The principal documentary source for the project was a report prepared by members of the inter-disciplinary Social Services Buildings Research Team (SSBRT) entitled 'Care of the Elderly'.[10] This report brought together many of the sociological and architectural aspects of caring for old people, by examining the background of the elderly in society, assessing types of accommodation provided; discussing specialised services provided for the elderly, handicapped and psychogeriatric, and concluding with a review of design standards and recommendations. For those students whose interest may have been aroused by this document, they were encouraged and aided to delve further into the problems of the elderly by appendices giving a comprehensive bibliography and a list of organisations concerned. The report, by examining and summarising various views and opinions rather than proposing any firm conclusion or recommendations, sought to introduce students to the many dimensions (only a few of which were architectural) of the problems of providing care for old people.

The Symposium

Twelve speakers, from almost as many disciplines, were invited to speak at a two-day symposium, organised by members of the Department of Architecture, Ian Davis and Nigel Hiscock, with a view to bringing together people concerned with the care of elderly people, and as a result to provide basic information for the students' project. The disciplines represented at this symposium were indeed diverse and included representatives from the Department of Health and Social Security, local Social Services departments, representatives of voluntary organisations, sociologists, a local vicar, architects, a town planner, a housing manager, a doctor and a director of a housing association.

The first day of the symposium discussed problems of the elderly at the national level, and also in Northern Europe – Sweden, Denmark, Germany and the Netherlands. Certain key themes emerged from this first day, evolving from the idea of the elderly being disadvantaged more by environmental and economic factors rather than old age itself, leading to a severe restriction of choice in all aspects of their lives. Possible ways to overcome these problems were discussed – the general trend being away from institutional care towards independence in their own homes (adapted if necessary), in sheltered housing with better standards and supportive care, creation of day centres, provision of domiciliary services, more money and concessionary travel.

The second day concentrated on a more detailed examination of problems experienced by the elderly in relation to a specific geographical area (Banbury), and also on examples of designs for old peoples' homes and sheltered housing. The symposium was then split into small study groups to discuss the issues raised, and then present them back to the meeting.

To the students of architecture, this multi-disciplinary introduction to the elderly in society, reinforced by the SSBRT report 'Care of the Elderly' and their own personal experiences, indicated the breadth and complexity of the problems and also the role, albeit a relatively small though important one, that architectural solutions had to play.

Summary

The range of information given to the students before they began work on the project was enormous, both in depth and breadth, spreading far beyond the boundaries of their own discipline. In addition the students were exposed to some generalised experiences and information far outside the narrow confines of an academic programme, bringing in factors and pressures that would be experienced in the real world. The personal experience gained from working in and visits to old people's accommodation gave the students the opportunity to meet and observe old people who could be expected to use any solution they might propose. Even though these meetings may have not been either pur-posive or structured, their value cannot be overstressed: first, it happens rarely in an academic situation, and secondly, more and more in practice architects tend to become divorced from contact with the potential users of their buildings.

The input of expert multi-disciplinary information, both documentary, and from discussion in the symposium, gave direction and emphasis for old people's needs and to problem areas for study. Also influential ideas were introduced in general terms such as independence, the need for choice, the need for services, and the concept of the elderly staying in their own home as long as possible. These ideas were taken up by students, and as will be seen later, developed in quite surprising ways.

Research and Brief Formulation

From being largely passive recipients of information, this stage marked the formal start for students' active involvement in the eight weeks project. The scheduled programme was extremely tight and demanding, for the research and brief writing period which had also to be supplemented with sketch designs, had to be completed within two and a half weeks. Because of the small amount of time available, the students were split into groups of approximately eight in order to prepare a brief, and the research was divided so that one member from each group could be assigned an area of study which would be common to all groups. These individuals combined to investigate their assigned study areas and their findings, when completed, were then reported back to their group to contribute to the formulation of the brief. The areas of study covered in this research period included: (i) old age in its widest social context; (ii) local and central government policy towards the elderly; (iii) employment and economic considerations; (iv) site feasibility – altogether a very ambitious programme. Necessarily, given the extreme time constraint, the research was largely superficial, but it did however represent a clear process of first, widening the students' knowledge of the problems and complex variables involved, which was reinforced by the multi-disciplinary pre-briefing period, then, secondly, to an application and narrowing down of this knowledge within a specific and defined geographical area leading, in turn, to a more detailed analysis of needs and an appraisal of the opportunities open for development, or improvements and then finally to specific policy proposals. These findings were incorporated into a written brief by each group.

The extremely wide and open-ended nature of the problems, and the complex and interrelated factors involved were handled confidently, though some might say rather unrealistically, by the students in putting forward policies in their briefs. Proposals for the elderly ranged from the realms of what might be called wishful thinking, such as the amalgamations of the Department of Health and Social Security and the Department of the Environment, the provision of organised shopping trips to London and Paris, and new bus services, to those based on a more careful examination of the local area's needs involving proposals for a special minibus service, day centres, rehabilitation, and a careful assessment of the accessibility of pedestrian routes. The problems that the students were most concerned with were the trend towards independent living and the need for choice. The proposals to meet these problems, especially where a built solution seemed appropriate, were often relatively quite feasible.

It is hardly surprising that the more realistic proposals were in the form of architectural solutions despite the amount of information which might have suggested answers which lay outside the orbit of the built environment. Three factors may have contributed to an architectural emphasis: first, that within the time the students were unable to gain the necessary knowledge to evaluate proposals that lay outside their own discipline; secondly, the structure of the programme given

Table 1

Proposals	Group 1	Group 2	Group 3	Group 4	Group 5	Group 6
New housing		Bungalows to mobility standards Bed-sits	Infill to mobility standards	Recommended but type not specified	Flexible housing to meet changing needs	
New sheltered housing	Proposed but no. of units not specified	30 units	20-30 units	30 units	Proposed but no. of units not specified	30 units
New sheltered housing + care unit			8-12 units		Unit incorporated	Unit incorporated + disabled units
Residential accommodation		Linked to sheltered housing			Linked to sheltered housing	
Rehabilitation	To mobility standards		To mobility standards	To mobility standards	To mobility standards	To mobility standards
Community centre	Day care + social facilities	Day care + social facilities	Day care + social facilities	Day care + social facilities	Day care + social facilities	Information centre
Medical centre	Included in community centre	Included in community centre	Included in community centre	Included in community centre	Included in community centre	Included in information centre
Sheltered workshops	Included in community centre	Included in community centre	Included in community centre			
Alarm system			All above accom linked to warden	All above accom linked to warden		All old people in locality linked to warden
Transport		Special service		Mini bus service to community centre	Mini bus service	Mini bus service
Pedestrian routes		Improved and made accessible			Improved and made accessible	Improved landscape made accessible
Shops					Chemists	General store

to the students had teaching objectives involved with the detailed design of buildings, though no specific building types were mentioned; and thirdly, opinions from the symposium speakers that expressed articulately and forcefully, and were subsequently reinforced in group discussions with the students, that the problems of old age were associated more with environmental factors such as bad housing than any other cause.

Table 1 shows the range of specific proposals put forward by each group in their brief. The areas of more general concern are not included as they were in the form of more vague propositions rather than firm proposals.

Themes from the symposium and 'Care of the Elderly' such as the possibility of integration to reduce old people's isolation; the need for independence and choice; the concept of continuing care; and in addition a local area that had no obvious problems except a lack of social facilities, only a small proportion of housing which was suitable for the elderly, and no medical facilities, led to the proposal of policies on a broad front often common to each group of students.

The major problem noted in respect of Grimsbury was the lack of any centre either for the community as a whole, or for the old people and this inevitably led to the proposal for a community centre. The general assumption was that, besides being an interesting architectural problem, the building would go some way towards solving problems of loneliness, provide opportunities for the elderly to meet other people, and where sheltered workshops were provided, give the elderly something useful to do. To meet these objectives the proposals combined, in all cases, a day care centre for the elderly, with social facilities for the whole community in the evening and also included some form of medical centre, either a group surgery or visiting doctor's room.

The concept of choice was almost universally taken to mean a choice of living accommodation which manifested itself primarily in proposals for new sheltered housing schemes on selected sites, reinforced by some new housing to mobility standards,[11] and rehabilitation of elderly people's houses to make them more suitable and barrier free.*

---

* The mobility housing concept arose from a DOE circular (74/74) which suggested the idea of increasing the choice of accommodation for the disabled as an integral part of the normal housing stock by either conversions or the incorporation of new standards into a proportion of the new housing stock. The standards included requirements that entrances should be accessible for wheelchairs, internal planning should allow for space for wheelchairs including wider doorsets, and that there should be at least a bathroom, WC and one bedroom at ground floor level.

A number of groups explored the possibilities of continuing care units, for the increasingly frail or temporarily ill either by incorporating such a unit within a sheltered housing scheme, or attaching residential accommodation to the housing. The problems of elderly people becoming increasingly frail was in fact a major area of concern to the students and it was realised that continuing care as a solution was only a partial one, but on the whole this problem, although well understood by the end of the programme, was left largely unresolved.

Independence for the elderly was closely related generally to the housing proposals, and specifically in detailed design, as well as to the deliberate policy of not building any residential homes. A number of groups introduced the idea of connecting all the old people's dwellings to an alarm or intercommunication system with some form of warden service in case of emergency. Transport was also conceived in terms of providing a form of independence by giving the elderly a service to enable them to get out and about.

It can be seen from the foregoing that although the solutions proposed were almost entirely related to the physical environment, the areas of concern were primarily social. The students first examined the problems, identified the needs of a particular community in relation to a particular section of the population, and then put forward a whole series of related proposals to try to meet these needs. Without the initial multi-disciplinary input to widen the students' horizons at the beginning of the project, it is undoubtedly clear that such a wide range of proposals, attempting to solve complex variables, would not have been even considered.

Design

During the period allotted for brief preparation, the groups were required to produce outline sketch designs to explain and illustrate their proposals. These group designs were assessed by members of staff and also by the specialist advisers, the majority of whom had been speakers or were involved in running seminar groups at the symposium. The expert knowledge of the advisers had been drawn upon at all stages of the project, that of discussion about policy for the briefs, for the preparation of the sketch designs, and at a group assessment which gave the students formal feedback on their ideas.

The sketch designs represented an outline policy framework within which individual students were then expected to choose, develop and design in detail one of their policy decisions. The design was programmed for four weeks and the students were in that short time expected to produce a fully developed final design as well as ideas for landscaping, and a specialised technical study. A further week was set aside for a constructional study and for preparing the final presentation of their schemes.

The level of detail that was included in the designs depended, individual ability aside, largely on the project chosen. At one extreme the choice of a community centre meant, almost invariably, that design time was spent investigating the complex internal planning arrangements and making appropriate decisions about multi-purpose rooms that had to serve the needs of old people as well as those of youth clubs. In the case of this building type, design for the disabled tended at the detailed level to include the appropriate door widths, ramps and barrier free planning. At the other extreme students that chose to look at the rehabilitation of older property had to investigate detailed design for the handicapped, involving ergonomic data, designs for kitchens and bathrooms, details for widening doors, and ground floor conversions. Designs for new housing tended to fall between the two extremes requiring an investigation of internal planning as well as detailed design.

The project was characterised by a heavy emphasis on the input of information drawn from many disciplines, an emphasis that to some concerned with the creative act of design could be viewed as a hindrance to the generation of their own ideas. The nature of this conflict between creativity and information has been explored in a number of sources[12,13] questioning how ideas are arrived at, and the necessity for information to act as a firm base from which to generate design concepts. However this theoretical explanation was not generally understood by the students as a whole, whose training for the first two years tended to concentrate on an intuitive rather than an analytical approach to design. What then was the student's process of design, and how and where in this process did the specialist advisers with their expert knowledge provide the most effective assistance?

Many suggestions have been made regarding the use of the scientific method, which with its stages of analysis, hypothesis formulation and testing, leading to further hypotheses may be seen as an iterative process which many have argued is applicable to the process of design. It is here that the analogy with the design process fails as essentially design has to be a decision-making process at varying levels of detail at specific times, thus leaving little time for the rigorous scientific reappraisal as implied in an iterative approach. However where the analogy works best is in the various stages of a design process, as each stage can be represented as having three dimensions – those of analysis, synthesis and appraisal – dimensions which have recently found common agreement in principle if not in application among a number of theorists.[14,15] These three dimensions, ending in appraisal lead to a decision, or series of decisions which, in the simplest terms, enable the designer to proceed to another level of detail, e.g. from overall design to detailed design, to the working drawing stage and so on. Both analysis and appraisal are dependent on information, whereas synthesis is generally seen as a creative act whereby the masses of often conflicting information are combined into one solution or a series of solutions which with luck and considerable skill will meet, by a system of trade-offs, most of the major objectives that were set out in a brief. Necessarily with complex and conflicting objectives any physical proposal will offer solutions to some parts of the problem, will trade-off against other aspects of the problem, and may ignore other problem areas altogether. Appraisal can assess the relative values of the results of this creative synthesis and lead to modification, occasionally rethink, and inevitably some sort of decision.

A recent study[16] of students' design processes in this department reinforced the validity of this theoretical explanation of design. The study tended to show that the students proceeded from a stage of analysis to one of 'conceptualisation', essentially a problem exploration at a general level of building form, space and function leading to a 'Eureka Point' (closely drawn from Koestler's idea of 'bisociation'[17]) resulting in an overall design concept – this stage paralleling that of synthesis. The next stage was found to be one of 'formalisation' where the overall concept was worked up in more and more detail involving successive stages of analysis, synthesis and appraisal, until a finalised solution emerged.

In addition to a generalised view of the design process of the student body as a whole, the study also analysed the particular emphasis placed on the stages of design by each year. It was discovered that the third-year students tended to spend 'more time . . . on organising and analysing the problem' and placed 'far more emphasis on trying to find an overall concept for each scheme'.[18] The time spent on detailed design was consequently proportionately less as the complex problem and number of variables involved made overall design a difficult task.

Within this scheme of design it can be argued where the specialist advisers' most effective role lay. Their most important contribution was in the group briefing stage where a widening problem area could be discussed, and complex and varied opinions incorporated into

general arguments in a brief. However when the design stage was
reached, and individuals had to assimilate the mass of information
discovered, the emphasis changed radically. This stage of
'conceptualisation' led students to avoid contact with the advisers,
who would, it was felt, make an already complex problem even more
complicated and difficult. The tendency was towards a rather more
private and individual process of problem exploration by bubble
diagrams of room relationships, sketches and immersion in the
complex social variables in order to reach a rather magic 'Eureka
Point' when a solution would emerge.

The following stage of 'formalisation' as mentioned above tended
in most cases to be rather short. This was regrettable in that the
specialist advisers had an extremely valuable role to play in providing
information and experienced knowledge on detailed design for the
elderly. A number of students who had the time to explore design
details expressed the value of this assistance, and the influence was
demonstrably beneficial in the final designs.

Feedback

For the students, assessments of their work came in three stages:
first, a formal assessment by staff of the department and the specialist
advisers; secondly, comments from local people in the community of
Grimsbury where an exhibition of the final work was held; and thirdly,
a seminar held in the department for the students to express their
views on the project as a whole.

The formal assessment of the students' work was conducted by
panels of members of staff, most of whom were approaching the
project for the first time, and specialist advisers. Each student
presented and explained their work to one of the panels, who then
discussed the concepts with the student, and made constructive
criticism where it was felt to be appropriate. As a method of feedback
this system had many problems. First, there were approximately
ten panels, each with only one of the specialist advisers, so it was
inevitable that students would get differing points of view and levels
of criticism depending on which panel they were assessed by. Secondly,
the assessment took place on one day leaving only an average of
between half to three quarters of an hour for each student, a very
short time to get to grips with a complex project. Thirdly, there was
inevitably a defensive attitude to contend with in that the students
were less happy to be subjected to criticisms than the panels were
to criticise, that being their role.

The exhibition took place in a church hall in Grimsbury and was opened by Lady Young, the then opposition spokesman for social services in the House of Lords, and was attended by the local press. The exhibition only lasted a few days but in that time excited considerable interest, and drew a surprising number of local people. During that time there were some students present to answer any questions that were raised. Subsequently a number of the ideas expressed in the students' work were taken up by the community with the intention of putting them into practice — though whether this was a direct result of the exhibition or that the ideas were there already, is debatable. However, one scheme in particular was certainly inspired by students' work and that was for the conversion and rehabilitation of a Methodist Chapel, where the students concerned were consulted on the proposed design.

The seminar held after the project was attended by one of the specialists who had come to give his views and generally congratulate the students for their excellent work. The seminar in fact was used as an opportunity by the students to give vent to their own feelings on the project, perhaps for the first time. These opinions ranged from some who expressed extreme enthusiasm, saying that it was the best programme they had ever been involved in, to those who were highly critical and had found many problems with the project. These comments are discussed later.

The Advisers

The project organisers' intention was, it will be remembered, to expose the students to a large number of views from outside advisers and experts. In this way, it was thought, the students would gain a wider approach and orientation to tackling complex social problems and thus would be engaging both in the briefing and the design processes in a more open and complicated context and background than is normally the case in schools of architecture.

Almost all the advisers whose views it was possible to obtain, in most cases some years after the event, agreed that the underlying idea was a good one. By bringing those involved either in the preparation of the brief for the building, or those with relatively expert views, in close contact with the students, especially at this formative stage in a student's career could, it was generally agreed, do nothing but good. The intention of making the students aware of the background social context and its attendant social and economic influences as well as questioning whether, in fact, a building or buildings would provide a solution was generally favoured. Indeed one adviser felt it 'should be put into practice with quite different forms of building . . .' for it would help 'future users to know that those who design buildings . . . have had personal experience through those who will actually have to use them'. This idea of trying to give the students involved some idea of the complexities of the social and economic policies, problems and alternative solutions that must be taken into account, both in considering a building as a possible solution, and then in detailed design solutions, was undoubtedly approved by all the advisers. Commenting on the failures of architectural design generally one adviser commented, 'closer liaison in the future can do nothing but good'.

Certainly at first sight, it appears that bringing the users – or some of their representatives or those who could be regarded as experts on the users' needs – in closer contact with the architectural students could only improve the situation. But there were also criticisms.

In the first place, many architects, especially those with a largely artistic background, have an inclination or liking for new ideas which can then be incorporated into their designs. As a conceptual technique this approach has many advantages providing that the ideas are so relatively simple that only a slight background and structure of knowledge and, perhaps, intellectual techniques, are necessary both to understand, analyse and then incorporate this knowledge into a conceptual understanding. But with the ever increasing mass of social, psychological and sociological data, concepts and theories and with the resulting complex approaches to the understanding of human behaviour it can be argued that the analysis and ordering of this information is a difficult task even for the full time student of the social sciences.

Perhaps in this problem lies many of the difficulties and reasons for the criticisms and failures of architecture today. With ever increasing and sophisticated knowledge of complex users' needs, as well as the growing awarness by the users of their own requirements, it is perhaps no longer possible for architects either to base their designs on peripheral surface knowledge or to believe that 'good ideas' can be incorporated into their designs without they, in turn, having both a detailed understanding and knowledge as well as the intellectual techniques necessary to understand and absorb this knowledge.

The students, in effect, were over a very short period indeed exposed to the views of a large number of specialists and, as one adviser put it 'Not only will each [specialist] have their own particular

personal axe to grind . . . but will offer a very different orientation'
and a number of different approaches and the students are required to
'sort out these different orientations and the implications for
architectural design'. This barrage of knowledge, orientations and views
expressed by the different advisers was, as one adviser put it, on such
a scale that, in the discussions which took place during the seminar,
the students often 'couldn't get a word in edgeways'.

Another view expressed doubts about the validity of the project
organisers' objective of asking the student to consider whether the
social problems involved could in fact, be met by a building of one
sort or another. Only really confident students, it was argued, would
be able to ignore the idea that 'the architect's work is to build buildings'
though, in general, the idea of widening the context of considerations
was thought to be an excellent educational and training aim.

Given the amount and complexity of data and the detailed
recommendations and orientations that the students were exposed
to, in a very short time period indeed, it was not surprising that some
of the schemes that the students concerned put forward caused one
specialist to write, 'Some of the . . . projects I recall were architects'
pipe dreams'.

In retrospect, it is clear that whilst the input of user-data on
detailed design considerations such as window catches, door design
and heights of working surfaces can make not only a definite
contribution and can also be absorbed by the students concerned, on
the other hand, when such questions as the choice between alternative
social policies and the consequent design solutions are posed then many
other factors and different levels of objectives must be taken into
account in considering the organisation of such projects.

The Students' Point of View

'I never saw architecture in its social context before this project' and
'I tended to concentrate on the aesthetics and the design of form,
but in this project I designed for needs', were typical comments made
by students reflecting on the project. If there was any consensus of
opinion among the students it was that this project effectively
changed their attitude and approach to design. For some students it
reinforced ideas that were already germinating about the need for a
social input into design, for others it represented the need for a larger
input of information and a widening of their horizons in directions
not previously recognised as having relevance, and for a small minority
it represented the chance to undertake some basic research and the

opportunity to question in some depth a number of the assumptions made when considering the role of buildings in meeting people's needs. The change in attitude, it appears, was not a temporary phenomenon induced by a special project, but represented a much deeper and lasting shift, as nearly three years later the students in question (now in their fifth year) have remarked on the project being a turning point in their approach to design, an approach that has in most cases been developed since. Indeed one student is proposing to undertake a research project in his final year to develop some of the ideas put forward in the earlier project. The project in fact could lay claim to being instrumental in altering the student's approach to design from a consideration of primarily aesthetic, planning and technical factors to the incorporation of these factors with other wider real world variables that included a social input and attempts to understand users' needs in a wider context than that of just a building.

Opinions varied as to the value of the specialist advisers, though there was much agreement regarding the importance of their role during the period of brief formulation. Here the advisers were included in the group discussions to help with policy decisions, and their specialised input of information was appreciated and incorporated in the main. The response to this input was not completely uniform, for 'one man's meat is another man's poison' and the wide variety of views expressed by the different specialists was, in some cases, found to be extremely stimulating and involved some students in protracted discussions and arguments in order to arrive at a decision. For others the conflict of opinion was too overwhelming and resulted in confusion and even in some cases resentment. These extremes of response correlated largely with the abilities and strength of the group in question. Obviously student individual abilities vary enormously, but it is surprising how often randomly selected groups, rather than deliberately chosen balanced groups of skills and talent, tend to produce extremes of on the one hand groups with a high proportion of more talented students that work well together, and on the other those with a higher proportion of weaker students. The stronger groups were able to use and develop the multiplicity of views expressed into positive and creative policies, whereas there was a tendency for the less successful groups to take guidance from a single adviser to obtain a more consistent view from which to develop policies. However, despite these differences in groups and approaches, in the final analysis, overall policies tended not to vary as significantly as might be expected, except in the depth and nature of the detail. One exception was a splinter group who arrived at a very different strategy of very small scale and detailed design, generally rejecting architectural solutions, and in the process this group reckoned that they got more out of the programme than any of the other students. This was a small group of highly motivated and articulate students who were able to compete with the specialist advisers in discussion and as a result found their expert contributions of immense importance. Discussions in this group tended to question and evaluate the advisers' contributions much more before arriving at a decision.

At other stages in the project there was general acceptance of the value of the multi-disciplinary input of the advisers at the symposium and of 'Care of the Elderly' – as being a good general introduction to the problem areas involved, and as being both stimulating and a process of widening horizons. As indicated earlier, the effect of the advisers in the detailed stage of design was limited to the extent that few students had the time to embark on this stage. Those that did seek advice at this stage reported that such practical guidance was of great value, and introduced them to new and challenging areas of detailed design – such as gardens for the disabled, design for wheelchair use, details for kitchens and bathrooms suitable for increasingly frail elderly people, and so on – considerations that had not been raised in detail before.

On the positive side the students generally felt that the specialist advisers were on the whole useful though sometimes confusing in their differing opinions, and that they were welcomed particularly by the groups preparing a brief. Perhaps the proof of their influence can be seen by reference to Table 1 showing policies from each group indicating the broad similarity of overall proposals. The students attributed their change in attitude and approach to design – a change seen by most as enduring, beneficial and worth developing – to the project and its associated multi-disciplinary input.

However, despite much praise and many benefits, the project was not received by the students as overwhelmingly enthusiastically as might be implied from the comments above. Indeed some deeply felt criticism was levelled at the project. This criticism often varied greatly between students, but on one issue there was almost complete agreement, and this evolved from the pressure inherent in the written programme, and also from the architectual staff, to produce a building. The introductory programme sheet giving some background to the project opened the way for a wide area of study, citing such factors as the differing pattern of family life, economic deprivation, lack of mobility, changing social conditions and so on as being possible causes of problems experienced by elderly people. It gave the possibility of investigating solutions outside a narrow architectural context by stating that a 'radical reappraisal of solutions within the present [social] context is urgently required', and it was 'hoped that a variety of different approaches to the problem' would be made. The background statement was included with the main programme giving detailed teaching objectives and requirements with a timetable. The stated objective particular to this programme was: 'To study buildings generated by a social need.' This was reinforced by a timetable that gave nine days to examine user needs, investigate design criteria and analyse sites, followed by a further eight days to produce a group brief and sketch designs. Four and a half weeks were then given to develop a final design with the mandatory requirement to produce a landscape design and a technical study. A final week was set aside for detailed constructional design and for the final presentation of a design. Clearly a building was required!

This conflict between what the students were led to believe by the large multi-disciplinary input of information, a sizeable proportion of which almost precluded purely built solution, and what they were given to do, led to a fairly lively expression of views at the seminar at the end of the project. The emphasis to produce a building was further reinforced first by ideas expressed as early as the symposium of the need in the local area for a community centre which gained a general acceptance, and secondly by fairly heavy criticism (reported by some students) of solutions that did not produce a new building, criticism that might be characterised by the phrase – 'that's all very interesting, but where's the building?' A further complication, if one is needed, was that although there was some genuine resentment that the possibilities for exploring other than architectural solutions seemed largely denied, the majority of the students, in the end, wanted to design a building.

Given the emphasis to produce a building and the underlying desire by the students to design a building, another commonly expressed criticism was that the information received was too open-ended, could not easily be moulded into a brief for a building and that the decision of what to desgin was made difficult by the lack of definition of problem areas and a specified schedule of accommodation. Obviously if these criticisms were overcome the result would have been a reversion to a traditional project comprising a single solution on a predetermined site with a predetermined brief – the complete opposite of what was intended.

The criticism which on the one hand argued for greater openness, freedom and flexibility of solutions, and on the other for the need of clear boundaries and a defined brief — and these conflicting views were often expressed by the same groups — could be viewed positively as a valuable experience. As an experience (with hindsight) it could be seen as a partial microcosm of the 'real world' where problems are hard to define, information can be overwhelming and often conflicting, and people's needs do not fit into neat packages, thus decisions are extremely hard to make and solutions difficult to arrive at. Perhaps what the experience did do was to enable students to perceive, through the complexity, possible roles where the architect could be effective in helping to meet the needs of the elderly.

Conclusions

It is perhaps evident from the foregoing description that a number of questions can be raised. How did the multi-disciplinary input of information affect the students' final designs? Did the project represent a reasonable simulation of the complexities of the real world? Arising from these questions is the extent to which the project's objective of closing the gap between architectural students' designs and the requirements of users was achieved.

The Effect on Design

There is little doubt that the answer to the first question is that the information input had a considerable effect at both the general and detailed levels of design. It is not easy to assess the effects of an information input into a complex process that results in the production of a single solution, but even so there are indicators that give some direction. First, there is the content of, and areas of concern covered by, the information given, secondly there is the evidence of the completed designs themselves, and thirdly there is a comparison, albeit one of doubtful reliability, between the designs in question and designs from a previous project. The information given, both by the specialists and 'Care of the Elderly', operated at a general level of conceptual and policy considerations which were largely drawn upon to formulate policies in the preparation of group briefs. At a detailed level, this information which related more to building design was used in drawing up design criteria within the group briefs and developed in more detail by individual students in their designs. The incorporation of the information at a more general level and its translation into proposals has been discussed earlier, and as can be seen in Table 1 resulted in fairly uniform proposals to attempt to solve the complex problems raised.

Information at the more detailed level was concerned with issues such as designing for increasing disability with age, difficulties in mobility outside the home, loneliness and isolation, the problem of hypothermia and so on. This type of information was expressed by specialists during group briefing discussions and throughout the design process, and was reinforced in 'Care of the Elderly' by reference to various design guides and relevant books. Even a superficial analysis of some of the designs would indicate the influence of this specialist input, and in outline the design features that were incorporated as a result of this information included the following.

1. Outside the Building

The provision of shelter and a concern over micro-climate, the provision of seating, the integration of the elderly into the community by designing units in physical proximity to local facilities, the choice of more level sites and the use of shallow gradient ramps in place of steps where necessary, a general concern over the accessibility of pedestrian routes and a concern over the use of appropriate hard surfacing materials, and the provision of private gardens suitable for working on from a wheelchair.

2. Inside the Building

A general incorporation of mobility standards (wider door openings, ramped access, bathroom and WC on ground floors) to ensure continuing use of property should the elderly house owner/tenant become wheelchair bound, the design and location of units and windows to give views out into areas of activity, the recognition of a need for privacy affecting window design, detailed designs based on anthropometric data for bathrooms and kitchens for the disabled, and a concern over such small but important details as the height and position of light switches and electric sockets.

These considerations were incorporated into designs for converting existing properties, as well as for purpose-built schemes.

Though the lists are by no means comprehensive, their specialised and detailed and sensitive nature is apparent and, by inference, represented attempts to meet, by the built form, the objective to help the elderly maintain their independence. Comparisons with earlier designs show that few, if any, of the above features were taken into consideration – the concentration of design being more on aesthetics, building form, planning arrangements and technical factors. It is indeed doubtful if this detailed and sensitive approach to design would have occurred without the input of the specialised multi-disciplinary information. The effects of this approach, it is interesting to note in passing, reached further than just the students, as after this project the criteria for judging students' designs often included such questions as accessibility for wheelchair use – considerations that had rarely been raised before this project.

A Simulation of Reality?

The briefing, design, construction and commissioning of a building, and the involvement of people from many disciplines in this process is, in the real world, extremely complex. How then does this complex reality compare with the student project? Some recent research[19] has indicated that when designing for the elderly there are, *inter alia*, four significant areas of concern that relate to the production of a satisf-factory building and these are: the definition of need; documentary sources; the briefing and design processes; and feedback of information from previous solutions.

Although the definition of need at a general level is often successfully undertaken by government (and sometimes voluntary) organisations, who respond by providing financial and medical aid, social services and housing, on the other hand when such needs are related to buildings the task of definition is more difficult at the necessary detailed level. The relationship of needs to built form is largely undiscovered. For example, can the needs of the elderly be satisfied by features such as the size and scale of a building, or by grouping smaller units together, by concentrating on a 'domestic' style, by decorating corridors in identifiable colours, or by providing communal facilities? All these features have been tried, but the basic questions remain unanswered, for perhaps only by a multi-disciplinary or inter-disciplinary research approach will it be possible, eventually, to discover the relationship of needs to built form. As a specific problem this was on the whole not perceived by the students who were largely presented with, or sometimes discovered, a series of identifiable problems faced by the elderly, and tended to assume that development of designs would go some way towards solving these problems. The need to test these designs did not become apparent to the students, though there was an understanding of the limited nature of architectural design in meeting people's needs.

The mass of documentary sources, often conflicting in their advice, often not completely relevant, and sometimes unintelligible, presented a second area of difficulty. This information was derived from numerous government design bulletins and circulars, from design guides by voluntary organisations and pressure groups, and from research. It could be argued that in the case of the students they were presented with more documentary evidence, of greater complexity and wider in boundary, than is likely to be available to the architect in practice with constraints of time and resources that mitigate against undertaking basic research.

The briefing process, in theory at least, is a complex, detailed and cyclical process, which in practice all too often only consists of a written document or schedule of accommodation presented by a client department to an architect. Despite this apparent simplicity even at this level of practice the briefing is still complex. In an ideal form the function of the briefing process is to transmit information and objectives about clients' and users' requirements and needs to the architect by discussion, meetings and documentation, and to incorporate into the process the views of building users and experts from other disciplines, but this function is hindered by a number of problems.

For most buildings designed for the elderly in this country government financial aid is generally sought, resulting in the briefing process being subjected to imposed procedures and requirement to obtain loan sanction, procedures that often affect the efficiency of the briefing process and dictate the timing and consideration of information required. Further complications are added, particularly in larger client organisations, where there is a general lack of understanding by the client of the architect's working methods and needs for information (and vice versa), and this often leads to late or inappropriate decisions by clients that hold up the design process and cause expensive delays in building. Finally, the briefing process is an information seeking process, this information being sought by the client and transmitted to the architect, so clearly the reliability and validity of the information to be incorporated into a design is of primary importance. Information, in practice, tends to be less than adequate, as it is derived from design guidance that it often out of date and rarely evaluated, especially in terms of previous built solutions which are almost never appraised in the necessary detail to obtain reliable feedback to the briefing process. For essentially, the briefing process and the design process run in parallel for a time in which exchanges of information between client and architect take place, but the design process then moves into a further stage of production drawings, construction and commissioning where the client's role is diminished. These earlier stages of design have been described in detail elsewhere (pp. 262-265).

The final dimension in reality is the stated need, if not the practice, of appraising a building in use, to test if it meets the needs of those for whom it was designed, and the objectives of those that designed it. This feedback information would clearly be of immense value in the briefing process, but it is seldom undertaken and in reality represents a large and significant gap in our present knowledge. As opposed to the deficiencies in the system of feedback from appraisal in the real world, feedback is an integral part of the process of education so the students in this project received the expert comments of architects, specialists and the general public to give an appraisal of their completed designs. Although comment on a design is very different from the objective appraisal of a building in use, nevertheless it was based on the experience of those who were closely involved with buildings and caring for elderly people, and consequently was of great value.

In addition the students' experience differed in that they were their own client organisation, having the job of defining the problems and writing a brief, and were then required to take the role of architect and designing within the discovered parameters. Where their experiences did correspond with reality was in the involvement of discussion with specialists, and of the difficulties of making decisions based on the large amount of conflicting information.

From the foregoing it can be seen that although the project was not an accurate simulation of the process as it exists in the real world, a number of the dimensions of the process were experienced by the students. The process of problem definition, the accumulation of information, analysis and the preparation of a brief, discussions with a variety of specialists, the need to make informed but rapid decisions, the process of designing for needs and the inclusion of feedback on their final designs, could certainly be viewed as a more than adequate introduction to the complexities of reality than is normally possible for students of architecture.

The Objectives

There is little doubt the project organisers' objective to attempt to bridge the gap, at least partially, between the architectural students and the users' representatives or specialists on the users' requirements was largely achieved. As a complete change from the largely artificial and necessarily limited academic world the students were, over a brief period, brought face to face with the complex architectural considerations of the real world. But, in addition, the students were given a small glimpse of the social, economic and political forces which work, largely via a bureaucratic process, to give form to a complex and often diffuse series of social policies from which, on occasions, there emerges a specific building design. This small glimpse of the real world was afforded not only by representatives of local and central government but by members of interest and pressure groups as well as enthusiastic individuals and thus the students became partly aware of the often confusing and conflicting interests, attitudes and orientations which continually beset social policy choices. By this widening and expansion of the hitherto largely limited area of problems surrounding any design solution the students were brought face to face with the immensely complex framework within which architects, in reality, have to work.

At the same time the subject of the project, elderly people, gave expression to many individual students' personal concern with social problems and thus achieved the project organisers' objectives of providing an understanding and means of expressing many individual student's social concern and conscience.

The extent to which many of the students addressed themselves to the problem of whether a building would provide an effective solution is conjectural. Nevertheless the project again provided an opportunity for students to consider the role a building can play in the overall context of examining and analysing a social policy and afforded a limited opportunity of expanding the student's vision and perception outside the normal architectural considerations, inherent in a school of architecture.

Thus to a large extent the project organisers' objectives were largely met and it is only in detailed considerations of the project that some criticisms emerge. One must, at this stage, draw a clear distinction between on the one hand detailed design considerations and on the other hand the largely conceptual, and often amorphous, policy considerations which were part of the subject of the project. Though even recommendations regarding detailed design features such as door widths, height of working surfaces, narrowness of stairways are often disputed, it was clear that these considerations, put forward in the seminar document 'Care of the Elderly', were heavily reinforced by the often urgent strictures of the advisers and specialists. In this case, then, making the students aware of the often, literally, crippling effect that these detailed design features can have on the elderly residents and thus indirectly reinforcing the need for the sensitivity of design required – the project organisers' objective was largely achieved.

However when one turns to the social policy questions involved, the success of the project becomes questionable. Such questions as national resources allocation; methods of bureaucratic process and structure; the use made of voluntary organisations; the degree to which the ageing process and increasing frailty should be taken into account; the extent to which the community should be or would wish to be involved; the use of supportive services and the location of further and extensive care facilities are immensely complex questions on which experts are often, to say the least, diffident in prognostication.

To expose the students to these intricate problems in such a short time period and at the same time have particularised views put forward by a small number of advisers as definitive opinions, whilst certainly expanding the students' area of perception and knowledge, was, to say the least, of doubtful value. Certainly only a few students, at the beginning of the project had any clear idea of the complexity of the questions that they were about to tackle, especially when those questions had to be considered in interaction with the constraints that inevitably affect design solutions. By the end of the project, many of the students, especially with the limited time available, had had either to turn to 'pipe dreams' or to limit the scope of their considerations by rigorously excluding all but a few of the many factors which had been brought to their attention.

Summary

In retrospect the criteria for projects of this nature seem apparent. First, the number of advisers and other forms of what might be called input data must be limited to the extent that peripheral and extensive factors must be replaced by deeper and intensive knowledge which can be analysed and ordered. Secondly, the scope of problems to be taken into account by the students must either similarly be more structured, or alternatively should be regarded as background knowledge which might inform, but not necessarily affect, the project objectives.

It is, of course, accepted as an alternative view that to throw

students into a problem area which they are not prepared or trained
to consider is an acceptable part of the educational process, but clearly
the parameters of the problem must be clearly set to avoid either
creating despair and a lack of confidence, or students who are thus
conditioned to believe that even a sparse and peripheral knowledge of
social problems and user needs are sufficient background for a design
solution. In this latter alternative perhaps lay the greatest criticism
of the project?

Thirdly, to a layman it would seem obvious that the structure of
architecture courses must be changed in order to strengthen both its
intellectual and analytical basis as well as its understanding and
emphasis on social, including user needs, content. The difficulty here
lies in the fact that the courses for gaining an architectural
qualification are already very long and there are already such an
inordinate number of other subjects each student has to master.
However a recognition of the importance of a much clearer understanding of building users and their activities is slowly gaining ground
amongst the more aware members of the architectural profession and
this awareness is slowly being reflected in the content of the courses
run by schools of architecture.

Fourthly, there is a need for non-architects to recognise how
difficult and complicated the architect's task often is, especially when
faced by a client or client committee which in turn has not thought
through its requirements and objectives, or the purposes for which the
building is intended. In many cases, the architect, despite his lack of
the specialised intellectual and other skills necessary, has no alternative
but to make some sort of attempt at discerning a social objective or
purpose and designing to that end. The greatest assistance that could
be given to architects asked to design buildings of great social
complexity would be for the client or client group to have a clearly
defined and agreed social policy and objective, with a clear understanding of the needs of the user-groups involved, and then indeed,
the situation would be transformed.

Finally, there can be little doubt that the project was a most
worthwhile and largely successful undertaking which, if the few
criticisms made of the project are taken into account, could with great
value, be taken and used as a basis for similar design projects by other
schools of architecture.

Notes

1. M. MacEwen, *Crisis in Architecture* (London, RIBA Publications, 1974), p. 51.
2. R.J. Newman, *The Basis of Architectural Design – Intuition or Research* (Oxford Architectural Research Paper, Oxford Polytechnic, Headington, Oxford), Dec. 1974.
3. A. Rapoport, 'The Design Professions and the Behavioural Sciences', *Architectural Association Quarterly*, vol. 1, no. 1 (Winter 1969), p. 23.
4. J.E. Reizenstein, 'Linking Social Research and Design', *Journal of Architectural Research*, 4/3 (December 1975), p. 29.
5. M. MacEwen, *Crisis in Architecture*, p. 33.
6. M. Broady, 'Social Theory in Architectural Design' in R. Gutman (ed.), *People and Buildings* (New York, Basic Books Inc., 1972), p. 174.
7. O. Newman, *Defensible Space* (London, Architectural Press, 1972).
8. M.P. Lawton, 'Research in Environmental Design for Deprived User Groups', *Journal of Architectural Research*, 3/2 (May 1974).
9. Social Services Buildings Research Team (SSBRT): (a) *A Study of the Briefing Process for the Design of Social Services Buildings – a Case Study of Oxfordshire County Council*, May 1976; (b) *The Appraisal of Buildings – An analysis and review of existing architectural and sociological approaches*, June 1976; (c) *The Appraisal of Buildings – Social Services Buildings; a proposed method of approach*, July 1976.
10. R. Newman, M. Jenks *et al.*, 'Care of the Elderly', Oxford Polytechnic, 1974.
11. Department of the Environment, *Housing for People who are Physically Handicapped*, DOE Circular 74/74, HMSO, London 1974.
12. R.J. Newman, *The basis of architectural design – Intuition or Research?* (Dec. 1974.)
13. T.A. Markus, 'Design and Research: are they in conflict, unrelated, or complementary?', University of Strathclyde, BPRU, Paper GD/34/TAM/MM, June 1969.
14. Geoffrey Broadbent, *Design in Architecture* (J. Wiley and Sons, London, 1973), pp. 252-71.
15. Building Performance Research Unit (BPRU), *Building Performance* (Applied Science Publishers, London, 1972), pp. 21-5.
16. T.O. Eggen and J.H. Hicks, 'Planned and Perceived Order in Architecture', unpublished thesis, Department of Architecture, Oxford Polytechnic, 1973.
17. A. Koestler, *The Act of Creation* (London, Hutchinson, 1964).
18. Eggen and Hicks, *Order in Architecture*, pp. 144-5.
19. (a) SSBRT, *A Study of the Briefing Process*; (b) R. Newman, M. Jenks and I. Smith, 'Some design problems', a paper given at the Institute of Social Welfare Seminar 'Some Unresolved Aspects of Sheltered Housing for the Elderly and Disabled', University of Nottingham, April 1977.

INDEX

activity theory of ageing 93
Age Concern 173, 186, 223, 229
Age Discrimination in Employment
Act (USA) 43
age structure: Japan 50, 51, 68;
United States 15, 38; Western
Europe 15, 37, 50, 51
ageing: and the architect 249-79;
and education 117-43; and the
environment 73-108; and health
149-71; and the mind 197-221;
and social work 172-95; and the
spirit 222-45; ecological model
82-5; future of 37-43; in eastern
society 45-70; in western society
15-43
Aging in American Society 223
Alexander, C. 76
All-University Gerontology Center
(Syracuse University, NY) 123,
132
American Association of Retired
Persons (AARP) 36, 43, 132
American Gerontology Society 124
anaemia, among old people 156, 164
Andrus Gerontology Center (Univ.
of S. California) 119, 123
antidepressants 204, 207, 209
anxiety and old people 202-3, 207,
208, 211
architecture, and ageing 76, 249-79
Argyle, Michael 241
arthritis, among old people 26
arts and hobbies, among Japanese
old people 66-7
Asia, old people in 33, 52
Association for Gerontology in
Higher Education (USA) 124,
143
atheroma 154, 155, 160
atherosclerosis 153-4, 155
arthrosis 160
Australia, and geriatric medicine
165

Banbury, old people's housing project
254-79
Barker, Roger 80

bedfast old people 26, 161, 237
Beit-Hallahmi, Benjamin 241
Bernanos, Georges 245
bereavement, and old people 158,
206, 241
Bexton, E.F. 74
Birren, J.E. 141
birth rates: Asia 52; Japan 48, 52,
68; USA 23
Blake, Richard 122
boarding-out, for old people 220
Bolton, Christopher R. 130
Bonn, retirement survey 31
brain disease, among old people
211-14
Brody, E. 96
Bromley, D.B. 156
Bureau of Census (US), and old
people's housing 106
Burgess, Ernest W. 21, 22
Butler, Robert N. 141

Caggiano, Michael 92
California, retirement housing study
96
Canada 123; education of old people
126-7; employee exchange 142;
and geriatric medicine 165;
social gerontology 120, 122
Canadian Executive Service Overseas
(CESO) 138
cardio-respiratory system, and
ageing 152
cardio-vascular disease, among old
people 26, 156
Care of the Elderly, SSBRT report
256-7, 258, 261, 270, 272, 273,
278
Carp, Frances M. 77, 78, 92
cataract, among old people 155
catheters, use of 162
Centenarians of the Andes 156
central nervous system: and ageing
150-51; diseases, among old
people 156, 160
Chicago: old people in 24; retirement
survey 31
Chicago University, gerontology

CONTRIBUTORS

Elizabeth Falor Bexton, Administrator and Co-Director SAGE (Senior Actualization and Growth Exploration) and a member of Gerontologic Facilities Inc.

Paul Brearley, Senior Lecturer, post-graduate Social Work Course Department of Social Theory and Institutions, University College of North Wales.

John Brocklehurst, Professor of Geriatric Medicine, University of Manchester.

Paul Gaine, Director, Liverpool Institute of Socio-Religious Studies.

Robert Havighurst, Professor of Education and Human Development University of Chicago.

David Hobman, Director of Age Concern England.

M. Jenks, Research Associate, Department of Architecture, Oxford Polytechnic.

Daisaku Maeda, Chief, Social Welfare Section, Sociology Department Tokyo Metropolitan Institute of Gerontology.

Lotte Marcus, Associate Professor, School of Social Work McGill University, Montreal.

Robert J. Newcomer, Associate Professor, School of Nursing, Department of Social and Behavioural Sciences University of California, San Francisco.

R. Newman, Senior Lecturer, Department of Architecture Oxford Polytechnic.

Tony Whitehead, Consultant Psychiatrist, East Sussex Area Health Authority.